GENDER HURTS

It is only recently that transgenderism has been accepted as a disorder for which treatment is available. In the 1990s, a political movement of transgender activism coalesced to campaign for transgender rights. Considerable social, political and legal changes are occurring in response and there is increasing acceptance by governments and many other organisations and actors of the legitimacy of these rights.

This provocative and controversial book explores the consequences of these changes and offers a feminist perspective on the ideology and practice of transgenderism, which the author sees as harmful. It explores the effects of transgenderism on the lesbian and gay community, the partners of people who transgender, children who are identified as transgender and the people who transgender themselves, and argues that these are negative. In doing so the book contends that the phenomenon is based upon sex stereotyping, referred to as 'gender' – a conservative ideology that forms the foundation for women's subordination. *Gender Hurts* argues for the abolition of 'gender', which would remove the rationale for transgenderism.

This book will be of interest to scholars and students of political science, feminism and feminist theory and gender studies.

Sheila Jeffreys is Professor of feminist politics in the School of Social and Political Sciences at the University of Melbourne, Australia.

GENDER HURTS

A feminist analysis of the politics of transgenderism

Sheila Jeffreys

Routledge
Taylor & Francis Group

LONDON AND NEW YORK

First published 2014
by Routledge
2 Park Square, Milton Park, Abingdon, Oxon OX14 4RN

and by Routledge
711 Third Avenue, New York, NY 10017

Routledge is an imprint of the Taylor & Francis Group, an Informa business

British Library Cataloguing in Publication Data
A catalogue record for this book is available from the British Library

Library of Congress Cataloguing in Publication data
Jeffreys, Sheila.
   Gender hurts : a feminist analysis of the politics of transgenderism / Sheila Jeffreys.
      pages cm
   Includes bibliographical references.
   1. Transgenderism.   2. Transgender people–Political activity.   3. Feminism.
   4. Feminist theory.   I. Title.
   HQ77.9.J44 2014
   306.76'8–dc23
   2013042861

ISBN: 978-0-415-53939-5 (hbk)
ISBN: 978-0-415-53940-1 (pbk)
ISBN: 978-1-315-77826-6 (ebk)

Typeset in Bembo
by Out of House Publishing

Printed and bound in Great Britain by
TJ International Ltd, Padstow, Cornwall

This book is dedicated to Ann Rowett with my love and with gratitude for her support and advice throughout this project.

CONTENTS

ACKNOWLEDGEMENTS

I am indebted to Janice G. Raymond for her pioneering book, *The Transsexual Empire* (1994, first published 1979). Her work is the foundation on which feminist criticism of transgenderism has been built, and continues to inspire radical feminist thought. I am grateful to all those friends who have read and commented upon chapters of this book: Lorene Gottschalk, Lynne Harne, Kathy Chambers, Ruth Margerison. Lorene Gottschalk's contribution was particularly valuable. She was much involved in the initial stages of this project and contributed to the writing of half of the chapters, and she conducted the three interviews that have been so important to Chapters 3 and 4. I am grateful, too, to the new wave of radical feminism both online and offline. Radical feminist bloggers such as Gallus Mag from 'GenderTrender' (n.d.a) and Dirt from 'Dirt from Dirt', among others, have provided invaluable factual material, references and ideas on their blogs, without which it would have been harder to write this book. Indeed, over the period that this book has been incubating, radical feminist bloggers strengthened and clarified my analysis. Radical feminist activists have provided venues at which I have been able to test out my thinking, these being the two very successful radical feminist conferences in London – Rad Fem 2012 and Rad Fem 2013. I owe much to these brave women. I salute the courage and tenacity of those radical feminists who are making it possible for radical feminists to speak, and furthering radical feminist analysis. I intend this book as a contribution to the considerable struggle that is presently taking place between mainly male transgender activists and radical feminists over who has the right to define what a woman is: women, or men who fantasise about being women. I am thankful for the support I continue to receive from the University of Melbourne, which has provided a crucible over the last two decades in which to develop my ideas, research and write.

INTRODUCTION

This book will explore the harms created by the ideology and practice of transgenderism, a phenomenon that developed in the mid to late twentieth century. Transgenderism has only been an accepted disorder for which the treatment of choice is the administration of hormones, and perhaps amputation or other surgery, for a comparatively short time. Many US physicians contested the idea of such treatments for the condition until the 1970s, and some still do (Meyerowitz, 2002). In the 1990s, partly as a result of the potential for networking created by the Internet, a political movement of transgender activism was created to campaign for transgender 'rights'. Considerable social, political and legal changes are occurring in response, and there is increasing acceptance by governments and many other organisations and actors of the legitimacy of such rights. These changes have ramifications for lesbian and gay existence and the lesbian and gay community; for the health and life chances of transgenders themselves; for the possibilities of women's equality; for organisations, workplaces, services and the law. There is now a copious literature on transgenderism, on its history, treatment, theory and practice. But this literature is generally positive towards the phenomenon, seeing transgenders as constituting an essential category of persons that has been denied rights and needs recognition. Some of this literature makes the claim that transgenderism is transgressive and part of a revolutionary process of social change, because it destabilises the 'gender binary'.

This book takes a quite different approach. It argues, from a feminist perspective, that transgenderism is but one way in which 'gender' hurts people and societies. Transgenderism depends for its very existence on the idea that there is an 'essence' of gender, a psychology and pattern of behaviour, which is suited to persons with particular bodies and identities. This is the opposite of the feminist view, which is that the idea of gender is the foundation of the political system of male domination. 'Gender', in traditional patriarchal thinking, ascribes skirts, high heels and a love of unpaid domestic labour to those with female biology, and comfortable clothing, enterprise and initiative to those with male biology. In the practice of transgenderism, traditional gender is seen to lose its sense of direction and end up in the minds and bodies of persons with inappropriate body parts that need to be corrected. But without 'gender', transgenderism could not exist. From a critical, feminist point of view, when transgender rights are inscribed into law and adopted by institutions, they instantiate ideas that are harmful to women's equality and give authority to outdated notions of essential differences between the sexes. Transgenderism is indeed transgressive, but of women's rights rather than an oppressive social system.

This book is necessary now because the practice of transgendering adults and children has been normalised in Western cultures but very little critique exists. There is evidence of an increasing criticism of the practice both from within a developing new wave of online feminism and from within the medical profession, but this is met with considerable resistance from transgender activists. Critics are labelled 'transphobic', subjected to Internet campaigns of vilification, and, in some cases, there are attempts by transgender activists to expel such insubordinate persons from their jobs or threaten their reputations. Nonetheless, the understanding of transgenderism is at a tipping point and there is evidence of a desire to rethink approaches to the practice. For instance, a conference was organised by the Royal College of Psychiatrists' Gay and Lesbian Special Interest Group for 20 May 2011 in London, entitled 'Transgender: Time to Change', which might have provided a platform for critical voices. Unfortunately, it was cancelled because of pressure from transgender lobbyists (Green, 2011).

There are attempts to censor all expressions of dissent towards malestream transgender ideology and to prohibit speaking platforms to those seen as heretics. This campaign against free speech is particularly directed against the burgeoning of an online radical feminist movement that is incisively critical of transgenderism. This includes feminists who operate under their own names and a far greater number who use pseudonyms, keenly aware of the severe harassment they face if their identities are revealed. These include Gallus Mag from GenderTrender (GenderTrender, n.d.b), and Dirt from the blog, The Dirt from Dirt, Change your World, Not your Body (Dirt from Dirt, n.d.), and many other critical voices.

An indication of the campaign being waged against feminist critics by transgender activists is the way that I have been prohibited from speaking not just on this issue, but on any issue at all. I was disinvited from a major feminist conference, 'Feminism in London' in November 2011, which, subsequently, did not take place because of concerns about offending transgenders. I was banned from speaking at a feminist conference in July 2012 in London, which had to take place at a secret venue, after a campaign of vilification by transgender activists (Jeffreys, 2012a). But this suppression of debate cannot continue indefinitely, since there is mounting interest in airing the contro-versy more publicly. Indeed, in early 2013, the issue exploded into public view as a result of an article in the *Observer* newspaper in the UK by col-umnist Julie Burchill, which was critical of the harassment of her colleague Suzanne Moore by transgender activists (Young, 2013). Burchill's piece was censored and removed from the website, only to be posted on many other websites sympathetic to her critique. Transgenderism was in the public eye and this time it was clear the practice was no longer beyond dispute. This book, therefore, is timely.

The idea and practices of gender have the potential to hurt many. In transgenderism the hurt can take several forms. People who feel that their 'gender' does not fit their bodies may suffer psychological hurts, and they then get physically 'hurt' by the medical profession that diagnoses and treats them. They are further hurt after treatment when they find themselves mar-ginalised and excluded, and some may even consider that they have made a mistake that cannot be easily rectified. This book goes further than other lit-erature on the topic, by exploring the wider social and political context and implications of the phenomenon of transgenderism. It looks at others who are hurt too, such as the wives who find their husbands now consider them-selves to be women; lesbian partners whose lesbianism is thrown into doubt when their girlfriends become 'men'; and the mothers who grieve for their lost daughters or sons. All these categories of persons who are hurt by trans-genderism are women, and this is the case whether the aspirants are male or female. Transgenderism hurts lesbian communities, which are fractured over the entryism of men who transgender, and the disappearance of their mem-bers to the chemically and surgically constructed heterosexuality that trans-genderism offers to increasing numbers of lesbians. The feminist movement, too, is harmed as transgender activists and theorists savagely criticise feminism and seek to destroy women-only spaces and services by their entryism. The success of the destabilising campaigns against feminism and the women-only principle depends upon confusion about what 'gender' means.

Gender and women's equality

Transgenderism cannot exist without a notion of essential 'gender'. Feminist critics argue that the concept of 'gender identity' is founded upon stereo-types of gender, and, in international law, gender stereotypes are recognised as being in contradiction to the interests of women (Hausman, 1995; Jeffreys, 2005; Raymond, 1994). The United Nations Convention on the Elimination of all Forms of Discrimination Against Women (CEDAW) (1979) was drawn up before the language of gender and the idea of 'gender identity' came to dominate international law discourse and to stand in for women as a sex category. It spoke instead of 'stereotyped roles' and recognised these stereotypes as the basis for discrimination against women. Article 5 says that States Parties should take

> all appropriate measures [to] modify the social and cultural patterns of conduct of men and women, with a view to achieving the elimination of prejudice and customary and all other practices which are based on the idea of the inferiority or the superiority of either of the sexes or on stereotyped roles for men and women.
>
> *(CEDAW, 1979: Article 5)*

The idea of 'gender identity' relies on stereotypes for its meaning and is in direct conflict with the understanding in CEDAW that such stereotypes are profoundly harmful to women.

The term 'gender' itself is problematic. It was first used in a sense that was not simply about grammar by sexologists – the scientists of sex such as John Money in the 1950s and 1960s – who were involved in normalising intersex infants. They used the term to mean the behavioural characteristics they considered most appropriate for persons of one or other biological sex. They applied the concept of gender when deciding upon the sex category into which those infants who did not have clear physical indications of one biological sex or another should be placed (Hausman, 1995). Their purpose was not progressive. These were conservative men who believed that there should be clear differences between the sexes and sought to create distinct sex categories through their projects of social engineering. Unfortunately, the term was adopted by some feminist theorists in the 1970s, and by the late 1970s was commonly used in academic feminism to indicate the difference between biological sex and those characteristics that derived from politics and not biology, which they called 'gender' (Haig, 2004).

Before the term 'gender' was adopted, the term more usually used to describe these socially constructed characteristics was 'sex roles'. The word 'role' connotes a social construction and was not susceptible to the degeneration that has afflicted the term 'gender' and enabled it to be wielded so effectively by transgender activists. As the term 'gender' was adopted more extensively by feminists, its meaning was transformed to mean not just the socially constructed behaviour associated with biological sex, but the system of male power and women's subordination itself, which became known as the 'gender hierarchy' or 'gender order' (Connell, 2005; Mackinnon, 1989). Gradually, older terms to describe this system, such as male domination, sex class and sex caste went out of fashion, with the effect that direct identification of the agents responsible for the subordination of women – men – could no longer be named. Gender, as a euphemism, disappeared men as agents in male violence against women, which is now commonly referred to as 'gender violence'. Increasingly, the term 'gender' is used, in official forms and legislation, for instance, to stand in for the term 'sex' as if 'gender' itself is biological, and this usage has overwhelmed the feminist understanding of gender.

Sex caste

In this book I have chosen to use the term 'sex caste' to describe the political system in which women are subordinated to men on the basis of their biology. Feminists have disagreed over whether women's condition of subordination is best referred to in terms of 'caste' or 'class'. Those who use the concept of women as a 'sex class', such as Kate Millett, are referencing their experience in left-wing politics and see the idea of 'class' as offering the possibility of revolution (Millett, 1972). Millett did, however, use the term caste as well, speaking of women's 'sexual caste system' (Millett, 1972: 275). If women are in a subordinate class in relation to men, as the working class is in relation to the bourgeoisie, then women's revolution can be conceptualised as overthrowing the power of men in such a way that sex class ceases to have meaning and will disappear as a meaningful category (Wittig, 1992). It also implies, as in left theory, that women's revolution requires the recognition by women of their 'sex' class status as the basis for political action. Nonetheless, the term sex class can be problematic because it implies that women could move out of their 'class', in the same way that individual working class people could change their class position by becoming embourgeoised. The term 'caste', on the other hand, is useful for this book because it encapsulates the way in which women are placed into a subordinate caste status for their lifetime (see Burris, 1973). Women may change their economic class status with upward mobility, but they remain women unless they elect to transgender and claim membership in the superior sex caste. Both of these terms can be useful in articulating the condition of women, but the term 'caste' offers a particular advantage in relation to studying transgenderism. The very existence of transgenderism on the part of women demonstrates the stickiness of caste subordination. The marks of caste remain attached to females unless they claim that they are really 'men', and only a very significant social transformation will enable change in this respect.

Postmodern and queer theorists share with transgender theorists the idea that 'gender' is a moveable feast that can be moved into and out of, swapped and so forth. Gender, used in this sense, disappears the fixedness of sex, the biological basis that underlies the relegation of females to their sex caste. Female infants are identified by biology at birth and placed into a female sex caste, which apportions them lifelong inferior status. The preference for biologically male children and the femicide of female infants, for instance, which has created a great inequality in the sex ratio in India and other countries, is based on sex and not 'gender'. Female foetuses are aborted and female infants are killed because of sex, not 'gender' discrimination (Pande, 2006). Foetuses do not have 'gender' or 'gender identity', because the forces of a woman-hating culture have not had a chance to affect the way they understand themselves. The inferior sex caste status of women is assigned with reference to their biology, and it is through their biology that their subordination is enforced and maintained through rape, impregnation and forced childbearing. Women do not pass in and out of wearing 'women's' clothing, as cross-dressers may do, indeed they may reject such clothing as inferiorising, but still suffer violence and discrimination as women. Though individual women may be successful in roles more usually arrogated to men, they are likely to be treated as interlopers and receive sexual harassment, as happened to the Australian Prime Minister Julia Gillard (Summers, 2013). Her caste status was continually thrown in her face by hostile male commentators, politicians and cartoonists. Women do not decide at some time in adulthood that they would like other people to understand them to be women, because being a woman is not an 'identity'. Women's experience does not resemble that of men who adopt the 'gender identity' of being female or being women in any respect. The idea of 'gender identity' disappears biology and all the experiences that those with female biology have of being reared in a caste system based on sex. Only one book-length critique of transgenderism was written in second wave feminism, Janice Raymond's deservedly well-known tour de force, *The Transsexual Empire* (1994, first published 1979). She usefully sums up the difference between feminist understandings of women and those of men who transgender thus:

> We know that we are women who are born with female chromosomes and anatomy, and that whether or not we were socialized to be so-called normal women, patriarchy has treated and will treat us like women. Transsexuals have not had this same history. No man can have the history of being born and located in this culture as a woman. He can have the history of *wishing* to be a woman and of *acting* like a woman, but this gender experience is that of a transsexual, not of a woman. Surgery may confer the artifacts of outward and inward female organs but it cannot confer the history of being born a woman in this society.
>
> *(Raymond, 1994: 114) (emphasis in original)*

Are women a figment of men's imagination?

Men have been adjudicating on what women are, and how they should behave, for millennia through the institutions of social control such as religion, the medical profession, psychoanalysis, the sex industry (Millett, 1972). Feminists have fought to remove the definition of what a woman is from these masculine institutions and develop their own understandings. Claims to the 'right' to self define 'gender', subject womanhood to men's power to define once again. The major task of feminist theory was to bring women out from under the weight of men's definitions and theories. Feminists developed what has been called 'feminist standpoint theory' to describe a new form of knowledge about women, that which is formed out of women's experience as an oppressed group and refined through struggle and collective process (Harding (ed.), 2004). The very basis of feminism is this declaration of independence, the rejection of men's 'knowledge' about women and the privileging of our own. Men's ideas about what women are have been formed from their ruling caste position, and have assigned women characteristics that would most advantage their masters, as well as justify men's rule over them. They do not represent 'truth' but have been promoted as if they were, with the backing of science and patriarchal views of biology. It is remarkable, therefore, that men's views of what women are, in the form of transgender ideology, have gained any traction whatsoever in any branch of feminist theory. But, as I shall explain in Chapter 2 on transgenderism and feminism, they have, to the point where men who have transgendered are invited as keynote speakers to conferences on women's experience.

Beyond all else, transgenderism on the part of men can be seen as a ruthless appropriation of women's experience and existence. The men who claim womanhood do not have any experience of being women, and thus should not have the right to speak as 'women'. Indeed, these men are often very conservative and hypermasculine. The American transgender helicopter pilot, Bob Tur, explains this point well:

> Well actually true transgenders do hypermasculine things. Kristin Beck the Navy Seal is not atypical of what's going on. There are a lot of airline pilots, a lot of military pilots. I've known all kinds of pilots, I've known spies, I've done quasi-military flights overseas. So, um, its not, its not atypical. It's a fairly standard thing. The typical transgender tends to be 30 IQ points above average, they tend to be left handed, they tend to be fairly conservative, they've been married, have children. And they, you know, in some cases have hypermasculine traits.
>
> *(Tur, 2013)*

Tur's interesting confessions suggest that there is nothing progressive about men's fantasies of being women, quite the reverse.

Definition of terms

The meaning of the term transgender is constantly being extended. Before the 1990s, the term used to refer to someone who wanted to change their 'sex' was transsexual. In the 1990s the term transgender was commonly adopted to refer to those persons who did not want to go so far as having surgery for the removal of their secondary sexual characteristics but wanted to change their 'gender', generally understood as appearance markers such as clothing. By the late 1990s, the term transsexualism was falling out of favour, and the term transgenderism had been adopted in the academy and in outreach services to refer to those would previously have been considered transsexuals, to the new category who wished to change 'gender' without surgery, and even to effeminate gay men and cross-dressers. It has also transmogrified into a very general term indeed, to include occasional cross-dressers or even those who are seen as not having a 'gender'. The development of this term, and its fast change in meaning, has been so profound as to allow arguments by some transactivists that homosexuals are themselves simply a subcategory of transgenders (Whittle *et al.*, 2007: 14). In the last decade the term transgender has been adopted into policy documents and into the law.

Transgenderism has become an umbrella term for a great variety of persons who are uncomfortable with traditional gender roles, but who, without a feminist analysis that gender itself is the problem, seek to act out their discomfort through adopting elements of the opposite gender stereotype. The increasing vagueness of the category has in no way impeded the swift adoption of the term transgender, and the idea of the 'right' of transgenders to exercise their 'gender expression', within state legislatures and regional forums such as the European Union. All the forms in which the term is used depend upon the idea of an essential gender that can be played with, or 'transed', but not dispensed with, and so all forms of transgenderism are equally problematic from the point of view of feminist theorists. They all give oxygen to a concept, gender, which forms the foundation and justification for the subordination of women. This book will seek to keep up with all the transmogrifications of transgenderism, while pointing out the harms that issue from it.

The physical transformations created by hormones and surgery do not change the biological sex of the persons upon whom they are visited. For this reason, in this volume, persons of the male sex who transgender are referred to as men who transgender, or male-bodied transgenders, and those of the female sex as women who transgender, or female-bodied transgenders, in order to indicate their biological sex. The more common terms male-to-female (MTF) and female-to-male (FTM) are not used here because they give the mistaken impression that sex can be changed when, in fact, it cannot.

Transgenderism is not connected with intersexuality. Persons who are intersex are born with 'a reproductive or sexual anatomy that doesn't seem to fit the typical definitions of female or male' (ISNA, n.d.). Intersex activists do not campaign for sex-reassignment surgery, and are often incisively critical of it, on the grounds that it has been traditionally employed to cut intersex infants up to fit one sex caste category or another, with harmful effects on their functioning (Dreger, 1998). Some transgender online personalities proclaim that they are intersex to make out that they are not biologically male, but intersexuality and transgenderism are different phenomena (ISNA, n.d.). Intersexuality has a biological basis, whereas this book will argue that 'gender identity' is a mental condition.

Pronouns

Pronoun use is a great concern of persons who transgender. They wish other people, including their wives, partners and children, to call them by their new, adopted pronouns. The disagreement over pronoun use is a political one. The masculine pronoun may no longer, acceptably, be used as if it were generic and included women, for instance. I have chosen to use pronouns that indicate the biological sex of the persons whose work is discussed here for a number of reasons. The first is that the biological sex of transgender persons does not change and use of the pronoun of origin indicates this. This is politically important, since it is useful for feminists to know the biological sex of those who claim to be women and promote prejudicial versions of what constitutes womanhood. Also, use by men of feminine pronouns conceals the masculine privilege bestowed upon them by virtue of having been placed in and brought up in the male sex caste. If men are addressed as 'she', then all this privilege, which affects their speaking position and may be crucial to their choice to be 'women' in the first place, is disappeared.

Another reason for adherence to pronouns that indicate biology is that, as a feminist, I consider the female pronoun to be an honorific, a term that conveys respect. Respect is due to women as members of a sex caste that have survived subordination and deserve to be addressed with honour. Men who transgender cannot occupy such a position. This argument is used by female partners of men who transgender in Chapter 4. They often find it impossible to accept that their husbands have become women, and cannot use pronouns for them that they understand to be specific to their own experience as women. As this book will argue, the perspectives of wives and female partners are important and should be respected. Also, sticking to the pronouns of origin avoids the difficulty of adjudicating on which men should be referred to as female, those who simply occasionally cross-dress, or those who take hormones, or those who undertake sex-reassignment surgery. Creating such distinctions is an odious task, and since they all retain male biology it is more straightforward to retain pronouns that indicate their sex. Also, persons who regret transgendering may decide upon a return to their pronouns of origin, or they may in some cases go back and forth a number of times with complex changes of pronoun at each turn. Use of the pronouns of origin avoids the need for potentially numerous changes over time.

Structure of the book

The two opening chapters of the book show how the idea of transgenderism developed and was able to gain traction from the mid-twentieth century onwards. Chapter 1 examines the construction of transgenderism by medical specialisms such as endocrinology, surgery and psychology. Chapter 2 analyses the factors that have enabled swathes of the feminist and lesbian and gay movements to support transgender rights, such as the development of queer and postmodern theory, which promoted the idea that there was really no such thing as 'woman' and that playing with and switching 'gender' was a transgressive practice. The third chapter 'Doing transgender: really hurting' examines the most immediately harmful impact of the construction of transgenderism. It will analyse the literature on the psychological and physical effects of transgender surgery and long-term hormone use on transgenders themselves. It will describe the harmful practices involved in transgender practice from breast binding to genital surgery, and repeated facial surgeries, and who profits from them.

The following chapters examine the social, political and legal effects of the construction of the phenomenon. Two chapters look at the harms to the wives, girlfriends and lesbian partners of transgenders, whose lives are substantially affected when their partners transition. Increasingly, women whose husbands have transgendered are speaking out and engaging in resistance. A majority of men who transgender (Lawrence, 2004) have histories of cross-dressing for sexual excitement, and these men are frequently married and have children before they make the decision to go further. The wives suffer from having their identities challenged by husbands who claim to be lesbians and may require their female partners to identify as lesbians too. Similarly, the lesbian partners of women who transgender have to redefine themselves as heterosexual women if they wish to remain in relationships with women who now see themselves as heterosexual men. In both cases, non-trans partners find themselves taking on considerable amounts of unpaid labour to support their trans partners, such as the need to be more feminine to help a lesbian partner feel more masculine. Partners have to provide unpaid nursing services, perform injections, arrange appointments, take their partners shopping, save up and pay for the surgeries. They have to manage exposure, or the need to, as they put it, remain in the closet about their partners' practice. They receive little support or acknowledgement for the psychological harm they endure, which some psychologists are now likening to post-traumatic stress. Another chapter details a very worrying effect of transgender activism and the lobbying of the medical profession, the transgendering of children.

The final two chapters examine the practical effects of the campaign for transgender rights for all women, including entry of men who transgender into women's toilets and prisons, and into women's spaces such as domestic violence refuges. Chapter 7, entitled 'A clash of rights' examines the way in which the demand for recognition in law of the 'right' to gender and to 'gender expression' constitutes a clash with the rights of women. This chapter will explore the ways in which the law is being changed in Western countries to accommodate 'gender rights' and the implications of these changes. One of the primary aims of transgender activist groups is to enable men who transgender to access 'gendered spaces' such as women's festivals, women's refuges, sexual violence services, women's sheltered housing, toilets and prisons. These spaces have been set up to service the interests of women as a subordinate group, to allow for social and political organisation separate from male control, for privacy and security from men's violence. The determination to enter these spaces by men who consider themselves transgender has led to considerable stress within women's communities. In some cases this has led to the suspension of women's festivals or abandonment of attempts to create women's centres, in ways that are very problematic for the communities of women that they were intended to serve.

Reading against the grain

There is very little critical literature about transgenderism that could form the foundation for this book. Since Janice Raymond's groundbreaking *The Transsexual Empire* in 1979, there has been an almost complete absence of feminist critical work, amid an avalanche of research and writing that takes a positive, if not celebratory, approach to the topic. For this reason it has been necessary to read the celebratory or supportive literature that does exist 'against the grain', that is to extract the copious evidence of the harm of transgenderism that is plain even in that which purports to promote the practice. As well as reading against the grain, I have used analogies in two chapters, and three key interviews carried out by Lorene Gottschalk, in order to reveal what the academic and popular literature does not.

In two chapters I have used analogies to show similarities between transgenderism and either homosexuality or eugenics, with the objective of demonstrating the harms amid a desert of any form of criticism. For the first chapter on the historical and sexological construction of transgenderism,

I found it very helpful to make an analogy with the construction of homo-sexuality as a category. In the absence of critical approaches to the construc-tion of transgenderism in academic or popular literature, this offered a useful way in, especially since the two practices are very connected in obvious ways. Similarly, I used an analogy in the chapter on the transgendering of chil-dren, likening it to the practice of sexual surgeries that were carried out by those inspired by the ideas of eugenics, in order to highlight the harm in the absence of any critical literature.

I had to develop my criticism of transgender theory without any help-ful pointers from other critical literature because published material of this kind does not exist. But the growing critical commentary by online radical feminists has been very useful in this respect. I am grateful to my sisters both for the factual information they provide on websites and blogs, and for their theoretical contributions. It is about time that academic feminism caught up with the bloggers of the new wave of radical feminism and produced more critical writing and research.

For Chapter 3, which deals with the harms of transgenderism to transgen-ders themselves, two interviews were conducted. There is very little critical literature about the process of transgendering from those who have gone through it, because the problem of transgender regret, in which men and women speak and write about de-transitioning back to their original sex because of their profound dissatisfaction, has only recently been moving into the public domain. Two interviews were conducted for this book with per-sons who have de-transitioned – a man, Walt Heyer, and a woman, Heath Russell.

Another interview was also conducted to provide first-hand evidence of the harms of men's practice of transgenderism to their wives. Collections of the accounts of their experience by wives and mothers of transgenders, and individual biographies by women whose husbands and male partners have transgendered, though not intended to be critical of the practice nonetheless contain a great deal of material that demonstrates the ways in which it hurts them severely. I have used this material here. There is one biography of a wife who is unequivocally critical and this has been very useful (Benvenuto, 2012). The interview with the female partner of a man who has transgendered was helpful in gaining a picture of her experience from someone with a critical eye and a developed critique of the phenomenon. All three interviewees used in this book were sourced through the online networks that are beginning to form of those critical of the practice. They have been a vital resource in the absence of critical literature.

There is beginning to be interesting research carried out on women who transgender and their partners by feminist academics, which has been useful to Chapter 5 of this book (Brown, 2007, 2009, 2010; Pfeffer, 2008, 2010). This work does not state that it takes a critical approach and, indeed, evinces no negative views regarding the practice of transgenderism itself, but does offer most useful information towards understanding the harmful impact of the transgendering of lesbians on their female partners. It may be that this issue is of concern to feminist and lesbian feminist academics because it is happening in their communities and is close to home.

In relation to the law on transgender rights, I discovered no critical literature and no literature that offered caveats as to the potential clash with women's rights. In this area much work needs to be done. There is also no literature on the impact of transgender inclusion in women's services and spaces, apart from that of Lorene Gottschalk, which is used in Chapter 8. There is a need for a great deal more research in these areas. To supplement the scanty critical literature that exists on several of the themes in the book, I have had recourse to the websites and blogs of transgender activists themselves, which have been a rich source for showing the rapid development of the transgender rights movement and some of its more bizarre outer reaches.

The importance of social construction

To place all of these issues in context, it is first necessary to examine how the phenomenon of transgenderism was constructed, historically and politically. This is the task of Chapter 1. I am very aware that new generations of feminist, lesbian and gay activists and thinkers may find the idea of social construction difficult to accept. The idea that homosexuality and transgenderism are innate has become quite dominant today, whereas at the time of second wave feminism, the understanding that gender and sexuality were socially constructed was a commonplace. This book is premised on the understanding that transgenderism is a social construct, and for this reason I have chosen to deal with the issue of social construction in some detail.

1

THE CONSTRUCTION OF TRANSGENDERISM

This book argues that transgenderism is a social construction of the mid to late twentieth century. The concept of 'transgenderism' was, as the anthropologist David Valentine puts it, 'institutionalised' in the 1990s (Valentine, 2007). Since that time, a new transgender history has been created to support the ideas and practices of transgender activists. This new history states that there have always been people who were essentially 'transgenders', throughout history (Prosser, 1998; Stryker, 2008). Transgender persons, these activists say, were aided in the twentieth century by the development of medical specialisms that enabled them to 'come out' of the transgender closet and realise their need to change sex. This chapter will contest this version of history, a history that only makes sense if transgenderism is understood to be based upon an essential quality, that which some sexologists call the 'feminine essence' idea (Dreger, 2008). If that premise is rejected, it is necessary to explain how the phenomenon of transgenderism has come about, and this chapter will attempt this task. I will argue that, far from being a constant in history and across cultures, transgenderism is a quite recent construction. This chapter will focus on men who transgender because the ideology and practices of transgenderism were invented by men. While women formed a small minority of those seeking to transgender before the 1990s, they have become an increasing proportion since that time, and have sought to slot themselves into a set of ideas constructed by male scientists of sex, and the men who were the main demanders of sex reassignment (Jeffreys, 2003). The differences between men and women's transgender behaviour will be considered in detail in a later chapter.

Origin of the term 'transgender'

The term transsexual was coined in the 1950s to describe those persons who wished to change their sex, and popularised by the endocrinologist Harry Benjamin in his book, *The Transsexual Phenomenon* (1966). The term transgender was coined by the male – and according to his protestations, heterosexual – cross-dresser Virginia Prince, who sought to distinguish himself from those identified as transsexuals, and to create a more acceptable face for a practice previously understood as a 'paraphilia' – a form of sexual fetishism (Prince, 2005b). Prince's adoption of the term was part of what I will call here the 'move to gender', in which both cross-dressing and transsexualism came to be understood as expressions of an internal or essential gender, rather than simply being hobbies carried out for sexual excitement. The term 'transgender' was then normalised through the queer politics of the 1990s, when it was adopted to convey a wide meaning encompassing all those who were seen as engaging in behaviour most usually allotted to the opposite sex, from butch lesbians to cross-dressing, gay, prostituted men. Presently, the term transgender is used in common parlance to refer to those who would once have been called 'transsexual', a word that is no longer much in use. This chapter will seek to explain why this most important change in terminology has taken place. The term transgender is used in this book in the way it is most commonly used in the present, to refer to those who consider themselves to have a 'gender identity' that differs from what, in male-supremacist societies, is associated with their biological sex.

The construction of the homosexual

The idea that transgenderism is socially constructed will be controversial. In transgender ideology, persons who transgender are seen as being in possession of an 'essence' – consisting of clothing or habits – of the 'gender' more usually associated with the opposite sex. This essence is understood to be the result either of an accident of biology, or as the product of some other mysterious and not usually identifiable process, and therefore 'natural'. For instance, in her book *Second Skins*, Jay Prosser specifically rejects the constructionist approach, arguing that transgender persons existed prior to and outside the forces of construction that I shall outline here (Prosser, 1998). Accusations of 'transphobia' and 'transmisogyny' are regularly directed at anyone who questions the essentialist discourse that such transgender activists subscribe to. But, interestingly, similar accusations of 'homophobia' were not, and are not, directed at those lesbian and gay historians and researchers who argue that the 'homosexual' is a social construction. The idea that the homosexual is not someone innately destined to be sexually attracted to their own sex is also controversial in large parts of the gay community, but has not led to such vitriol and invective. The invention of the homosexual is instructive in demonstrating how the 'transgender' also came to exist, because the idea that there is such an entity as a transgender person follows the script for the construction of the concept of the 'homosexual' by male sexologists, or scientists of sex, in the nineteenth century.

The construction of transgenderism in the late twentieth century resembles, in important respects, the construction of the homosexual. The 1960s and 1970s were the glory days of social constructionism in the social sciences. Lesbian and gay theorists and historians, educated in the values of those times, argued that the idea of the homosexual, as a particular kind of person who was destined by a congenital abnormality to be exclusively attracted to others of the same sex, was in fact a social construction (Mackintosh, 1968; Weeks, 1977). The social constructionist approach was not without its critics in lesbian and gay academia. There were some who argued that the construction of homosexuality owed something to biology as well as to culture (Dynes, 1992). Some of the constructionists themselves recognised that individual homosexuals did not experience their identities as socially constructed, so there must be some recognition in social constructionist theory of the cogency of personal experience (Epstein, 1992). But for most lesbian and gay academics it was well understood that history, culture and politics constructed the homosexual.

There are disagreements as to when this construction primarily took place: in the late seventeenth century, when homosexual men gathered in Molly houses and clubs in London, as Mary Mackintosh (1968) argued; or in the nineteenth century, as Michel Foucault (1978) argued. However, it is clear that it was in the nineteenth century that significant social institutions became involved in the construction of homosexuals as a distinct category of persons. The homosexual was constructed, in this understanding, from two main sources, the law and medicine, both of which, I will argue here, have been fundamentally important to the construction of transgenderism too. Lesbian and gay scholars explain that in the early part of the nineteenth century sexual behaviour was still regulated by the church courts (Weeks, 1977). There was no concept of the homosexual as such, but particular sexual practices were seen to be unacceptable, notably, in this case, sodomy. As church courts went into desuetude, the criminal law took over as a regulator of correct sexual practice. Thus, in the late nineteenth century in the UK, the Criminal Law Amendment Act of 1885 was promulgated, which specifically made homosexual male sexual behaviour illegal. Under this legislation, Oscar Wilde was prosecuted in the 1890s, and his trial was widely publicised. All of this helped to crystallise the idea of the homosexual. In the same period the science of sexology took over from religion to provide prescriptions of acceptable and unacceptable sexual behaviour.

The first detailed articulation within sociology of the idea that homosexuality was not a 'condition' but a 'social role' was by the lesbian sociologist Mary Mackintosh in her path-breaking article, 'The Homosexual Role'

(1968). She applied understandings from labelling theory to homosexuality, and argued that conceptualising the homosexual as a certain kind of person who suffered from a condition operated as a form of social control, which 'helps to provide a clear-cut, publicised, and recognizable threshold between permissible and impermissible behaviour' (Mackintosh, 1968: 183). Mackintosh explained that, in relation to homosexuality, '[t]he creation of a specialized, despised and punished role of homosexuality keeps the bulk of society pure' (Mackintosh, 1968: 184). She says that psychologists and psychiatrists take part in the labelling process in relation to homosexuality and thus in the 'mechanisms of social control'. This way of seeing homosexuality is useful for understanding transgenderism too. The creation of the transgender role can be seen as a way of separating off unacceptable gender behaviour, which might threaten the system of male domination and female subordination, from correct gender behaviour, which is seen as suitable for persons of a particular biological sex. In the case of homosexuality, the effect is to shore up the idea of exclusive and natural heterosexuality; and, in the case of transgenderism, the naturalness of sex roles.

Mackintosh points out another aspect of the homosexual role that is relevant to the 'role' of the transgender, which is that 'homosexuals themselves welcome and support the notion that homosexuality is a condition' (Mackintosh, 1968: 184). This is because it removes the possibility of 'drifting back into normality' and 'removes the element of anxious choice'. Thus the homosexual, and perhaps the transgendered person today, can see themselves as acting in a way that is legitimate for them, and they can continue to behave in that way without 'rejecting the norms of the society'. Michel Foucault produced his own version of the social constructionist analysis in *The History of Sexuality: Volume 1*, asserting that, in the nineteenth century, the homosexual 'became a personage, a past, a case history, and a childhood, in addition to being a type of life, a life form, and a morphology' (Foucault, 1978: 43). When this book was translated into English in 1978, his ideas created a new wave of gay, social constructionist history and scholarship.

There was no outburst from other gay men and lesbians in the 1960s and 1970s that such social constructionist accounts of homosexuality were 'homophobic', but similar arguments about transgenderism today are attacked as 'transphobic'. Within the social sciences they were well accepted, and Mackintosh's analysis is now regarded as a classic in the field (see Stein, 1992). However, in relation to transgenderism over the last two decades, during which time the construction of this practice has been at its peak – with certain notable exceptions (Gottschalk, 2003; Hausman, 1995; Jeffreys, 2006, 2008) – there has been no such social constructionist analysis. This, in itself, presents a puzzle.

Similarities between the construction of homosexuality and the construction of transgenderism

One important reason why the social construction of homosexuality is instructive in understanding this process in relation to transgenderism is that the sexologists who were involved in creating the idea of the homosexual as a particular type of person in the late nineteenth and early twentieth centuries did not clearly distinguish homosexuality from what would later be understood as transvestism, transsexualism or transgenderism. A prime similarity in the sexological construction between the homosexual of the nineteenth century and the transgender person of today is that they are both understood as biologically determined to act in the way that they do. Henry Havelock Ellis's *Sexual Inversion* (1927, first published 1897) is a good example of this. Ellis, whose work included detailed consideration of the work and conclusions of the many sexologists and psychoanalysts who preceded him, stated that homosexuality, or sexual inversion was a 'congenital abnormality' (Ellis, 1927: 318). He considered that the abnormality arose as a result of the 'latent organic bisexuality' of each sex (Ellis, 1927: 310). Ellis included in this understanding cross-dressing by men, which he called Eonism, after the Chevalier D'Eon. In his opinion, Eonism, or transvestism, was separate but under the same umbrella and created by the same biology. The invention of the term 'transvestite' to describe a practice different from homosexuality is attributed to the sexologist Magnus Hirschfeld, in a publication in 1910 (Blanchard, 2005).

The other significant similarity is that both the homosexual of sexological discourse and the 'transgender' person of today are seen as biologically destined to adopt the behaviour culturally associated, at a particular time in history, with the opposite sex. The 'inverted person', Ellis explains, had 'subtle approximations to the opposite sex … both on the physical and the psychic side' (Ellis, 1927: 310). Another similarity is that there is little evidence to support the belief in biological determinism in either case. With no scientific evidence to support his belief, Ellis simply made an assertion about the existence of male or female 'germs': 'at conception the organism is provided with about 50 per cent of male germs and about 50 per cent of female germs, and that, as development proceeds, either the male or the female germs assume the upper hand, until in the maturely developed individual only a few aborted germs of the opposite sex are left' (Ellis, 1927: 311). In the homosexual, he considered, something goes wrong with the process 'on account of some peculiarity in the number or character of either the original male germs or female germs' with the result 'being a person who is more fitted for the exercise of the inverted than of the normal sexual impulse' (Ellis, 1927: 310). This person may show no physical signs of inversion, but the congenital abnormality may be evident in behaviour. Such behaviour may include, in Ellis's view, being left-handed, having a high feminine voice, feminine handwriting or, in women, masculine handwriting. Many of the male cases he recounts showed the inability to whistle or, in female cases, the ability to 'whistle admirably' (Ellis, 1927: 291). Ellis argued that 'inverted women' also expressed behaviours more usually associated with the opposite sex, that is they 'frequently, though not always, convey an impression of mannishness or boyishness' (Ellis, 1927: 251).

Historically, those who loved and engaged in sexual relationships with persons of the same sex were likely to engage also in cross-dressing and cross-gendered behaviour, camp, drag and effeminacy in relation to male homosexuals, and butchness and masculinity for lesbians. Mary Mackintosh quotes a description from 1729 of the way that homosexual men behaved in Molly houses where 'members of the clubs adopt(ed) all the small vanities natural to the feminine sex to such an extent that they try to speak, walk, chatter, shriek and scold as women do, aping them as well in other aspects' (quoted in Mackintosh, 1968: 188). The expression of behaviour seen as 'belonging' to the other sex was an ordinary, if not the major, form in which homosexuality was practised. For this reason, lesbian and gay historians have routinely included those exhibiting this behaviour in gay history. As John D'Emilio put it in his 1983 history of 'sexual communities' in the United States from 1940–1970: 'During the first two decades of the twentieth century, male homosexual transvestites and their ordinary-looking comrades made their liaisons in saloons and clubs scattered through the least respectable parts of town' (D'Emilio, 1998, first published 1983: 12). His book was published before transgender activists and academics made a land grab for effeminate gay men and butch lesbians to be included in transgender as opposed to 'gay' history. D'Emilio characterised drag balls as being a part of gay history too, though they would likely be seen as expressions of 'transgenderism' today (D'Emilio, 1998: 12).

In the work of transgender activists and theorists today, those engaged in same-sex relationships in previous historical periods, and who cross-dressed, are separated out from the category homosexual and placed in the category 'transgender'. Jay Prosser, for instance, identifies the character Stephen, in the novel *The Well of Loneliness*, as an archetypal transgender (Prosser, 1998), though she has been characterised as a lesbian by lesbian historians (Doan, 2001; Newton, 1984). A more recent person to have been 'transnapped' by Prosser and other transgender activists is Brandon Teena, the young woman who dressed sometimes in male attire and was murdered in Nebraska in 1993. Prosser says that it was quite wrong for the media to identify her as either female or as a lesbian, and shares the outrage of the transactivist group Transsexual Menace, which formed in reaction to this perceived 'queering' of transgender experience. The anthropologist, David Valentine, on the other hand, says that 'the unquestioned inclusion of people like ... Brandon Teena into the encompassing category of "transgender" produces a representational colonisation of those lives' (Valentine, 2007: 229). Carolyn Gage, the US lesbian feminist playwright, has written eloquently about her concerns at the transnapping of Brandon (Gage, 2010). She explains that crucial information is missing from the movie *Boys Don't Cry* – made about Brandon – and from the writings by transgender activists that heroise her. The information includes the facts of her severe sexual abuse for years in her female childhood by a male relative. Gage draws similarities between Brandon's mental health problems, her eating disorder and her identification with a male abuser with the experiences of other girls sexually abused in similar ways. All of this makes her more typical of a young female abuse survivor, she says, than of a man.

I will argue that the category 'transgender' was created by forces of male power, i.e. that it was created not just socially but politically. David Valentine says that the task of his research on the development of transgenderism was to investigate the 'set of power relations whereby' new categorisations are created and people are forced to adapt to 'the political, social, cultural, and economic processes which underlie such power relations; and what effects such requirements have' (Valentine, 2007: 243). I will seek to identify the forces of male power that constructed transgenderism as a category separate from homosexuality in the twentieth century.

Medicine creates transgenderism

Transgenderism, when understood as the possibility of physically changing sex, only became thinkable as the result of developments in medicine in the twentieth century. In her social constructionist account of the emergence of transgenderism, Bernice Hausman explains that this association has not been well understood, as

> these links between medical technology, medical practice, and the advent of 'sex change' in the twentieth century have been ignored by most scholars who study the subject, who more usually understand transsexualism as representative of a transhistorical desire of some human subjects to be the other sex.
>
> *(Hausman, 1995: 2)*

Endocrinology was the medical specialism that played the most significant role, and the two most influential doctors in advocacy for sex changes in the mid-century were the endocrinologists Harry Benjamin and Christian

Hamburger. Bernice Hausman argues that it was the 'public dissemination of scientific knowledge of the human endocrine system' that enabled 'certain human subjects' to 'understand themselves as members of the "other" sex' (Hausman, 1995: 26). Endocrinology, she explains, 'provided medicine with the tools to enforce sexual dimorphism – not only to examine and describe it' (Hausman, 1995: 38). Endocrinologists developed expertise with hormones, which were originally, in the first few decades of the twentieth century, introduced into the bodies of men who wanted to improve their virility by the insertion of goat testes. Later, artificial hormones that mimicked the natural hormones produced by the human body proved more efficacious. These hormones were used on intersex patients whom the sexologists considered should be made to resemble more closely the sex category into which the doctors had placed them at birth. They were then used on patients who wanted to change sex. Another medical specialism needed to be at a particular stage of development to enable the plastic surgery to be performed – and this was anaesthesia (Stryker, 2008). The third medical specialism that enabled transgenderism was plastic surgery itself.

The development of these medical specialisms was so important to the construction of transgenderism that the historian of sexuality, Vern Bullough, comments that he 'once presented a paper', in 1973, suggesting that transsexualism might be 'iatrogenic', that is a health problem created by medicine itself. It might exist, he says, 'simply because surgeons could now do sex changes not possible before' (Bullough, 2006: 4). Hausman explains that when there was public knowledge about medical advances and technological capabilities, individuals could then name themselves as 'the appropriate subjects of particular medical interventions, and thereby participate in the construction of themselves as patients' (Hausman, 1995: 23). These medical developments enabled the construction of the idea of 'gender identity'.

The demanders

It would be wrong, Hausman argues, to see the patients who sought sex changes as the passive victims of the treatments; rather 'transsexual subjects' played a defining role in the construction of transgenderism, through 'demanding' surgery and drugs that they considered might help them in their aspirations (Hausman, 1995). She says that it is 'important' to 'underscore the agency of transsexual subjects insofar as they forced the medical profession to respond to their demands' (Hausman, 1995: 110). Hausman sees the alliance of transgenders with doctors as the defining element in the construction of transgenderism. In 1980 it had led to the inclusion in the *Diagnostic and Statistical Manual* of gender identity disorder, which paved the way for treatment (ibid.). It recognised their desires as a form of mental illness caused by being possessed of an anomalous, but essential, 'gender'.

The identity of transgenders, therefore, depended on the medical profession, and it was their demand for surgery that distinguished them from the other categories of sexual deviance that sexologists were involved in diagnosing and regulating, such as homosexuality. Whereas homosexuality is simply a form of behaviour that anyone can adopt, for the vast majority of its acolytes, transgenderism represents a pilgrimage towards a goal that can only be realised through doctors because transsexuals 'needed the services of professional physicians to achieve their goals' (ibid.). As the historian of sexuality, Vern Bullough, points out, these medical developments 'forced medicine and transsexuals to have a close alliance in the 1960s and 70s' at the same time as 'gays, lesbians, bisexuals, transvestites, and later even intersex individuals' were seeking to extricate themselves from medical control (Bullough, 2006: 4).

The demanders were overwhelmingly male, though there was always a sprinkling of women among those demanding sex change, including Reed Erikson, a rich American woman who was able, through the Erikson Foundation, to fund and influence sexological research on transgenderism (Meyerowitz, 2002). Before the most recent expansion of the category, the sexologists estimated there to be three men demanding surgery to one woman. This ratio remains largely in place, with applicants for the UK Gender Recognition Certificate under the 2004 Gender Recognition Act being in precisely the same ratio (Ministry of Justice, 2012). The male demanders fell into two categories: homosexual men who felt unable to love men while remaining in a male body; and men who were overwhelmingly heterosexual, and transgendered as a climax to their interest in cross-dressing (Blanchard, 2005).

A wave of publicity that alerted men to the possibilities open to them occurred in relation to the sex change of Christine Jorgensen, who falls into the first category. The historian of transgenderism, Joanne Meyerowitz, states 'In the 1950s Jorgensen made sex change a household term' (Meyerowitz, 2002: 51). Jorgensen's case generated huge media interest in the United States. In his *Transgender History*, the transgender activist Susan Stryker says that 'Jorgensen's fame was a watershed event in transgender history' (Stryker, 2008: 49). Jorgensen was homosexual, and said in his memoirs that his 'emotions were either those of a woman or a homosexual' (Meyerowitz, 2008: 54). His preference was to consider himself a woman, perhaps because he considered homosexuality immoral: 'it was a thing deeply alien to my religious attitudes' (quoted in Meyerowitz, 2008: 57). In a letter to a psychiatrist in 1950/1951, Jorgensen described himself as a 'homosexual' with a 'large amount of femininity' (quoted in Meyerowitz, 2008: 59). Within a few years both Jorgensen and the doctors who treated him would emphasise the difference between his condition and that of homosexuality, and stress that his problem was 'glandular' (Meyerowitz, 2008: 61). But early in his career, the concept of transgenderism had not been constructed with which Jorgensen could identify. Meyerowitz explains that it was Jorgensen's endocrinologist who told him that he was not homosexual but had a condition called 'transvestism', which was 'deep-rooted in all the cells' of his body (Meyerowitz, 2008: 66).

Opposition to transsexual surgery from psychiatrists

The idea of transsexualism as a condition that required treatment by hormones and surgery was not well accepted in these early years. Indeed, as Bullough points out, when Christine Jorgensen went public with his experience in the 1950s, a 'turf war' broke out in the medical profession about the correct treatment for men like him. The turf war was between those who dealt with the mind – and considered the fantasy of being a woman to be best treated by psychotherapy and surgery to be a 'mutilation'; and endocrinologists and surgeons – who considered that the best treatment was physical, in the alteration of the body (Bullough, 2006: 7). In a 1968 paper, the psychiatrist Donald Hayes Russell voiced his opposition to what he called 'sex conversion'. He referred to 'trans-sexualism' as a 'newly described abnormality', saying that '[t]raditionally, homosexuals and transvestites are known for their proclivities to act like their opposite sex. Differing from these conditions is the relatively newly described abnormality – that of "trans-sexualism"' (Russell, 1968: 355). He weighed into the controversy by saying that the condition 'is generally considered to be psychiatric, having its roots in early emotional development' but that 'some few observers', erroneously, 'entertain the notion of some constitutional mystique' (ibid.).

Today the 'feminine essence' theory is much more pervasive. But in the 1960s this idea had not taken hold, and Russell considered those seeking sex change to be delusional, with the transsexual hoping to 'really be transformed – through medical science – into something that he is not' (ibid.). Russell explained that there were extremely serious ethical issues involved in carrying out surgery on aspirants, because

> [p]hysicians generally consider it unethical to destroy or alter tissue except in the presence of disease or deformity. The interference with a person's natural procreative function entails definite moral tenets, by which not only physicians but also the general public are influenced.
> *(Russell, 1968: 356)*

He identified transsexual surgery as 'harm' and says '[t]he administration of physical harm as treatment for mental or behavioral problems – as corporeal punishment, lobotomy for unmanageable psychotics and sterilization of criminals – is abhorrent in our society' (ibid.). Moreover, he considered, physicians should be careful because they could be sued for malpractice. Little did he know at that time that these scruples would be so overwhelmingly overturned in the next few decades. Before long, the explanation of the causes and appropriate treatment for transgenderism had been effectively taken over by the patients themselves to suit their interests, and criticism of their schema had come to be seen as unacceptable hate speech.

Paul McHugh, another psychiatrist opposed to sex reassignment, was responsible for putting an end to sex-change operations at Johns Hopkins University in 1979. He explained his reasoning in an article in 1992 entitled 'Psychiatric Misadventures', one of which was accepting that those with troubles about 'gender' should have hormonal and surgical treatment (McHugh, 1992). He said he saw men who felt they were in the 'wrong body', 'not uncommonly'. He recommended that the patient's claim that his feeling is lifelong should be checked by speaking with those who knew him as a child, because it might not be accurate. Another problem was, he argued, that the 'feeling like a woman' was often based simply on sex stereotypes, 'something that woman physicians note immediately is a male caricature of women's attitudes and interests'(McHugh, 1992; 502). He expressed his frustration by comparing the recommendation of surgery for transgenders with interventions such as liposuction for those suffering the delusion that they are obese. 'We don't do liposuction on anorexics. Why amputate the genitals of these poor men?' (McHugh, 1992: 503). He also compared it with lobotomy, 'the most radical therapy ever encouraged by twentieth-century psychiatrists' and said that neither treatment resulted from 'critical reasoning or thoughtful assessments' (ibid.). He reiterated his opposition in 2004 saying, 'I have witnessed a great deal of damage from sex-reassignment ... We have wasted scientific and technical resources and damaged our professional credibility by collaborating with madness rather than trying to study, cure, and ultimately prevent it' (McHugh, 2004: 38). This kind of forthright opposition is rarely voiced in the twenty-first century, when transgenderism has become, as McHugh describes it, 'fashionable' (McHugh, 1992).

Transgenderism and cross-dressing

Apart from unhappy homosexuals such as Christine Jorgenson, the other major category of demanders derives from male, ostensibly heterosexual, cross-dressers. Although cross-dressing is a fairly common pursuit of heterosexual men, most do not seek to change their sex but dress at home, occasionally venturing out in public 'dressed'; or in some cases, seeking to live full-time as women but eschewing surgery or hormones (Woodhouse, 1989). It is, however, from this constituency of men that the term 'transgender' arose, and although there is much fuss about the boundary between cross-dressers and those who choose to transition, the difference seems neither clear nor fixed. The historian of sexuality, Vern Bullough, like many other researchers of transgenderism, considers that there is little difference between cross-dressing and transsexualism; some cross-dressers simply go further than others and end up either living permanently as a woman, or elect to have surgery (Bullough, 2006). A social movement of male cross-dressers developed in the 1960s and 1970s, which formed another conduit in the construction of transgenderism. The movement was spearheaded by Virginia Prince, to whom the first use of the term 'transgender' is attributed. Prince created the journal *Transvestia*, for men interested in cross-dressing as women, in 1960. Vern L. Bullough says that the term was 'first used by Virginia Prince to describe those individuals who, like her, elected to change "gender" and not "sex"' (Bullough, 2006).

The pool of interested men, cross-dressers, from whom the increasing numbers of those seeking to change sex are drawn, is quite considerable. In an article that points out the connections between cross-dressing and transgenderism, transgender psychologist Anne Lawrence gives figures from a survey to indicate the ubiquity of cross-dressing interests in men. This showed that 2.8 per cent of men reported having experienced sexual arousal in association with cross-dressing (Lawrence, 2007: 507). Other studies, he says, found a rate of 2 or 3 per cent. The interest of publicly heterosexual men in cross-dressing in garments more usually associated with women has a long historical pedigree. Cross-dressing is understood by sexologists as a sexual interest of heterosexual men and they are agreed that there is no analogous practice for women, heterosexual or lesbian, as women are usually not afflicted by unusual paraphilias (Bailey, 2007). Cross-dressing is engaged in by groups of men for fun, as well as being practised secretly at home. Marjorie Garber, in her examination of this practice in the United States, points out that it has been commonly engaged in by privileged, upper class men in colleges and universities, which gives an indication of its respectability. She explains that dressing up as women, even to the extent of using prostheses to imitate female body parts, takes place in all male bastions of the American upper class, such as the Tavern Club in Boston and the Bohemian Club in San Francisco, where, she explains that '[f]ar from undercutting the power of the ruling elite, male cross-dressing rituals here seem often to serve as confirmation and expressions of it' (Garber, 1997: 66).

Virginia Prince, who has been described as the 'pioneer' of transgenderism, played an important role in the development of cross-dressing from a hobby into a movement (Ekins, 2005). He had a PhD in pharmacy and lived as a woman for part of his life, after two marriages. He did not, however, consider himself a transsexual and did not have sex-change surgery. The *International Journal of Transgenderism* dedicated an issue to him – at ninety-two years old – in 2005, to celebrate the importance of his work in creating the field. Prince had the classic history of a cross-dresser, which today would be likely to lead to a diagnosis of gender identity disorder and make him a candidate for surgery. He began cross-dressing at the age of twelve, using his mother's clothes, and as a teenager sometimes 'dressed' in public, seeking to pass himself off as a girl. He sought out the advice and support of psychiatrists about his interest, and in 1960 he published the first issue of his magazine for cross-dressers, *Transvestia*, which stated that it was directed to 'sexually normal' – that is heterosexual – cross-dressers. He formed a transvestite support group from subscribers to the magazine, *Hose and Heels*, in Los Angeles in 1961, to which homosexuals and transsexuals were not admitted. The group became national and was renamed Foundation for Full Personality Expression (FPE). It gained subscribers from outside the United States, and in 1965 a European regional group of FPE called the Beaumont Society was formed in London. Prince also published transvestite fiction, some written by himself, and sold aids such as artificial breasts. After his second marriage ended he began to, as he puts it, 'personate' women in public, had electrolysis to remove his beard and gained breasts as a result of hormone treatment, but he retained his penis. Prince became the spokesman for the transvestite community and claimed to have coined the terms 'transgenderism' and 'transgenderist' to describe men such as himself who 'have breasts and live full-time as a woman but who have no intention of having genital surgery' (quoted in Ekins, 2005: 9). Prince considered the development of transgender surgery, and its wide dissemination and promotion, to be problematic because he thought it caused susceptible transvestites to be seduced into taking that route; an insight that was prophetic.

In 1978 Prince wrote an article for his journal *Transvestia*, which presages the ways in which queer and transgender theorists were to write about transgenderism twenty years later. He explained the usefulness of the suffix 'trans', and that a 'transcendent is a person who climbs over and goes beyond some sort of limitation or barrier' (Prince, 2005b, first published 1978: 39). Transgenders, he claimed, have to climb over the barrier of gender, and quotes the sexologist John Money on the definition of gender as '[a]ll those things that a person says or does to disclose himself or herself as having the status of boy or man, girl or woman respectively' (Prince, 2005b: 40). Interestingly, Prince considers that gender isn't 'biological, it's cultural' (Prince, 2005b 41), and his understanding of what femininity consists of comes from the culture of the 1950s, 'a world of silk and satin, of lace, and perfume, of grace, beauty and adornment and, ideally, of virtue' (2005a, 23). Prince's work is an indication of a move to understand cross-dressing and transsexualism in terms of 'gender' that was under way. This culminated in the inclusion in the *US Diagnostic and Statistical Manual*, the bible of mental health professionals, of the diagnoses of 'gender identity disorder' and 'gender identity disorder in childhood', which form the foundations for treatment of this mental health problem by hormones and surgery. Gender identity disorder becomes the new language for what was previously called 'transsexualism' (Zucker and Spitzer, 2005). In the new 2013 edition of the *Diagnostic and Statistical Manual*, the nomenclature was changed again, and gender identity disorder became 'gender dysphoria', resulting from the arguments of transgender activists that their problems with gender did not constitute a disorder, a term that has connotations of poor mental health.

The move to gender

The construction of the idea of 'gender' was necessary in order to justify and explain sex-change treatment. The taking up of this new idea led to an important staging post in the history of this practice, when, in the 1990s, the term 'transgender' began to crowd out the term 'transsexualism' from common understandings. The move to the language and idea of gender in conceptualising cross-dressing and transsexualism began with the sexologists of the 1950s and 1960s. During this time, the doctors who offered transgender treatments created a notion of gender – which previously had only a grammatical meaning – as the ideological foundation for their practice. Hausman explains that sex-change surgery was predicated upon the notion of gender: 'the idea of an identity prior to and within the body that theoretically should dictate the physical appearance of the subject' (Hausman, 1995: 70). The idea of gender was developed by the sexologists, John Money and others, in the 1950s and understood as 'the social performance indicative of an internal sexed identity' (Hausman, 1995: 7). It arose from their work using surgery and hormones in the treatment of intersex children, and was used to determine which children should be treated and in what ways. As Hausman observes, there was a heterosexist bias from the beginning in the medical construction of intersexuality and transsexualism, because the physicians were concerned to construct appropriately gendered persons who would act out in acceptably heterosexual ways. Through the study of the history of transsexualism, Hausman argues that the 'production of the concept of gender in Western culture' can be analysed (Hausman, 1995: 11). All of the medical 'interventions', as Hausman refers to them, depended upon 'the construction of a rhetorical system that posits a prior gendered self necessary to justify surgical interventions' (Hausman, 1995: 71). She calls the doctors the 'gender managers', and stresses that opposition to homosexuality fuelled their work and justified the sterilisation that was a component part of the treatment, as they considered that it was 'more important that the patient is not homosexual than that the patient is fertile' (Hausman, 1995: 74).

The development by the sexologists of the idea of gender was to make possible a considerable linguistic and ideological move for the men who were seeking to change sex. As an increasing number of sexologists, psychologists and philosophers of science are now pointing out, the idea of gender enabled the demanders to wrap their practice and desires in a new framework, which they then sought to justify as essential or even biologically determined (Bailey, 2007; Blanchard, 2005; Dreger, 2008; 2011; Ekins and King, 2010). The idea of gender offered a way out of the difficult situation in which such men would otherwise be seen as sexually motivated by a 'paraphilia' to cross-dress or change sex. The association with sexuality created problems for their access to treatment, and to the seriousness with which they were regarded in the public world. The idea of a 'gender' mistake, in which they mysteriously incorporated a 'feminine essence', washed them clean of sleaze and enabled them to constitute themselves as a confident rights-bearing minority who were just born different. The move from sex to gender was accomplished with the increasing acceptance of a new language – transsexualism became transgenderism.

Cross-dressing and transgenderism as paraphilias

The biographies of cross-dressers and the descriptions of their excitements and interests are very similar to those provided by those who go on to access surgery and hormones. Cross-dressing is rather clearly a sexual interest, but spokespersons for cross-dressers, and most of those who go on to transition, reject the idea that their practice is related to sexual excitement. Prince specifically rejected the notion that cross-dressing was driven by a pursuit of sexual satisfaction; rather he said it was based upon 'gender' and allowed men to express their full personality including their 'love of the feminine' (Ekins, 2005: 11). This claim, the sociologist Richard Ekins argues, was to gain acceptance from family, friends and society. There is an increasingly vocal opposition to the idea that the desire to change sex is based upon gender, rather than being a sexual interest, among some of those most involved in theorising transgenderism. This group of professionals, which includes the psychologist Professor Michael Bailey (2003), the philosopher of science Alice Dreger (2008), the transgender psychotherapist Anne Lawrence (2004), and the sociologists Richard Ekins and Dave King (2010), favour the understanding of transgenderism developed by the sexologist Ray Blanchard (2005). Blanchard argues that there are two types of transsexual: those who love men and are basically homosexual; and those who are sexually attracted to the idea of themselves as women, whom he calls autogynephiles. Autogynephilia, he says, constitutes 'a male's propensity to be attracted to the thought or image of himself as a woman' (Blanchard, 1991: 235). Critics have responded that these two categories do not account for all transsexuals, and that many do not easily fit the criteria for one or the other, but the supporters say that the schema of there being two such types is overwhelmingly correct, and fits the evidence. They reject the idea that transsexuals have a biological condition in which their 'gender' has been wrongly allocated: 'It is unfortunate that the public face of MTF transsexualism is so different from reality' (Bailey and Triea, 2007: 531). Blanchard, Bailey and their colleagues consider that non-homosexual transsexualism, autogynephilia, is a sexual interest, or paraphilia.

The sociologist, Ekins, who has made cross-dressing and transgenderism the subjects of his research and his life's work, describes the erotic interests of what he calls 'male femalers'. He makes no real distinction between cross-dressers and men who go further in their practice and seek to change sex, and they are all, in his view, male femalers. Ekins explains that, for the male femaler,

> the desire, or excitement, is aroused ... by his own femaling, and/or through the awareness of others of his own erotic femaling ... The femaler [may experience] intense orgasm following a dressing sequence, while at the other end, the femaler might find himself mildly enjoying the sensual feel of his bra strap against his shoulder as he makes the minor movements necessary to eat a meal or drink a cup of coffee.
>
> *(Ekins, 1997: 56)*

This example usefully demonstrates the difference between the cross-dresser's fantasy of what it is to be a woman and what women actually feel, as there is an absence of accounts by women of feeling sexually aroused by the feel of their bra straps. But his characterisation of the practice also offers an insight into the importance attached by some men who transgender or cross-dress to appearing in public, to women in toilets, for instance, and seeking a reaction from them. Bailey and Triea argue that this is a common aspect of autogynephilia, describing it as 'the erotic fantasy of being admired, in the female persona, by another person' (Bailey and Triea, 2007: 523). Ray Blanchard explains that a signal difference between autogynephiles and homosexuals – to whom they are often compared – is that homosexuals do not seek a reaction from passers-by for their sexual satisfaction, whereas the heterosexual men who progress from cross-dressing to transgenderism act as if they are in a perpetual 'movie' into which other persons, such as wives, are inducted, however unwillingly, to play the part of audience (Cameron, 2013).

The concept of autogynephilia is useful in explaining how men's sexual interest in that which, in their minds, appertains to femininity, can go further than cross-dressing to incorporate inscribing womanhood on their bodies by physical means. Bailey and Triea explain that 'one common manifestation of autogynephilia is fetishistic cross-dressing', but some may not cross-dress but rather 'fetishise about being a nude woman by focussing on desired anatomical features', and some 'experience erotic arousal at the idea of becoming a woman, and this arousal motivates them to become women' (Bailey and Triea, 2007: 523). They explain that not all autogynephilic males choose to become transsexuals, and their 'interests run a gamut from cross-dressing to engaging in stereotypic female activities (e.g. knitting alongside other women) to possessing female breasts and genitals' (ibid.). There is no 'obvious' difference, they argue, between those non-homosexual cross-dressers who will go on to transgender and those who will not. Bailey and Triea have no truck with the notion of a 'feminine essence' or innate gender.

Though an increasing number of sexologists are saying that cross-dressing and autogynephile transsexualism are based on a sexual orientation, or paraphilia, rather than misplaced gender, they seldom venture to explain exactly what the sexual excitement is based upon. Bailey and Triea imply that this sexual interest is a form of masochism, pointing out that '[o]f men who die practising the dangerous masochistic activity of autoerotic asphyxia, approximately 24% are cross-dressed' (Bailey and Triea, 2007: 524). I have argued elsewhere that the fact that the excitement is masochistic is clear in the pornography of cross-dressers, and in the statements of cross-dressers themselves (Jeffreys, 2005). The excitement that the idea of being a woman, and the excitement that the accoutrements of womanhood hold when placed upon a man, result from the fact that womanhood represents a subordinate position. When a man is forcibly cross-dressed, or able to imagine himself as a woman, he experiences the delicious excitement of being unmanned, deprived of the superior status of manhood and demoted to the subordinate status of womanhood. It is an excitement derived from the hierarchy of gender, the caste system of male dominance and women's subordination, and would not be imaginable outside that framework. Women's clothing is not sought out because it is prettier or more delightful, but because of its symbolic meaning. This understanding of men's practice of cross-dressing, and the transsexual impulses that can result, is not likely to meet with the approval of women, for whom being feminine is an often arduous and burdensome aspect of their lowly status rather than a source of orgasm. Perhaps for this reason, the feminine essence theory, the idea of a misplaced 'gender', is much more acceptable than the eroticising of women's subordination by men. Bailey and Triea offer an explanation for the enthusiasm for the feminine essence theory among many men who transgender, saying that those who promote this idea may consider they are more likely to be accepted for treatment if they are not seen as sexually deviant. They may find the idea 'intrinsically appealing' even if it is 'implausible' (Bailey and Triea, 2007: 528).

Blanchard and his supporters argue that there is plentiful evidence of the existence of autogynephilia whereas there is none for feminine essence (Blanchard, 2005). It lies in the narratives that Blanchard has heard from his many patients, and from the fifty-nine narratives that transgender psychotherapist, Anne Lawrence, has collected. Blanchard offers some examples from Lawrence's collection to show how autogynephilia manifests itself. One narrative describes the author's sexual excitement at being taken for a woman: 'In the early days I would become aroused whenever anyone, a sales clerk, a casual stranger, would address me as "Ma'am" or perform some courtesy such as holding a door for me' (Blanchard, 2005: 440). Another explains that both before and after sex-reassignment surgery (SRS) he liked to pretend to menstruate: 'it was and still is sexually exciting for me to have female body "functions." Before my SRS, I would pretend to menstruate by urinating in sanitary pads. I particularly enjoyed wearing the old fashioned belted pad with long tabs' (Blanchard, 2005: 440). Blanchard uses one quote from a narrative to explain why autogynephiles might seek out sexual encounters with men. While not seeing themselves as homosexual, such incidents may serve to gain recognition of the womanhood of the transgender: 'I felt I was confirming my womanhood by being a passive partner … I have never been interested in sex with a man when I was presenting as a man, myself' (Blanchard, 2005: 441). The motivations of ostensibly heterosexual men who transgender are fairly well explained by these sexologists as arising from masochism, and the desire to obfuscate the sexual nature of cross-dressing and transgenderism was one of the forces constructing transgenderism in the late twentieth century.

Importantly, Bailey and Triea argue that the sort of attacks on their reputation received by any person who publicly challenges the feminine essence idea serves to prevent any alternative being voiced. Two prominent proponents of the theory, transgender activists Lyn Conway and Andrea James, called the 2003 book, in which Bailey was critical, *The Man who would be Queen*, 'Nazi propaganda' (Bailey and Triea, 2007: 528). Bailey was subjected to a campaign of vilification, which included placing photographs of his children on a website with insulting captions (Dreger, 2008). He says that many untrue accusations were made against him, and these were 'precisely an attempt to punish the author for writing approvingly about Blanchard's ideas, and to intimidate others from doing so' (Bailey and Triea, 2007: 529). Bailey and Triea argue that advocates for the feminine essence narrative, and against Blanchard's theory, are non-homosexual transsexuals who 'incorrectly deny their autogynephilia' (Bailey and Triea, 2007: 529). These men are supported in their mistaken ideas by many 'gender physicians' who may be unwilling to disbelieve or displease their patients, and who are more comfortable with facilitating sex reassignment for 'reasons related to gender than eroticism'.

Transgenderism and homosexuality

Another force in the construction of transgenderism, according to David Valentine, is the conservatism of a gay male politics concerned to reject and sideline effeminacy. Whatever the balance of forces that constructed transgenderism in the late twentieth century, one puzzling element is the lack of criticism by male gay scholars, particularly since hatred of homosexuality so clearly played a role, and one group of those who aspire to transgender are men who love men. As we have seen, the doctors who were involved in constructing transgenderism, and the demanders themselves, were determined to avoid any association of cross-gender practices with homosexuality. The absence of any critique of transgenderism from within the male gay community is sufficiently conspicuous as to need explanation, and David Valentine seeks to offer one (Valentine, 2007). He argues that the lack of protest by gay men points to the useful function that transgenderism performs for a new breed of conservative gay men post gay liberation. These conservative gay men assert their concordance with normative masculinity and seek to deny and exclude effeminate gay men by casting them into the category of 'transgender'. This ploy protected the normality of the gay man and helped in his campaign to be accepted legislatively and socially as just another jock.

He argues that effeminacy was separated off from homosexuality and placed in a special category of its own as a result of a range of impulses, one of which was the normalisation of male homosexuality by those he calls 'accommodationist' activists after gay liberation. At the time of gay liberation there was a radical critique of what were called 'sex roles' emanating from the influence of the feminist movement that was contemporaneous. At the height of the gay liberation movement there was a rejection of both masculine and feminine role playing, as symptoms of a harmful patriarchal system that oppressed homosexuals (Jeffreys, 2003). Gay male theorists argued that gay men should not be sissies or butches because these roles were an imitation of that which they identified as the oppressive rules of patriarchy. The behaviours of masculinity and femininity in general were understood as backward, and they should, it was argued, be jettisoned.

Gay liberationists and feminists in the 1970s provided explanations as to why male homosexuality was associated with femininity and lesbianism with masculinity not only in medicine, but also by homosexuals themselves. They argued that in male-supremacist societies, heterosexuality was enforced through the excoriation of same-sex sexual behaviour. Masculinity was, and is, so strongly correlated with male, aggressive penis-in-vagina sex, that deviation from this norm, to the extent of engaging sexually with the same sex, was seen as unmanly and therefore a representation of femininity. In the same way, women who made love to women were seen as unwomanly because this was a masculine role and lesbians were seen as embodying a form of masculinity. These messages were sufficiently strong enough to influence the way that those who loved the same sex thought about themselves. There is a wealth of material to suggest that these messages were thoroughly imbibed (Gottschalk and Newton, 2003). In 1950s lesbian culture, for instance, lesbians were likely to adopt male names, bind their breasts to hide them, and even evince their desire for penises (Jeffreys, 1989). But there is no suggestion that these women saw themselves as 'really' being men; rather, they wished to enact a male role towards those they loved.

As the radical edge of gay liberation was worn down, and a much more conservative era of neo-liberal consumerism dawned in the 1980s, this political critique of 'sex roles' was abandoned. In its place there developed among gay men a cult of masculinity, in which effeminacy was eschewed and a new camped-up extreme masculinity was adopted and venerated, represented in sadomasochism, in cowboys and construction workers and all the types of the gay pop group Village People. Gay sociologist, Martin Levine, is one of the male gay writers to have criticised this burgeoning masculinity – he called this the 'butch shift' (Levine, 1998). This shift is understandable as a reaction against the association of homosexuality with effeminacy and representative of a new self-confidence, but it created problems for gay men's health and lives through the promotion of a masculinist and aggressive sexual culture involving large numbers of sexual partners and harmful practices such as fistfucking and anal sex without condoms (Jeffreys, 2003). Feminist critics have argued that male gay masculinity was an obstacle in the way of the need to abolish 'gender roles', create an egalitarian sexuality, and challenge pornography and the sex industry.

Valentine explains that as a result of all this, transgenderism was 'institutionalised' in the 1990s 'in a vast range of contexts, from grassroots activism, social service provision, and individual identification, to journalistic accounts' such that 'transgender identification' was understood 'to be explicitly and fundamentally different in origin and being from homosexual identification' (Valentine, 2007: 4). The patriarchal state invested heavily in the concept with funding to social service agencies and centres designed to cater to the 'transgender' community. The concept was developed in the academy, with transgender studies and transgender publishing. Despite these developments, Valentine argues that when he did his research in the late 1990s in New York, he found, much to his surprise, that there was no transgender community. He carried out his research while employed as a safe sex educator for the transgender community and found that the majority of those to whom he was directed for outreach work either did not know the term transgender or did not relate to it. Even those who lived full-time in clothing usually associated with women, and those who had had surgery to remove parts of their bodies saw themselves as gay men. Valentine argues, persuasively, that most of the varieties of behaviour now commonly placed by scholars and social workers under a transgender umbrella, such as drag artists, feminine gay men and butch lesbians, have historically, and in the present, been understood by themselves and others as 'gay'. How, he asks, did the category 'transgender' get created and what are the implications of its construction? 'What is the reason for the incredibly rapid dissemination of "transgender" in the United States since the early 1990s which has cemented the distinction between gender variance and sexual orientation?' (Valentine, 2007: 6). The sidelining of effeminate gay men, he argues, is a result of the separation of 'gender' and 'sexuality' that has taken place in the academy and in gay communities and has 'effectively required the birth of a new category – transgender – for those who are not identified primarily in terms of "sexuality"' (Valentine, 2007: 236). Another element in the creation of the idea of 'gender identity' as separate from sexuality is that 'gender' is conceptualised as a form of 'social difference' rather than, from a feminist perspective, 'a site of power relations' (ibid.).

Transableism

Another force in the construction of transgenderism is the way in which the development of the Internet has enabled groups of mainly men to create online communities around their sexual proclivities. This happened in relation to cross-dressing and transgenderism, but also in relation to another practice that has some close connections with transgenderism – 'transableism'. The example of transableism shows how an 'identity' can be built online, but also shows the problems of this kind of identity politics, in which categories of persons who suffer disadvantage – in this case persons with disabilities – can be the subject of appropriation and imitation for sexual excitement using the justification that an identity, however peculiar, should be respected. In this practice, which was originally labelled 'apotemnophilia' (Money et al., 1977), now more usually called Body Integrity Identity Disorder (BIID), aspirants seek amputation of one or more limbs (First, 2004; First and Fisher, 2012). The aspirants have been busy online creating identities and campaigning for amputation by medical professionals (Davis, 2011). They have their own terminology for their interest, transableism, which references transgenderism, in order to make themselves look more respectable. These transableists include both those who seek satisfaction from amputation and those who seek disability in other forms, such as paraplegia, deafness or blindness. In recent writings by sexological experts, gender identity disorder and BIID are seen as fundamentally similar, particularly in relation to the sexual satisfactions involved. Michael First, for instance, editor of the *US Diagnostic and Statistical Manual*, who has been advocating for BIID to be added to the *Diagnostic and Statistical Manual* so that those seeking amputation can access treatment, argues that transableists in general should be placed in the manual under a heading of identity disorder that includes only two categories, gender identity disorder and BIID (First and Fisher, 2012). First explains that, because of the similarities, he uses the diagnostic criteria for gender identity disorder as the model for the twelve criteria he offers for a diagnosis of BIID. Voluntary limb amputation has achieved a surprising degree of normalisation through Internet networking and campaigning, and this offers insights into the way in which transgenderism has flourished as a practice and a movement.

Conclusion

The critical scholarship on transgenderism has scarcely begun, and this book seeks to encourage its development. The theme this chapter has explored, of how the concept came to exist, is an important place to begin. Much more critical research on the construction of transgenderism is needed, but this work cannot take place while this practice is seen as an essential phenomenon that is beyond question. The assertion that an essence of gender is the explanation for transgenderism prevents any exploration of the history and construction of this practice. Such investigative scholarship is represented as 'transphobic' and met with resistance. The idea that 'gender' is quite separate from 'sexuality' and has a logic and essence of its own is commonly stated in queer and transgender theory, and this effectively prevents the history of the entanglement of hatred of homosexuality in the construction of transgenderism from being voiced or analysed. The lessons that critical lesbian and gay, and feminist scholarship contribute to the understanding of transgenderism are that its construction serves the political agenda of shoring up heterosexuality and maintaining a correctly gendered citizenry. Janice Raymond expressed this succinctly in *The Transsexual Empire*. 'What we have here is a very sophisticated form of behavior control and modification, on both the individual and the social level' (Raymond, 1979: 131).

Another force in the construction of transgenderism was queer theory in the academy, which destabilised academic feminism and led to claims that there was really no such thing as a 'woman', so, of course, men who transgender could be women too. The weakening of feminist theory by the advent of queer politics undermined the criticism of transgenderism by those persons most affected by the phenomenon – women and feminists. The impact of queer politics will be considered in the next chapter.

2

TRANSGENDERISM
AND FEMINISM

Transgender theory and practice contradict the very basis of feminism, since feminism is a political movement based on the experience of persons who are women, born female and raised in the female sex caste. In the last decade there has been a considerable campaign, mainly by some men who consider themselves transgender, to establish that they are feminists, and that their practice is not only compatible with feminism, but exemplary of its proper aims. This campaign has had some success in being accepted by parts of the feminist movement and academic feminism, because it resonates with the queer and poststructuralist theory that has overwhelmed feminist understandings of 'gender'. This acceptance made the idea that men can be both women and lesbians, and that some women who transgender who were previously lesbians are really 'men', seem reasonable. This chapter will examine the way that feminists have theorised transgenderism, the impact of queer theory, and the development of transgender theory and transgender feminism. It will consider, also, the way in which transgender activism has sought to silence the feminists who challenge transgenderism.

At the height of second wave feminism in the 1970s, transgenderism was a much less common practice. Nonetheless, there was a quite general political rejection of the practice by feminists on the grounds that transgenderism, called transsexualism at that time, replicated the sex role stereotypes, now called 'gender', that were seen as the building blocks of the subordination of women (Morgan, 1978; Raymond, 1994).

Such 'stereotyped roles' are, according to feminist critics of the practice, the very foundation and *sine qua non* of transgenderism. The transgenderism that feminists did come in contact with in the 1970s consisted of a few individual males seeking to 'personate' women, as the influential theorist of cross-dressing in the 1960s and 1970s, Virginia Prince (2005b), called his practice. Before the 1990s, the organised transgender activist movement that was facilitated by the Internet did not exist. At that time, the phenomenon of women seeking to 'personate' men was much less common, and not visible in lesbian communities.

Forty years ago radical feminist thinkers and activists were very clear in their view that persons who were born biologically male and raised as males, but sought recognition as women in the women's liberation movement, were engaged in a form of colonialism and should be ejected. Males were understood to be members of the oppressive sex caste that benefited from women's subordination. Robin Morgan explained this clearly in her speech to the West Coast Lesbian Conference in Los Angeles in 1973 (Morgan, 1978). She changed her speech to include the issue of transgenderism in response to the problematic presence of a cross-dressing man, whose attendance caused grievous damage to the conference:

> [A]ll hell broke loose that very first night, caused by the gate-crashing presence of a male transvestite who insisted that he was (1) an invited participant, (2) really a woman, and (3) at heart a lesbian. (It is, one must grant, an ingenious new male approach for trying to seduce women.) The conference promptly split over the man. More than half the women there Friday evening demanded he be forced to leave an all-woman conference; others ... defended him as their 'sister'. Some women left the conference for good.
>
> *(Morgan, 1978: 171)*

Feminists at the time objected to what she calls 'the obscenity of male transvestism' because they saw it as an insulting practice in which men caricatured stereotypes of women for their own amusement or pleasure. They compared it to other ways in which members of dominant groups mocked those they considered their inferiors, as happened in the black and white minstrel shows of the period when white men performed in blackface. As Morgan put it, '*We know what's at work when whites wear blackface; the same thing is at work when men wear drag*' (Morgan, 1978: 180) (italics in the original).

Morgan says that the transvestites, as she called them, were 'men who deliberately reemphasize gender roles, and who parody female oppression and suffering' and is firm about rejecting their entryism:

> No, I will not call a male 'she'; thirty-two years of suffering in this androcentric society, and of surviving, have earned me the title 'woman'; one walk down the street by a male transvestite, five minutes of his being hassled (which *he* may enjoy), and then he dares, he *dares* to think he understands our pain? No, in our mothers' names and in our own, we must not call him sister.
>
> *(Morgan, 1978, 180) (emphasis in original)*

The particular 'transvestite' at the 1973 conference had a history of demanding entry to women's spaces despite the destruction and division that this clearly caused. He had already, she explained, 'four years ago tried to pressure a San Francisco lesbian into letting him rape her' and had done great damage to the lesbian group Daughters of Bilitis by his entryism into that organisation. He had threatened the conference organisers with legal action if they sought to exclude him; 'when personally begged by women *not* to attend this conference, [he] replied that if he were kept out he would bring federal suit against the women on the charges of "discrimination and criminal conspiracy to discriminate"' (ibid.). Morgan accuses the transvestite of narcissism, of wanting to be the centre of attention and to use the conference to 'boost his opportunistic career' (ibid.). 'Transvestites', she argued, should form their own organisations and pursue their own interests rather than trying to barge into women's activism and spaces. They should 'band together and organize against that oppression, instead of leeching off women who have spent their entire lives *as women* in women's bodies' (Morgan, 1978: 181).

In the UK, the feminist response to transsexuals seeking to enter the women's movement was similar. In a 1979 paper for the Leeds Radical/ Revolutionary Feminist conference, Lal Coveney explained why transsexuals were not women:

> It needs to be stated loud and clear that being a woman is a long-term experience, and one that isn't summed up by a collection of female genitalia with some clothes draped over them. It takes years of constant pressure and lots of practice to achieve the accepted standards of femininity – we learnt the tricks (in order to survive) so presumably men can too. But the state of mind, the process of becoming – we didn't have any choice about that.
>
> *(Coveney, 1979)*

The paper ends, 'operations don't change the lining of your head'. In the London Women's Liberation Newsletter for 1979, the sentiments towards the entryism of transsexuals were overwhelmingly in the negative for all these reasons.

The only full book-length feminist critique of the practice of transgenderism in this period was Janice G. Raymond's *The Transsexual Empire* (1994, first published 1979). Raymond, a radical feminist theorist and professor of the Philosophy of Science, provided an incisive, feminist, political analysis of the problem: 'My main conclusion is that transsexualism is basically a social problem whose cause cannot be explained except in relation to the sex roles and identities that a patriarchal society generates' (Raymond, 1994: 79). She argued that transsexualism was a product of medicine as an industry, rather than a transhistorical and essential aspect of humanness, or a flaw in biological development that needs to be repaired by the kindly attentions of surgeons. Her work was a development of the sociological critique of medicine, which owes its origin to the work of Talcott Parsons (1951). Parsons argued that medicine was a social institution that regulated social deviance through the provision of medical diagnoses for nonconforming behaviour. Medicine was, in this understanding, engaged in social control. Another form of argument in this approach was the Marxist one of seeing medicine as a source and mechanism for extracting profits in capitalism and part of the medical-industrial complex (Riska, 2003). Both of these approaches have been employed by transcritical feminists in their critique of transgenderism.

These ideas lay behind the anti-psychiatry movement of the 1960s and 1970s, which focused on challenging the proliferation of psychiatric diagnoses and drug therapies to control forms of behaviour that should, they considered, be seen as politically and socially constructed rather than mad. In this view, the problematic behaviours should be seen either as social protest, or as the products of the inequalities and injustices of a classist, racist and sexist capitalist status quo (Illich, 1975; Szasz, 1960). It was not just radical feminist theorists like Raymond who were critical of transgenderism in the 1970s and 1980s. Social constructionist sociologists were too. Dwight Billings and Thomas Urban carried out research in this more critical period, using observation and interviews in a 'gender' clinic (Billings and Urban, 1982). As critical sociologists of the time, they engaged in a thoroughgoing critique of the medical practice of transgenderism. They argued that physicians created and promoted sex-change surgery, which would heal 'neither the body nor the mind, but perform a moral function instead' and that the surgery 'privatizes and depoliticizes individual experience of gender-role distress', which is a symptom of social change and challenge to the political construction of gender roles (Billings and Urban, 1982: 266). They conclude, powerfully, that '[b]y substituting medical terminology for political discourse, the medical profession has indirectly tamed and transformed a potential wildcat strike at the gender factory' (Billings and Urban, 1982: 282).

Feminist critiques of medicine and psychiatry developed these radical political ideas, but their work in relation to transgenderism, which would have seemed unremarkable at the time among those who saw themselves as progressive thinkers about medicine, is excoriated today by transgender activists as 'hate' speech and vilification, and results in campaigns of defamation and harassment against any women who are critical (Jeffreys, 2012a). The feminists who were critical of the practice of transgenderism in the 1970s tended to be some of the biggest names in radical feminist theory of the time, whose analyses of sexual politics provided the foundations of feminist theory in general, such as Mary Daly, Janice Raymond, Robin Morgan. They are subjected to strong critiques in the literature of transgender activists today (Serano, 2007; Stryker, 2008). The burgeoning field of transgender studies and the 'transgender feminism', which is now increasingly taught in women's studies programmes, pays considerable attention to debunking the arguments and actions of these most influential second wave feminist theorists in relation to the practice. The project of transgender activists is to replace this radical feminist theory, which seeks the abolition of sex role stereotypes, now called gender, with a version of 'feminism' more compatible with their interests. The feminist critique of transgenderism was sidelined, in common with all forms of radical feminist theory and practice during the 1990s, when queer theory swept aside feminism and lesbian feminism and formed a sure foundation for the burgeoning of transgender ideology and practice. To understand how the feminist critique of transgenderism was replaced by a politics that provides support for the practice, it is necessary to examine the development and ideas of queer theory, particularly in relation to gender.

'Gender' in feminist theory

Queer theory and politics inherited the term 'gender' from its usage by feminist theorists. The term 'gender' was not widely adopted by feminist theorists until the late 1970s or early 1980s (Haig, 2004). In David Haig's useful study of the adoption of the term through analysis of titles in feminist writings in journals and books, he shows that those feminists who used it in the 1970s clearly identified its origins in the work of sexologists such as John Money and Robert Stoller. Sexologists developed this term – from a usage that was purely grammatical, referring to the gender of words – to apply to sex-appropriate behaviour, and used it to facilitate their attempts to place intersex children in categories they considered suitable. It does not originate in feminism, but was adopted by feminists for its usefulness in delineating the process of social construction of women's subordinate role. Feminist theorists developed the usage of the term to describe the whole system in which women were subordinated, as in the expression 'gender hierarchy'. Unfortunately, the feminist usage has been buried in waves of confusion and obfuscation and in non-feminist contexts there is a conflation of 'sex' and 'gender' in everything from college application forms to the ideology of transgenderism. As Haig comments, 'gender has come to be adopted as a simple synonym, perhaps a euphemism, for sex by many writers who are unfamiliar with the term's recent history' (Haig, 2004: 95). The term has become so politically ambiguous that it is likely a new language will have to be created by feminists as they seek to dismantle the mess that its usage has created. One aspect of that mess is the way in which queer theory was able to deploy the term 'gender' so that a very conservative form of behaviour, male, heterosexual cross-dressing, came to appear transgressive.

The queer assault on feminism

The term 'queer' was adopted to describe a type of politics that developed in the early 1990s out of AIDS activism. Male gay activists who came out onto the streets to protest the wave of anti-gay hatred that accompanied the AIDS epidemic used the term 'queer' to differentiate themselves from what they saw as an older generation of men who used the term 'gay' and who were accommodationist and not sufficiently confrontational for the moment of emergency that the new activists saw themselves to be confronting (Jeffreys, 2003). The term queer did not emerge from lesbian feminist politics and was in clear opposition to them from the beginning. The new term was a big step back for lesbians and feminists, as it had taken two decades of struggle to reach the point where there was a recognition that lesbians needed to be separately acknowledged in the titles of conferences, books and campaigns. Generic terms such as 'homosexual' and 'gay' disappeared lesbians under male interests and concerns, and the male imaginary. The lesbian feminist movement in the 1970s showed that lesbians had quite separate and in many ways contradictory interests from those of gay men. Lesbian feminists developed a profound critique of gay male politics and gay male ambitions, as is clear in Marilyn Frye's work in *The Politics of Reality* (1983) and my *Unpacking Queer Politics* (Jeffreys, 2003). It became clear from the beginning that the new generic term would cancel out the hard-won visibility of lesbians within these politics, and that is what came to pass.

Lesbian feminist critics challenged the content of queer politics in a number of ways. They said that queer politics constituted a return to a male-dominated sexual freedom agenda that feminism and lesbian feminism in the 1970s and 1980s had sought to overturn (Jeffreys, 2003). They argued that queer theory arose out of a conservative time in the 1990s when the radical politics of lesbian feminism and gay liberation were being disavowed as unrealistic. These radical politics had challenged the existence of gender as a system of power, challenged marriage and heterosexuality as political institutions, and argued that homosexuality was not biological and could be a matter of political choice. These ideas were too radical for the 1990s, which were not daring times politically. In that much less revolutionary decade, individual bodies were challenged rather than the body politic, such that body modification, branding, cutting and tattooing came to be seen as progressive practices (Jeffreys, 2000). Queer politics coincided with the marketisation of many areas of life, including sex, and the queer consumer was born. More and more sex industry practices were incorporated into lesbian and gay social life, such as drag shows and strip shows.

Moreover, it was argued that doing unusual things to and with your genitals, including cutting them off as in transgenderism, was revolutionary (Jeffreys, 2005; 2008a). Even the cutting off of other body parts, or placing objects under the skin, and brutal forms of branding in different forms of 'body modification' were somehow given queer credentials (Pitts, 2001; Sullivan, 2001). Attacks upon the bodies of deeply troubled lesbians and gay men by themselves, by commercial cutters or by surgeons, were represented as 'transgressive' rather than destructive (Jeffreys, 2008b).

The most important aspect of queer theory for the development of a transgender movement, however, was its theorising of gender. While feminists had sought to use gender in ways that suited their revolutionary purposes and aimed to demolish gender differences, the queer approach was much less radical, and paved the way for transgenderism to be seen as an emblematic practice of queer politics. Queer theory developed as a subset of postmodern theory, and was devoted from its outset to a form of deconstructionism that disappeared the category 'woman' itself (Brodrib, 1992). Without 'women' feminism cannot exist, since feminism is a political movement for the liberation of a specific category of oppressed persons, and the disappearance of women renders feminism superfluous. 'Woman' was not a concern of queer politics, and 'gender' displaced any consideration of the fleshly reality of woman's existence. Queer theory created a gender politics which reduced gender to a form of personal expression or performance, and obscured the material power relations of male domination (Butler, 1990). The aim of queer gender politics was to make gender flexible and create more 'genders'. In these ways queer theory was in direct opposition to feminist politics and enabled the development of transgenderism as a practice and ideology.

Radical feminist theorists do not seek to make gender a bit more flexible, but to eliminate it. They are gender abolitionists, and understand gender to provide the framework and rationale for male dominance. In the radical feminist approach, masculinity is the behaviour of the male ruling class and femininity is the behaviour of the subordinate class of women. Thus gender can have no place in the egalitarian future that feminism aims to create (Delphy, 1993). In the predominant queer theory approach, however, gender is something that can be 'played with'. In this queer interpretation, gender is 'transgressive' when adopted by persons of one biological sex who would normally be expected to display different characteristics. There is, however, no way out of gender; it can be swapped but in this formulation it cannot be abolished. In this respect queer theory suited the socially conservative times of the 1990s when the idea of social transformation was forgotten and various forms of cavorting in line with the system were relabelled as fun and rebellious. Queer theory on gender, rather than being progressive, should perhaps be seen as coquettish, flirting with male domination and reproducing its contortions. It locks lesbians and gay men into precisely the old time sex role stereotypes that more progressive movements – gay liberation and lesbian feminism – sought to demolish.

Queer theory adopted the term 'transgender' to cover those engaging in 'transgressive' performances of gender. This included lesbian and gay role players alongside transvestites, drag queens and kings, and both old-fashioned transsexuals, mired in biology, and those who reject biological explanations for their transitioning. As Holly (now Aaron) Devor puts it, 'Under the rubric of queer sexuality, we have seen postmodern sensibilities come to the fore as more and more people come forward to claim their right to be whatever their hearts and groins tell them to be' (Devor, 2002: 16). In this respect, queer sexuality is about whatever turns you on, with no interest in the social construction and political implications of individual desires and practices. Queer theory's politics of identity represents a fierce individualism. Devor explains that the queer/transgender community is composed of 'transsexual lesbians, of tranny fags and the men who love them, of lesbians and gay men who enjoy sex together, and of dyke daddies who live out their fantasies as SM gay men' (ibid.). The transgender activist and academic, Susan Stryker, explains that transgender became 'articulated' with queer in the form of 'an imagined political alliance of all possible forms of gender antinormativity' (Stryker, 2008: 146).

Queer theory and politics became involved in a gender rescue mission against the radical feminist campaign to abolish it. This may be because, for most women and men under male dominance, sexual desire is constructed precisely from eroticising the power difference between the sexes that is embodied in gender. Equality is unsexy and the very idea of dismantling gender is, therefore, as Catharine MacKinnon explains, 'detumescent' (Jeffreys, 1990; MacKinnon, 1989). This has been a particular problem for those lesbians and gay men who are unable to challenge the gendered nature of their own experience of sexual desire. Same sex attraction does not immediately offer the eroticised inequality of heterosexuality, and those who need this form of sexual stimulation have to recreate the power difference of 'gender' through role playing. To this purpose, gender was embraced as a 'sex toy' by significant queer theorists and activists such as Pat Califia (now Patrick) (1994), and Judith (Jack) Halberstam (Halberstam, 1998), who pronounced that role playing masculinity and femininity was precisely what put the pizzazz into lesbian sex and should be celebrated. Role playing, it became clear, offered the sexual satisfactions of a mild form of sadomasochism (Jeffreys, 2003).

The eminent queer theorist, Judith Butler, whose work is most usually cited as arguing that gender is a 'performance', takes a similar approach, explaining that she is someone whose sexual desire is constructed out of

gender difference. In an interview she says that she 'situated' herself 'in relation to butchness' in her early twenties, and has had 'an active and complicated
relationship with both butch-femme discourse and S/M discourse probably
for almost 20 years' (More, 1999: 286). In *Undoing Gender* she explains that
'[t]here may be women who love women' who cannot do this 'through the
category women' and that 'they/we' are 'deeply … attracted to the feminine' (Butler, 2004: 197). She asks, 'why shy away from the fact that there may
be ways that masculinity emerges in women?' (ibid.). Butler's enthusiasm
for gender causes her to embrace transsexual surgery as a human right even
though this practice is not playful or flexible and goes way beyond performance, since amputated penises cannot be reattached. She goes so far as to
promote the right to transsexual surgery as a matter of justice and says that
she agrees with the transgender activist argument that transsexuality 'should
be a matter of choice, an exercise of freedom', so that restrictions on surgery
lead to 'a basic human freedom' being 'suppressed' (Butler, 2004: 88). She also
states that the aspirations of transgenders are about 'the ability to live and
breathe and move and would no doubt belong somewhere in what is called
a philosophy of freedom' (ibid.). In this way she seeks to tie the transgender
project into a vision of progressive social change.

The clear difference between this queer approach and that of radical feminism is demonstrated in the work of the radical feminist law professor and
feminist theorist, Catharine MacKinnon, who does not accept that gender
swapping makes gender somehow harmless. Of the sexualising of dominance
and submission, which makes the 'target or object' of sexuality 'subordinate'
and 'usually a female', she writes, 'hierarchy is always done through gender
in some way; even if it is playing with gender or reversing gender or same-
gendering, it is still using gender for sex. Gender hierarchy is either being
played with or played out' (MacKinnon, 2006: 273). For feminists who recognise gender as a hierarchy, playing with it cannot form part of a future
that is friendly to women's interests, because women's freedom requires the
abolition of gender.

'Gender' in transgender theory

The most dangerous legacy of queer theory and politics for feminism is the
way in which it paved the way for the politics of transgenderism, by creating the notion that transposing gender is somehow revolutionary. Although
queer theory is social constructionist, and posits that transgenderism shows
the mutability of gender rather than the reverse, it has been enlisted to justify a transgenderism that is essentialist and, for many of its adherents, seen
as based in biology. In the academy, where queer theory has become the
orthodox way to understand gender in women's studies and lesbian and gay

studies, there is no critique of even the most biologistic versions of trans-genderism. Transgenderism has been able to exploit the way in which queer theory has removed 'gender' from its basis in the subordination of women and made it into an aspect of consumerism, something to be assumed and played with, and inscribed on the body, something that can be bought and paid for through hormones and surgery.

Out of queer theory, the new discipline of transgender studies emerged, which is taking up the space once occupied by lesbian and gay studies or women's studies and is the new sexy kid on the block. In transgender studies, gender doesn't look very playful at all and is in fact represented as compul-sory, something that everyone has to have. Conscientious objection, that is the conscious and political rejection of gender, is not possible. Thus Rikki Wilchins, the spokesperson of the campaigning transgender organisation GenderPAC, argues, from his position as a man who has transgendered, that though feminists have problems accepting transgenderism as progressive they should do so because they all need 'gender', 'Because, right now, the women's community is not totally on speaking terms with the drag and transgender community … They don't yet realize that they all have a common stake in gender' (Drescher, 2002: 72). Wilchins opines that lesbians and gay men should be supportive and inclusive towards transgenders because '[g]ay people have always been about gender. That's how your mother "just knew" some-one was gay' (Drescher, 2002: 73). Psychotherapist David Seil, who works with persons who aspire to transgender, argues that lesbians and gay men are 'on a continuum with transgendered people … We all are on that continuum, including heterosexual men and women' (Seil, 2002: 33). Female-bodied transgender Jamison Green argues similarly, saying that it is not possible to question the need for gender since it is the necessary basis of human inter-action: 'Everyone uses gender to communicate' (Green, 1999: 126). Clearly, within these understandings, there is no way out of gender, and lesbian and gay conscientious objectors are seen as charlatans, failing to recognise the ways in which they too are inevitably and fundamentally gendered.

Genderqueers replace lesbians

The queer understanding of 'gender' has had a profound influence on les-bian communities, with young women in some parts of American queer culture, who would once have understood themselves to be both lesbians and women, now identifying as 'genderqueer'. It is from this milieu that the strongly developing trend for lesbians to transgender emerged in the last decade. The transgendering of lesbians not only fractures communi-ties but disappears lesbians themselves as they reject womanhood, and this impoverishes feminism profoundly since lesbian feminist politics was central to second wave feminism (Faderman, 1997). Lesbians were crucial to developing the theory, and doing the work of feminism. They were prominent in creating services to support women who suffered male violence, such as rape crisis centres and refuges, and in setting up the basic institutions that created a women's culture, bookstores, women's centres, presses, music groups and theatre companies. They provided, too, the ethical core of feminist politics on sexuality and relationships (Card, 1991; Raymond, 1986). Lesbian feminist ethics were based on creating and practising a sexuality of equality that eschewed the eroticising of power difference in the form of butch/femme role playing or sadomasochism. Lesbian feminists created a journal in the United States called *Lesbian Ethics* and wrote books on ethics (Hoagland, 1988). The lesbian core of second wave feminism created the culture and spaces in which all women could relax, strategise, and develop strength. Importantly, the core of lesbian feminism was separatism (Frye, 1983). Lesbian feminists chose to live separately from men and to socialise and develop community in spaces that were women-only. The takeover of women's spaces by queer and transgender politics has led to the erosion of the sense of solidarity and community that is so important to the strength of a feminist movement. The entryism of men who transgender into women's spaces has helped to fracture lesbian communities, by extirpating the environments that have nurtured women's resistance and rebellious thinking and their ability to love one another.

The effect of the rise of queer politics, combined with the decline of lesbian feminist politics, was the development of 'genderqueer' communities in place of lesbian communities in some areas of the United States in particular. For lesbian feminism – or indeed feminism – to exist, it is necessary for women to be able to think of themselves as women and as lesbians. But this is very hard for many young lesbians in the present, who come out into a queer community in which only manhood has value. They may have extremely fragmented identities, which make them unable to accept themselves as women and lesbians. This is clear in a study in which young women who once might have called themselves lesbians were interviewed (Bauer, 2008). The young women engage in sadomasochism, or BDSM (bondage, discipline and sadomasochism), and could 'choose and negotiate roles and identities for play' (Bauer, 2008: 234). They identified in the following ways: 'white bisexual femme', 'white pansexual genderqueer femme', 'white queer transgendered stone butch', 'white queer genderqueer femmeboy', 'white queer femme'. The study explains 'genderqueer' thus:

> While genderqueers do not identify full time as either men or women, they do not conceive of themselves as in the middle of the spectrum or androgynous either. Their gender is rather fluid (shifting) and multiple

at the same time, which means that their positioning within a variety of genders depends on the context. For example, a person might express a femme side in an encounter with a butch and express a fag partial identity with a gay transguy the next day.

(Bauer, 2008: 238)

The author defines herself as 'a white German, queer, polyamorous, BDSM top, and transfag with a working-class and activist background' (Bauer, 2008: 239). The term 'lesbian' does not appear in such self-descriptions.

Indeed, some lesbian academics argue that the 'lesbians' in the lesbian community may cease to exist as a separate category as '[m]any young people are embracing a more fluid role in terms of their sexual orientation and gender identity' (Weiss, 2007: 208). Their sexuality is described as 'fluid', meaning that '[q]ueer-identified young women are likely to have sex with queer-identified young men, and consider it a queer relationship. Masculine labels such as "boy" and "daddy" are not considered taboo by women's communities' (ibid.). This erasure of lesbian existence, to quote Adrienne Rich (Rich, 1980), is called a move 'away from essentialism and towards universalism' in which 'academics of this new generation' may not bother to 'distinguish clearly a field of "Lesbian" Studies, or any sexuality-based disciplines' (Weiss, 2007: 209).

Genderqueer 'fluidity' may create a problem for these young women as they seek to situate themselves in the world and attend to their health. A study of the problems that lesbians, and especially those who transgender, have in accessing health care suggests that their lack of a secure identity creates problems in this respect. They have difficulty defining themselves; 'Gender-queer-identified and Transmale-identified youth often struggle for language to describe their own or their transgender peers' or partners' understandings of themselves' (Welle *et al*. 2006: 46). The study suggests that it is the gender studies and queer studies programmes taken by these gender and transidentified young women that caused them to have such fragmented and complex notions of who they were, as they 'had all participated in critical gender studies and queer studies courses and referenced academic discourse to frame LGBT and queer identities' (Welle *et al*., 2006: 48). One respondent, Samantha, says that a 'fixed identity is limited and limiting' and that 'fag culture or style', or possibly some 'dyked-out version of it', represents what she does. The young people in the study who were involved in sadomasochist sexual practice used the language of tops and bottoms from gay male culture to describe what they did in sexual role playing. The article concludes that '"more complexity" may be accompanied by unique vulnerabilities' (Welle *et al*., 2006: 66). Such studies indicate that the clear feminist critique of what were at first called sex roles or sex stereotypes, and only later commonly referred to as 'gender', was undermined by the advent of queer and poststructuralist ideas in the 1990s. But they indicate the disappearance of lesbians too.

Lesbian feminist academic, Bonnie Zimmerman, has evinced concern about this, suggesting that lesbian feminism barely survives as a recognised way of being a lesbian today in the United States. She warns that lesbians could disappear because

> in many locations, and many ways the discourses of lesbians – and specifically, Lesbian Feminism, have been all but silenced. This leads to the appropriation of our work … the vilification of our values and continued existence, and the misrepresentation and ahistorical construction of the past thirty years.
>
> *(Zimmerman, 2008: 50)*

The understanding of themselves as women and lesbians that formed the firm and necessary foundation of organising by second wave feminists has dissipated, in a way that creates difficulties for a new wave of activism, but there is evidence from online radical feminism that a new generation of young lesbians are developing their own form of lesbian feminism for new times. However, as transgender activism developed, during the same period in which feminism was under attack from queer and postmodern theory, these new forms of theory were employed to build the ideology that underpins transgender studies, and enable an onslaught on varieties of feminism that threaten the importance of gender as a grail. It is in this context, in that the very existence of 'women' and 'lesbians' has become doubtful, that 'transgender feminism' has been able to create a place for itself.

Transgender 'feminism'

Transgender 'feminism' argues that gender difference and femininity must be protected from the feminists who seek to demolish them. These theorists model 'femininity' on their own view, as men who consider themselves transgender, of what 'womanhood' is, i.e. pleasure in acting out the female sex role stereotype. Feminist theorists of the second wave saw it as crucially important to wrench the idea of what a woman is away from patriarchal ideologies and institutions and recreate it in a way suited to women's liberation. In such feminist work, male ideologues were accused of appropriating and colonising women's experience and existence (Millett, 1972). The institutions and ideologies that were identified as mediating the subordination of women are religion and the church, psychoanalysis and the medical profession, the so-called sciences of sociology and anthropology and the institutions of the state (de Beauvoir, 1973, first published 1949; Wittig, 1992). All the disciplines of universities, as Monique Wittig points out, can be seen to constitute the 'straight mind', that is ideas based on seeing women as complementary to men within the framework of heterosexuality (Wittig, 1992). These theorists have examined how the idea of woman has been constructed, and pointed out that this idea serves to justify male dominance. Importantly, the idea of woman is founded in the notion of an inevitable – and essential, usually biological – difference between the sexes. This 'difference' meant that woman was to be a helpmeet to man, to pleasure him, live under this control, provide children and a home, and display certain qualities that delighted him, an interest in fashion, display of the body, deference, feminine gestures and deportment. In the light of this, it should be a matter of some concern that men who transgender are retaking the opportunity to state what women are and should be, shape what feminism is and promote similar stereotypes. Once again men are exercising their authority in defining what women are.

The upshot of an atmosphere of acceptance, and indeed welcome, of transgenderism within the queer and postmodern feminist academy was the burgeoning of 'transgender feminism', whose creators and exponents are mainly men who transgender and reject entirely the form of feminism that eschews gender, and, instead, construct feminism as a movement for the celebration of gender stereotypes. This male-designed feminism has become so prominent within the feminist academy that, in 2011, for example, Indiana University hosted a conference entitled Postposttranssexual: Transgender Studies and Feminism (CSGS, 2011), and in 2012 at the University of California there was a 'research cluster' entitled 'Queer, Feminist and Transgender Studies' (DHI Research Cluster, n.d.), as if these currents of thought were compatible. In 2013 the Department of Women's Studies and Feminist Research at Western University in Canada will offer a subject called 'An Introduction to Transgender Studies'. Moreover, men who transgender are increasingly engaged to lecture to women about feminism as keynote speakers at feminist conferences, an example being the 22nd Annual Women and Society Conference in Poughkeepsie, New York in 2013. At this event the keynote was given by Kate Bornstein, whose perspective on women and society, as a man who has transgendered, will inevitably be very different from that of women, that is, persons with female bodies who did not choose their subordinate status, but were placed into it at birth (Culture Lab, 2013).

One influential exponent of 'transgender feminism' is Julia Serano, author of *Whipping Girl: A Transsexual Woman on Sexism and the Scapegoating of Femininity* (2007). Serano has a classic cross-dresser profile. He explains that he did not consider himself to be female until he was eleven years old and did not want to do girls' activities at school, though he had a sexual fantasy life of being turned into a girl: 'I did not have the quintessential trans experience of always feeling that I should have been born female' (Serano, 2007: 78). He realised he was female when he had the urge to dress in a lace curtain at eleven (an experience unlikely to have been shared by many females): 'It wasn't until the age of eleven that I consciously recognized these subconscious feelings as an urge or desire to be female … I found myself inexplicably compelled to remove a set of white, lacy curtains from the window and wrap them around my body like a dress' (Serano, 2007: 79). This important force in the creation of transfeminism decided he was somehow female in the brain – 'it seems as if, on some level, my brain expects my body to be female' when he realised he was sexually excited by clothing associated with women, and by curtains (Serano, 2007: 80).

Serano seeks to reinvent 'feminism' to fit his erotic interests. Since he is turned on by the accoutrements of femininity, he is angry that many feminists are critical of it. He states that feminists misunderstand femininity, 'Even many feminists buy into traditionally sexist notions about femininity: that it is artificial, contrived, and frivolous; that it is a ruse that only serves the purpose of attracting and appeasing the desires of men'. It is not true, he says, 'that femininity is subordinate to masculinity', nor that it is 'artificial' or 'performance'; in fact, 'certain aspects of femininity (as well as masculinity) are natural and can both precede socialization and supersede biological sex' (Serano, 2007: 6). The job of feminism, according to Serano, is to 'empower' femininity, because '[n]o form of gender equality can ever truly be achieved until we first work to empower femininity itself' (ibid.). He explains, 'I make the case that feminist activism and theory would be best served by working to empower and embrace femininity, rather than eschewing or deriding it, as it often has in the past' (Serano, 2007: 9). He chastises feminists for having somehow got everything wrong.

Transgender activists such as Serano have developed a new vocabulary to advance their political agenda. One of these new terms is 'cis', which they apply to all those who are not unhappy with their 'gender'. In effect the term 'cis' creates two kinds of women, those with female bodies who are labelled 'cisgender', and those with male bodies who are 'transwomen'. Women, those born female and raised as women, thus suffer a loss of status as they are relegated to being just one kind of woman and their voices will have to compete on a level playing field with the other variety, men who transgender. In this ideology, everyone has a gender, and those who have a 'gender' that fits their 'biological bodies' have 'cisprivilege', which advantages them over transgenders who are not comfortable with what Serano calls their 'birth' gender. Transgenders, he says, are oppressed by ciswomen, who do not recognise their privilege and do not seek to work off their guilt by supporting the demands and needs of oppressed transgender people who are more oppressed than women. Cispersons, that is women, are often guilty of '*Cissexism*, which is the belief that transsexuals' identified genders are inferior to, or less authentic than, those of *cissexuals* (i.e., people who are not transsexual and who have only ever experienced their subconscious and physical sexes as being aligned)' (Serano, 2007: 12) (emphasis in original). Examples of cissexism, apparently, include 'purposeful misuse of pronouns or insisting that the trans person use a different public restroom'. The concept of cissexism is employed by transgender activists to guilt-trip women into silence or support for their cause, and the addition of a prefix has political effects such as precluding feminist analysis of the situation of women. Moreover, transgender activists adjure women to refer to themselves as 'cis' even when speaking among themselves, free from the presence of men who consider themselves transgender. The transgender blogger T-girl, for instance, tells women in a guide how 'ciswomen' should relate to men who transgender but retain their penises and wish to date them: 'Please adopt this language, even when trans people are not around' (Savannah, 2013). The article is published on *Autostraddle*, a website run by lesbians for the LGBT community. Feminism is a political movement that started from being angry at men telling women who they are and when and how they should speak. For this reason, this kind of advice from a man in possession of a 'lady stick' – as penises are referred to in the transgender community – that women should police their conversations and only describe themselves in ways that could give no offence to such men, could look rather quaintly old fashioned in its arrogance and should, perhaps, be seen as an exercise of male power.

The term misogyny is also redefined by transgender activists so that it means disparagement of the femininity that is attractive to cross-dressers, as Serano comments, '*misogyny* will be used to describe this tendency to dismiss and deride femaleness and femininity' (Serano, 2007: 14). According to this logic feminists are mostly misogynists because they seek to abolish femininity, the behaviour of the underclass, and gender in general. As Serano explains, 'When a transperson is ridiculed or dismissed', they become 'victims of a specific form of discrimination: *trans-misogyny*' (Serano 2007: 15) (emphasis in original). This kind of verbal sleight of hand is a good example of what radical feminist theorist Mary Daly describes as 'patriarchal reversal' (Daly, 1978: 79). Transgender ideology is full of such reversals, in which the material reality of biological and existential womanhood is usurped by men who fantasise about being women.

The new language silences women and feminists. Any statements or behaviours that offend men who transgender, such as political criticism or lack of enthusiasm on the part of lesbians for relationships with men with 'lady sticks', are labelled 'transphobia'. This word owes its origin to the term 'homophobia', which is not the most useful of terms because it implies that hatred of homosexuals is some form of psychological problem rather than a politics. Discussion of what transgender activists are doing or saying can thus be labelled irrational as well as discriminatory and hateful. Feminist criticism, of course, is far from irrational and based in decades of theorising and practice, but through transgender sleight of hand it can be buried in loud boos and hisses and accusations of transphobia before it can reasonably be heard or considered.

The transimposition of their particular version of politically correct language has the effect of making it difficult to mention women's bodily processes. Even the observation that menstruation is a function of persons who are female can be labelled transphobic. In a book on menstruation from 2010 this scientific fact is proclaimed unacceptable because it disturbs the sensibilities of women who transgender and like to think they are not actually women:

> radical menstruation activists have changed the language of menstruation to talk about 'menstruators' rather than 'women who menstruate.' This choice of language not only reflects a commitment to a more inclusive (including trans people) movement but also demonstrates the political importance of gender neutral language and dismantling the narrowness and restrictiveness of gender binaries.
>
> *(Worcester, 2013: 151)*

In similar advice in the newsletter of the environmental group Earth First, women are told not to describe their bodies and reproductive processes as female: 'I am a birth educator, and with a lot of practice I have been able to replace cissexist language with more neutral terms like "birthing person," "parent," "breastfeeding person" etc. ... Changing cissexist language may seem like a lot of work, but it makes such a difference for trans people. Just do it!' (Hollis, 2013). Serano refers to himself as an 'infertile woman' and claims to find 'contraception-focused' feminism 'alienating' (Scum-o-rama, 2012). Issues related to reproduction are of great importance to women, of course, but may be boring for men who want 'feminism' to concentrate on their interest in impersonating women.

A useful resource providing insights into how both men and women academics who transgender seek to reconfigure feminism to suit their interests is the collection *Transfeminist Perspectives* (Enke (ed.), 2012). It is edited by Anne Enke, a self-described 'transfeminist teacher and activist' who has a 'vested interest in keeping the categories woman, and trans★ [*sic*] wide open' (Enke, 2012a: 77). Enke says that he is someone who 'peed standing up as a child, who spent more than twenty years terrified that someone would discover that I was "really" male, and who passes almost consistently as a woman' (Enke, 2012a: 71). Enke grew back his beard in 2012 and now wears it with a braid/plait. He has the privilege of being able to use whatever toilet he wants without being queried because of his high status at the university but remains so angry at not feeling entirely welcome in the women's facility, that

> I go there, braided and bearded, and am furious to discover the options … I can walk through either door, and I will not be physically or verbally assaulted. I enter the one that says 'women' … I kick the door as hard as I can on my way out.
>
> *(Enke, 2012a: 73)*

Such an act of aggression may well undermine Enke's mission to be recognised as a woman.

Enke argues, as is common in the transgender version of feminism, that both gender and sex are socially constructed: 'Gender, and also sex, are made through complex social and technical manipulations that naturalize some while abjecting others' (ibid.). All bodies, Enke argues, are 'made', and the problem with many feminists is that they believe that there is a difference between men's bodies and women's bodies and that that difference of biological sex matters. In fact, he states, all bodies are 'made, one kind of body no more or less technologically produced than the other', and 'feminist, queer, disability, and critical-race theorists, trans studies' recognise this. Some feminists, though, 'preserve sex as a category' and presume 'that there is a knowable difference between male and female bodies' (Enke, 2012b: 6). It is quite hard to know what Enke means here, since the reproductive differences between male and female bodies, breasts that can lactate, wombs and menstruation, non-surgical vaginas, penises, testes, are all objectively 'knowable' except in the argument of someone trying to deny common sense. In fact, Enke points out that 'the vast majority of transsexual people and people with significant cross-gender identification will have no genital surgeries' (ibid.), so the differences will be quite clear to the naked eye. Transfeminism, it seems, is based on a rather mystical principle that there is no such thing as biology. Enke makes a land grab for feminism itself, arguing that it is but a variety of transgender practice: 'most feminists should be seeing feminism as a transgender phenomenon: Some version of gender self-determination and resistance to binary gender norms and oppressions has always been central to feminism' (Enke, 2012b: 5).

Feminism is not just under attack from men who transgender, however. Jean Bobby Noble, a female academic who has transgendered, demonstrates considerable hostility towards feminism for its focus on female bodies (Noble, 2012). Noble accuses feminists of 'panic' about gender and says there is 'incessant repetition of panic over *trans* entities in the house of feminism' (Noble, 2012: 59) (emphasis in original). Feminists, it seems, are hysterical rather than having well thought out ideas about women being the foundation of the feminist project. Noble adds another insulting term to the critique of feminism by arguing that feminists are 'fundamentalists'.

> Doesn't the gender-panicked imperative to 'remember the women' mark an unequivocal gender fundamentalism, where such fundamentalisms themselves – not unlike those of nationalism, military-state, white-supremacist, or Christian, to name only a few – function to ground a feminist imaginary and its methodology of social, moral, and biological coercive normalization?
>
> *(Noble, 2012: 50)*

Noble uses the language of warfare to describe the campaign to make feminists bow to transgender priorities: 'Trans entities' are having to 'slowly fight their way into institutionalized feminist spaces' (Noble, 2012: 57).

Another important exponent of transgender feminism is the much respected Australian professor and theorist of gender, Robert Connell, who transgendered late in life and now calls himself Raewyn Connell. Connell writes and lectures on transgenderism and feminism (Connell, 2011, 2012). He describes criticisms of transgenderism made by Jeffreys and other feminists as 'attacks'. Connell proclaims that the campaign by feminists to abolish gender is inappropriate because gender should be maintained:

> The current in metropolitan feminism that hopes to abolish gender or dissolve the gender order has had strong appeal in the past two decades. But in the long run, transsexual women will find more relevance in the attempt to create just gender orders.
>
> *(Connell, 2012: 873)*

In 'just gender orders', gender will be retained but there will be less inequality between genders. In fact, the idea of a 'just gender order' is an oxymoron since gender is a hierarchy and in the absence of inequality would not exist. It is hard to know how inequality can be rendered 'just'. Despite his status and the esteem in which his contribution to feminist theory has been held, he ends up on the same trajectory as Julia Serano, towards the necessary protection of femininity.

The silencing of dissent

Alongside the direct confrontation that transgender activists are staging with feminist theory, there are many other ways in which their campaigning damages the gains of second wave feminism. Some of these will be discussed later in this volume, such as the campaign to enter women-only spaces and women-only services and the promotion of the transgendering of children. Other direct onslaughts on feminism and feminists will be considered here, such as the vilifying of, and attempts to silence, the work of feminist activists and theorists. It is important to transgender activists that they should be able to silence the feminist, sociological and scientific criticism of their practice, because much of the critique is easily understandable and likely to be readily embraced by a critical public if it gains publicity. The main method adopted to effect this silencing consists of campaigns of hatred and vilification to destroy the reputations of critics and to deny them spaces to speak or publish their work. If a person is known to have ever been critical of the practice of transgenderism the transgender activists seek to get them banned from speaking about any topic at all or harass them at venues. I was banned from speaking at a conference in London in July 2012, which was due to take place at the well-known venue, Conway Hall, as a result of the campaigning of transgender activists (Jeffreys, 2012a). The organisers were informed by the venue operators that I would not be allowed to speak after the activists had applied pressure and accused me of hate speech. I was banned on the grounds that I fostered 'hatred' and was guilty of active discrimination. On being asked to provide proof for this, Conway Hall appeared to compare me to 'David Irving the holocaust denier'. The proffered evidence consisted of quotes from my work arguing that transgender surgery should be considered a human rights violation – hardly evidence of hate speech. The feminist academic Germaine Greer was glitter-bombed in New Zealand in 2012 at a book signing by transgender activists for being critical of the practice in her book *The Whole Woman* and in other remarks (Gray, 2012).

Influential feminist opinion columnists receive similar treatment. In January 2013 the *Guardian* columnist, Suzanne Moore, became the object of serious and aggressive bullying by transgender activists because she opined that women were expected, in their appearance, to resemble Brazilian transsexuals (Moore, 2013). This led to a quite vicious campaign against her on social media. Moore replied with exasperation and the campaign was ramped up, with violent insults and threats explicitly directed against her female biology. Tweets included the sentiments that Moore was a 'cunt', 'a completely horrific bag of trash', 'cunted cunt', 'transmisogynist arsehole extraordinaire', 'a piss stain on the pants of fascism'. She was told that she needed to be 'entered', and, 'Guess who secretly wants to fuck all the trans chicks'. One commented, 'I will cut your face off and feed it to the wolves' (GenderTrender, 2013). In defence of Moore, Julie Burchill, another well-known and controversial columnist, wrote a piece critical of transgenderism in the *Observer* newspaper (Young, 2013). The transgender activist campaign against the Burchill piece led to its removal from the website and the issuing of an apology to the activists (Sweeney, 2013). In response, many malestream newspapers and feminist blogs chose to publish Burchill's piece and complain that the censorship of her was unreasonable. Transgender views are well represented in the *Guardian* and the *Observer*, with a number of men who have transgendered, such as Jane Fae, Roz Kaveney and Juliet Jacques, having regular columns in which they promote transgender ideology, criticise feminism and describe their transitions in very considerable detail. But these liberal newspapers, which seek to be politically correct, very rarely publish material that raises any kind of questions about the practice.

This harassment is so abusive, including copious taunts of 'Die cis scum' directed at any feminists that are transcritical (They say this never happens, 2012), that it suggests considerable rage on the part of the transgender activists involved. In acknowledgement of this, transgender psychotherapist, Anne Lawrence, has provided an explanation (Lawrence, 2008). Lawrence argues that the level of anger and abuse, including threats of extreme violence including death, could be accounted for by 'narcissistic rage', that is a form of rage experienced by persons who have suffered from shame and react in extreme and aggressive ways when they are challenged because of their history of feeling inferior. Whatever the explanation, the very determined and vituperative campaigns against critics suggest a great anxiety by transgender activists about the possibility that their practice could be rethought, and that their interpretations might not be the only ones that should be allowed an airing in the public domain.

Conclusion

At a time when feminism was experiencing backlash from many directions, the impact of queer and postmodern theory undermined the possibility that academic feminists and feminist communities could stand up to the challenge posed by the entryism of men who transgender into the movement. Once queer theory had made the category 'woman' questionable and promoted the transgressive nature of playing with gender, the transgender project was hard to criticise. The result is that not only has there been no critique of transgenderism from feminist scholars in recent decades, but transgender ideology has been welcomed into the feminist academy where students may be taught to deride the important work of second wave feminists on this issue, learn new politically correct language that makes it very difficult to articulate women's interests, and become radically uncertain about their sex and sexuality. The transgender project of promoting femininity as the proper focus of feminism has made considerable inroads into an academic feminism, which has, to a large extent, lost its way and failed to support women and feminist scholarship. There has been no feminist scholarship in recent decades that is critical, for example, of the harmful hormonal and surgical treatments that are used to transgender women and men, despite much incisive feminist criticism of such treatments when directed at women in the form of cosmetic surgery and hormone replacement therapy. The next chapter will seek to show that such a critique is urgently needed and contribute towards opening up a transcritical space on the mental and physical health of those who are transgendered.

3

DOING TRANSGENDER

Really hurting

Written with Lorene Gottschalk

This chapter examines the harmful effects of the practice of transgenderism on the health and functioning of transgenders themselves. The transgender studies literature is generally celebratory and does not cover the harm to the health of individual transgenders from their medical treatment. Moreover, it disregards the increasingly common problem of 'transgender regret', that is the feelings of survivors of the treatment who consider that they have been wrongly diagnosed and may wish to have reconstructive surgery so that they can repair surgical harms. While feminist scholars have explored the harmful effects of other areas of hormone treatment and cosmetic surgery, and created sophisticated theoretical critiques of the medical industry that wreaks this damage on women (Haiken, 1997; Sullivan, Deborah A., 2001), there is no such critique, apart from the early pioneering work of Janice Raymond, of transgender treatment (Raymond, 1979/1994). This is the case despite the fact that many of the surgeries and treatments are the same as those that have harmful effects upon women. Prolonged hormone treatment, for instance, is used on women in the forms of the contraceptive pill and implants, and on postmenopausal women when it is called hormone replacement therapy (HRT), precisely the same term that is applied to similar drug regimes when used on women and men who have been transgendered. The surgeons who offer cosmetic treatments to enable women to play the feminine part also offer cosmetic breast and facial surgeries to men who wish to play a similar role. But the feminist critique of cosmetic surgery has not been extended to the similar treatment of transgenders.

This chapter will bridge this divide and criticise the harms to the bodies of its victims of what Janice G. Raymond calls *The Transsexual Empire* (1979/1994), which consists of those parts of the medical profession, and those pharmaceutical companies, that rely on transgendering men, women and children for their profits. In the early twenty-first century, sex-reassignment surgery (SRS) is common worldwide from small towns in the United States to developing countries. It is an important part of the medical tourism industry of Thailand and of the economy of the small town of Trinidad in the state of Colorado, for instance (Bucar and Enke, 2011). An example of the avoidance of such topics is a chapter in the collection *Transgender Feminist Perspectives* (Enke (ed.), 2012), ostensibly concerned with fitting the practice of transgenderism into political economy theory, and subtitled 'Notes on the Relationship between Critical Political Economy and Trans Studies' (Irving, 2012). I was intrigued and thought some of these problematic issues might at last be approached. But the chapter turns out to be concerned with who is able to afford the treatments, and contains nothing about the international medical tourism industry that services those seeking surgery, and nothing on who is making the profits, the drug companies, hospitals and surgeons, psychiatrists and therapists. Such considerations are not part of transgender studies, though they are an important part of feminist studies. This chapter describes the treatment options for both male and female-bodied transgenders and details the consequences and side effects. It uses information from the websites of transgender support organisations, medical literature, and interviews with one male and one female transgender regretter to gain an understanding of how the mental and physical health of those who transgender is affected.

The efficacy of sex reassignment – medical disagreement

Historically, there has been far from universal agreement as to the efficacy of treatment for persons identified as transsexual/transgender. The term 'efficacy' is widely used in the medical literature on the practice but not well defined. In this chapter I understand the 'efficacy' of treatment to relate to the degree of improvement in mental health without injury to physical health. Since the 1950s and 1960s when some endocrinologists such as Harry Benjamin were seeking to legitimise body changing treatment for transsexuals, there have been doctors and psychiatrists who did not agree that a problem of the mind should be treated with physical therapies. As early as the 1970s, Dr Jon Meyer conducted an evaluation of the success of the treatment at the Johns Hopkins Gender Identity Clinic, which led him to the conclusion that physical therapies were ineffective (Meyer and Reter, 1979). He does not see transgenderism as an innate condition that should be affirmed by surgery, but sees the request for sex change as essentially 'problematic', and he wants to 'step back from "normalization" of sex-reassignment procedures in order to look objectively at the long-range effects of surgery' (Meyer and Reter, 1979: 1010). Meyer and Reter document the findings of the small number of previous evaluations of the effectiveness of treatment, none of which support the overwhelmingly positive message that issues from transgender activists today. Meyer's conclusion after his evaluation of fifty persons, including a comparison between those who asked for surgery and got it and those who were refused, was that 'Sex reassignment surgery confers no objective advantage in terms of social rehabilitation, although it remains subjectively satisfying' (Meyer and Reter, 1979: 1015). Meyer's critique of transgender treatment contains no trace of a feminist perspective. Like other psychiatrists of his era he was keen to blame women, usually mothers, for the psychological problems of his patients. He attributes gender identity problems in women and girls to mothers who have 'significant character pathology', possess 'penis envy' and 'a sense of the unfairness of a woman's "lot" (penetration, menstruation, gestation)' (Meyer, 1982: 410).

Paul McHugh, who became Head of Psychiatry at Johns Hopkins University in the 1970s, upon seeing the lack of evidence for the efficacy of surgery stated, 'Hopkins was fundamentally cooperating with a mental illness. We psychiatrists, I thought, would do better to concentrate on trying to fix their minds and not their genitalia' (McHugh, 2004). McHugh stopped the practice of SRS at Johns Hopkins in 1979 and other university clinics followed suit. This critique continues in the present but has become much more muted as a result of the normalisation of the practice and the burgeoning of the 'transsexual empire'. Nonetheless, one strong contemporary critique comes from the psychiatrist Az Hakeem, who works at the Portman Clinic in London, specialising in therapy with those seeking to be transgendered, and those who have been transgendered but continue to suffer distress. In a book chapter aptly titled 'Trans-sexuality: a case of "The Emperor's New Clothes"', he calls the notion of persons seeking to be transgendered that they are really of the other gender or sex an 'overwhelming false belief' and a 'delusional disorder' (Hakeem, 2007: 184). He criticises the practice of treating transgenderism as a biological condition that resides in the body and can be cured through hormones and surgery, commenting that 'It seems strange that as psychiatrists we attempt to address an internal psychological conflict with an exterior surgical solution' (Hakeem, 2007: 183). He points out that psychiatrists who are 'psychoanalytically informed' are those most likely to be critical of the practice. One such critic is the French, feminist psychoanalyst, Colette Chiland (Chiland, 2004).

There is still a remarkable absence of recent studies that follow up those who have SRS to find out whether this treatment is efficacious despite the great expansion of the industry of transgendering. A 2011 long-term follow-up study from Sweden found that sex reassignment was not efficacious because after sex reassignment transgenders had higher risks of psychiatric morbidity, suicidal behaviour and mortality overall than the general population, when using controls of the same birth sex. The study concluded that 'sex reassignment' may alleviate 'gender dysphoria' but 'may not suffice as treatment for transsexualism, and should inspire improved psychiatric and somatic care after sex reassignment' (Dhejne *et al.*, 2011). The voices of critical medical personnel, and the problems revealed by the few long-term evaluations, have not been successful in dampening the enthusiasm of the medical profession and pharmaceutical companies for this fashionable and profitable 'disorder'. Indeed, the public health service of the UK, the National Health Service, has endorsed the practice not just for adults but also for children (Department of Health, 2008).

Identifying 'real' transgenders

Health professionals seek to identify those who have a 'genuine' gender identity disorder, or gender dysphoria as it is renamed in the 2013 *Diagnostic and Statistical Manual*, and assert its essential nature as the justification for treating it. This is despite the fact that transgenderism is becoming an increasingly slippery concept. And the idea that it is a disorder of any kind is in dispute by transgender activists themselves, some of whom argue that the hormones and surgery should be elective and constitute ways of contouring the body that everyone should have the right to access via the public purse. Moreover, many transgenders in the present make no effort to support the idea that they are essentially members of the opposite sex. In Kristen Schilt's study of female-bodied transgenders, for instance, she found that some of her interviewees did not consider themselves men or male (Schilt, 2006). They were simply women who had availed themselves of 'top' surgery, or may be taking hormones electively. Female-bodied transgender, Jean Bobby Noble, says that the borderlines between butches and transgenders are blurred and describes herself, a woman who was a lesbian and feminist for many years before she decided to transgender, as 'a guy who is half a lesbian' (Noble, 2012: 29). She says that she does not 'find my home in the word "lesbian" any longer (although that's often my dating pool)' (Noble, 2012: 21). The prominent US male-bodied transgender activist, Rikki Wilchins, now describes himself as a 'male-to-female-to-male transsexual', and has given up any attempts to look 'feminine', though he still uses the women's toilets (Wilchins, 2013). Wilchins is the founder of the transgender activist group Transsexual Menace; the campaigning group GenderPAC, which promotes the right to 'gender'; and the encampment that lays siege to the Michigan Women's Music Festival, Camp Trans. The understanding of who is genuinely transgender becomes more and more murky and insubstantial, at precisely the same time that more is being revealed about the harmful effects of the practice. The idea that there is such an entity as a 'real' transsexual has become increasingly difficult to support.

The task of identification is muddied further by the campaign by part of the transgender rights movement to defeat the idea that the desire to transition is a 'mental disorder'. Rather, activists argue that transgenderism is an ordinary expression of the human condition and should be available in the same way as other forms of cosmetic surgery in which people seek to express a desired appearance. Riki Wilchins is an influential exponent of this point of view and states that transgenderism should not be seen as a mental disorder and that SRS is similar to the variety of cosmetic surgeries that some women engage in. He complains that while his mother 'can go into the hospital tomorrow and she can get calf implants and chin implants, get her eyelids, her butt, and her tummy tucked, collagen put into her lips and collagen taken off her thighs', if he were to 'go into the same hospital for a "groin job"' he is seen as having a mental disorder (Drescher, 2002: 79). Despite this determination by some transgender activists to defeat the idea that transgenderism is evidence of poor mental health, there is considerable evidence that persons who transgender do suffer from a range of serious mental health problems before, and often after, they transition.

Psychological harms

The main argument advanced for the efficaciousness of transgender treatment is that it improves mental health, but there is a good deal of evidence that this is not necessarily the case. The severity of the mental health problems of persons who aspire to transgender are clear in the clinical literature, with patients who present at gender clinics having 'levels of anxiety and depressive disorders that are much higher than the general population' (Nuttbrock et al., 2010: 13). However, as a result of the normalisation of transgenderism that has taken place, the medical professionals who treat transgenders are reluctant to see the desire to transgender as a symptom of this mental distress. Rather, in order to match the trans ideology that the desire to transgender is an entirely sane and reasonable ambition that should not be managed by medical gatekeepers, the concept of 'minority stress' has been used in explanation of the psychological distress that transgenders experience. 'Minority stress' is a concept developed in relation to gay men, meaning the psychological distress they experience as a result of their minority status (Meyer, 1995). A form of this approach, adapted to transgenderism, is ubiquitous in the voluminous clinical literature. If persons who transgender were unhappy children, for instance, then it is assumed that this was because they were 'really' transgender even at that time. Mental health professionals are advised that they should abandon misgivings and be accepting of any claims by their patients to be transgender and avoid at all costs any negative responses or attempts to deter them from embarking on their quest. To suggest that the mental health problems that transgenders experience may be the cause of transgenderism would, according to this literature, be most reprehensible.

A similar approach, the 'disability model', is now being promoted as best practice for dealing with transgender patients in a guide for UK hospitals produced by the Royal Free Hospital in Hampstead: 'In understanding the great difficulties in trans people's lives, it is helpful to adopt the widely accepted disability model – that it is the barriers and obstacles presented in society that cause the problems and not being trans in itself' (Thom and Weeks, 2010). According to this model, as in that of 'minority stress', the distress that transgenders feel is the result of discrimination and prejudice against them. The 'minority stress' approach and the 'disability model' have a lot of work to do to explain why the severe distress of those who transgender is so long-lasting, both before and after transition. One study taking this approach, that the distress of transgenders is caused by abuse that is related to their gender identities and called 'gender-related' abuse, found that lifetime major depression in the male-bodied transgenders who were studied, at 54.3 per cent, was almost three times higher than the estimate for the general population (Nuttbrock *et al.*, 2010: 21). Lifetime suicidal ideation, at 53.5 per cent, was more than three times that for the general population.

The use of concepts such as 'gender-related' abuse, 'minority stress', and the disability model creates a context in which important questions cannot be asked. It closes out the possibility that violence and sexual and physical abuse may be causes of the desire to 'transition'. There is some support in the literature, though the research does not usually ask about this, for a connection between the experience of sexual violence and a determination to transgender. Holly Devor's study of women who had transgendered found a strong association in information volunteered by interviewees, but did not ask a question about violence (Devor, 1994). One study of attempted suicide among transgenders, which found that 60 per cent of participants were depressed, also found that 59 per cent had been forced to have sex or raped, which, the authors consider, is one of the factors related to the high rate of attempted suicide – 32 per cent in the sample (Clements-Nolle and Marx, 2006). The regretter who was interviewed for this book, Walt Heyer, whose website and publications have led to his networking with large numbers of survivors, considers that sexual abuse is an under-recognised contributor to the desire to transgender. It played a role, he argues, in his case as he was 'sexually molested by my uncle before I was 10 years old for a 2–3 year period of time'. The abuse took place after the uncle discovered that the grandmother was putting the boy child into feminine attire. In relation to female-bodied transgenders in particular, he says, 'in every case where I have had a personal involvement with the family or the parents the kid was abused, every one of them!' But recognition of this link would undermine the accepted belief in the medical profession that the distress of those who transgender is due only to 'minority stress', and so it is not the focus of research.

The assumption behind hormonal and surgical treatments is that these mental health problems will be alleviated but there is a good deal of evidence in terms of suicidality and depression, for instance, that this will not necessarily be the case. One reason for this may be that social functioning is impaired rather than improved by the practice, as persons who transgender may find it difficult to form relationships and may alienate their families. A German follow-up study after five years found that 30 to 40 per cent of the patients who had been very carefully selected for sex-reassignment surgery did not 'seem to benefit fully from SRS' in areas such as social, psychological, and psychiatric functioning (Bodlund and Kullgren, 1996: 311). As well as not providing redress for the psychological ills experienced by transgenders, the treatments by hormones and surgery are likely to create new and grave challenges for health and functioning.

Side effects of hormone treatment

Though some aspiring transgenders buy hormones on the black market, most will find physicians willing to prescribe them. An increasing percentage of transgenders do not undertake surgery on their genitals though they may have mastectomies, or breast implants. However, most do take hormones and the treatment is called 'hormone replacement therapy' or HRT. HRT was promoted to women as a way to alleviate the distress they experienced when their allotted sex role of looking desirable for men was undermined by the aging process, and it was touted as a way to prevent menopausal symptoms. It was severely discredited in the early 2000s (Writing Group for the Women's Health Initiative Investigators, 2002). But, with the increasing use of HRT by transgenders, the drug companies have found a newly profitable form of psychological distress to exploit. Hormone usage has to be lifelong for those who wish to maintain an appearance of the opposite sex, or who need to avoid the premature menopause and problems for bone health involved in being without hormones. Profits will be increased by rising numbers of diagnoses, particularly if these take place at young ages and hook children into seventy or eighty years of hormone use.

As a result of the remarkable lack of long-term follow-up studies there is little information on the effects of hormone treatment of transsexuals (Schlatterer *et al.*, 1998). One short-term follow-up study warns, however, that 'cross-sex hormonal treatment may have substantial medical side effects' (Futterweit, 1998: 209). It found that the main side effects of androgen therapy in female-bodied transgenders were: water and sodium retention and occasional 'cerebrovascular accidents'; increased erythropoiesis, i.e.

overdevelopment of red blood cells, which may require bloodletting; decreased carbohydrate tolerance; decreased serum high-density lipoprotein cholesterol, which is an indicator of diseased arteries; liver enzyme abnormalities, which can indicate cancer risk; obesity; emotional or psychiatric problems including 'very frequent early increased aggressiveness, fluctuating moods'; hypersexuality; 'affective and/or psychotic symptoms'; and depression (Futterweit, 1998: 215). The study warns against prolonged hormone treatment prior to surgery because of the risk of endometrial cancer. A study of two cases of long-term exposure to androgens leading to ovarian epithelial cancer concludes that androgen use is a risk factor for this form of cancer and recommends removal of ovaries in female-bodied transgenders (Hage, 2000).

A 1980s evaluation by a team from the Dutch transgender industry found very worrying results (Asscheman *et al.*, 1989). They studied 425 'transsexual' patients for the 'side effects of sex steroid treatment' (Asscheman *et al.*, 1989: 867). They found, as have other studies, a serious level of suicidality, with the number of deaths in men who transgendered being five times the number expected when compared with men who did not transgender. But the study also found significant adverse health effects from the hormone treatment. There was an increase in thromboembolic events (45-fold); in hyperprolactinemia, that is excessive production of the hormone responsible for milk secretion in women's breasts (400-fold); depressive mood changes (15-fold); and transient elevation of liver enzymes. The problems were different and not as lethal for women who transgendered, consisting mainly of weight gain and acne, but both groups had persistent liver enzyme abnormalities. The study concluded that the 'occurrence of serious side effects' was 'not rare'.

A study of the way in which the hormone treatment took place found that there was very considerable inconsistency in dosage: 'Typical transsexual estrogens were two to three times as high as the recommended doses for hormone replacement therapy (HRT) in postmenopausal women' (Moore *et al.*, 2003: 3468). The authors point out that this is a serious concern considering the findings of the Women's Health Initiative study where considerably lower levels of hormone usage were found to cause harm. The Women's Health Initiative study of 2002 found combined oestrogen and progestin increased the risk of coronary heart disease, strokes, pulmonary embolism and invasive breast cancers in postmenopausal women on HRT (Writing Group for the Women's Health Initiative Investigators, 2002). For this reason, sustained use of a progestin is warned against, though some practitioners are still using it for purposes such as enhancing breast growth (Moore *et al.*, 2003: 3469). The study on forms of hormone treatment concluded that the 'adverse effects of sex steroid therapy are real and apparent' and it states that 'gender reassignment ... should not be considered a cure' (ibid.). It found that some patients, who procured hormones from a variety of sources, were on regimes of hormones that were twenty-one or even thirty times greater than in postmenopausal women. The study found that there was little research on the effects on women who transgender because the numbers were usually too small, but the authors considered that the risks for this group may be 'underestimated' as the 'worrisome combination of increased weight, decreased insulin sensitivity, poor lipid profiles, and an increase in hematocrit (percentage of red blood cells) have raised the concern for cardiac and thromboembolytic events' (Moore *et al.*, 2003: 3470). Another serious effect for male-bodied transgenders seems to be the possibility of breast cancer, with one study noting increased risk of breast cancer, deep vein thrombosis and osteoporosis, especially for older male-bodied transgenders (Persson, 2009).

The National Health Service (NHS) in the UK admits that little research has been done on the long-term use of hormones in transgendered people, effectively admitting that this treatment is experimental. They write, 'Hormone treatment for trans people at reasonable dosages is remarkably safe' (NHS, 2007: 11) but then proceed to list the potential side effects. They point out that taking oestrogen is associated with thrombosis, stroke, pulmonary embolism and altered liver function, and that taking testosterone is associated with polycythaemia (overproduction of red blood cells) (NHS, 2007; Persson, 2009). The overproduction of red blood cells causes the blood to become thicker than normal and can cause breathlessness and phlebitis (inflammation of the veins), thus increasing the risk of heart disease and heart attack. For a practice that is 'remarkably safe', this is a surprisingly extensive list of serious side effects. All of these health problems are attached to a practice that, as we have seen, some authors have identified as 'iatrogenic', that is, caused by the faulty diagnosis that originated from the medical profession itself (Bullough, 2006). Though once what was called 'transsexualism' was understood to require sex-reassignment surgery as well as hormone consumption, this is not the case with transgenderism. Aspirants are likely to take hormones but may not proceed to surgery, and, indeed, the 2004 Gender Recognition legislation in the UK requires neither hormones nor surgery on the part of those receiving certificates to show they have changed their sex (Jeffreys, 2008). For those who do go on to surgery other serious harms are likely to result.

Surgery and self-harm

For those transgenders who seek to change their bodies there are a number of means that do not require access to the conventional medical system. Some transgenders may not have the resources to use doctors, or may be leading disorganised lives in which non-medical practices are more familiar and accessible. They will often self-harm before they transition, through practices such as using street-bought hormones, injecting silicone into chest tissue and breast binding, practices that are outside medical supervision. They may engage in cutting and piercing as other young people involved in body modification do (Jeffreys, 2000; 2008). Body modifiers have high suicidality and exhibit similar mental health problems to those who transgender (Jeffreys, 2008). Once body modifiers become involved with the medical profession, their self-harm becomes official and is directed by doctors licensed by the state. Doctors may be unlikely to recognise the legitimacy of a man's desire to be a nullo (i.e. a body modification practice of having all external genitals amputated) and he would likely have to find a professional piercer and cutter to do the job. They do, however, recognise transgenderism and put patients on regimes of hormones that will change their bodies, in some ways permanently, and direct them towards surgery to remove sexual characteristics. All of these practices inflict harms upon the body, which include scarring, loss of sensation, sterilisation, weight gain, acne, infection, necrosis of tissue and many more problems, alongside the risks involved in undergoing anaesthesia.

It is not always easy to distinguish the medical practices from those that self-mutilators carry out on themselves in private, or engage others to practise upon them. There can be a connection between self-harm in private, such as that which young women in particular are likely to perform in their homes, and 'self-mutilation by proxy', that is practices in which women and men seek out others to inflict dangerous physical harms to their bodies (Jeffreys, 2000). The proxies may be professionals in the cutting and piercing industry who brand and cut out designs from flesh and are paid to do so, or they may be tops in sadomasochism in which cutting, branding and piercing are common practices. They may also be medical doctors who legitimise self-mutilation by providing their services for a fee, such as cosmetic surgeons who do breast implants and facelifts for women and those who perform transgender surgery.

The first harmful practice that an aspiring female-bodied transgender is likely to adopt, without medical oversight, is breast binding. Breast binding is not a new practice, but was adopted by butch lesbians in the 1950s in the United States and United Kingdom as a way to make them look more masculine or to alleviate the dysphoria of loving women in clearly female bodies, in an era when that was socially forbidden (Jeffreys, 1989). While the advent of lesbian feminism in the 1970s enabled lesbians to have pride in loving women without having to ape men or negate female characteristics, the rebirth of butch and femme role playing, and now transgenderism, have meant that in the last two decades breast binding has returned to the lesbian community with a vengeance. Interestingly, breast binding is a practice that was a counterpart to foot binding in China until the 1920s (Chin, 2012). The practice was enforced on women to conceal their sexual characteristics and to conform with modesty requirements. Breasts were seen as too sexually explicit and exciting to men. Presently, it is a Chinese cultural context, Taiwan, that is now an important source of binders for aspiring female-bodied transgenders who are keen to conceal their female sexual characteristics (see for example, T-Kingdom, accessed 20 February 2013).

Among female-bodied transgenders, the desire to eliminate their breasts is strong and they are likely to use breast binding as a technique to hide their breasts in the lead-up to having them surgically removed. Breast binding leads to a number of serious health problems. The Transguys website offers advice on what it calls 'chest binding', which is perhaps a more appealing term for women who are denying that they have female body parts (Transguys, 2010). They warn against binding in ways that restrict breathing and create a lack of oxygen and warn that binders are uncomfortable and hot, causing sweat and skin irritation and sores that resemble open wounds. Despite the harms, Transguys explains, 'chest binding' can be 'very freeing for transgender men' as it can 'curb dysphoria'. A Stanford University student health website offers useful tips in relation to 'chest' binding, explaining that using 'Ace bandages, saran wrap, or duct tape' can peel skin and permanently damage ribs (Stanford University, n.d.). Rib displacement from the practice, which can lead to permanent physical harm, is a common source of concern on transgender 'health' websites (Ira, 2010).

Surgery for female-bodied transgenders

Surgeons have become active participants in the contemporary epidemic of self-mutilation. They act as proxies in the now mainstream and profitable practice of cosmetic surgery, mostly on women (Sullivan, Deborah, 2001), and it has now become routine for some of the same surgeons to perform sex-reassignment surgery so that those who cut women's labia to make them more socially acceptable, and tighten their vaginas for their husbands' pleasure, also create labia and vaginas for men who are transitioning to become 'women' (Jeffreys, 2005). Surgery for female-bodied transgenders, which can include mastectomy, hysterectomy and phalloplasty, creates a number of health challenges. Mastectomy can lead to severe scarring and, as Holly Devor explains, this type of amputation surgery can lead to serious losses, such as permanent loss of feeling in nipples (Devor, 1999: 480). The majority of female-bodied transgenders in Devor's study chose not to go on to phalloplasty, though such a decision can lead to them feeling incomplete in their sexual lives. They may, however, choose to engage in a variety of 'body modifications' that are promoted on transgender websites to increase the size of the clitoris, and make it more prominent and noticeable (Tenpenny and Cascio, 2002). These modifications may include 'pumping' the clitoris and using piercings to make it stick out. Piercings and metal rings may be inserted to close the vagina and make it clear to potential partners that that female area of the body is out of bounds (ibid.).

For those who want a closer simulacrum to a penis, there are two methods by which this can be accomplished: metoidioplasty and phalloplasty. Metoidioplasty can be carried out by surgeons or, in the body modification community, by non-professionals. When carried out by surgeons it takes place as follows: 'the enlarged clitoris, which is an effect of testosterone hormone replacement therapy (HRT), is relocated upwards to create a sensate and functioning micropenis' (Female to Male, n.d.). This is achieved by 'releasing' the suspensory ligament and creates a small imitation penis that does not allow urination while standing up. Phalloplasty creates a phallus through the use of a flap of flesh taken, usually, from the forearm, and is a lengthy, multi-stage procedure involving more serious risks. Neither procedure creates a phallus that is functional in the way that a penis might be, and there can be very serious side effects including lack of sexual feeling. A French study found that forty-six patients, or 83 per cent, had some feeling in the constructed phallus but 'only five (9%) had obvious erogenous sensitivity when touching their phalloplasty' (Leriche *et al.*, 2008). Other surgeries, such as hysterectomy, may occasion later regret as they lead to sterilisation and loss of the capacity for motherhood. Serious surgical procedures, such as those involved in reassignment that require the amputation of healthy body parts, involve the risks that appertain to anaesthesia and the problems of healing from complex surgery.

Surgery for male-bodied transgenders

Male-bodied transgenders who go further than the consumption of hormones seek a different palette of surgeries, which can include breast implants, amputation of penis and testes, construction of a penetrable orifice, facial surgeries, surgeries to 'contour' the body, or shave the Adam's apple, and an array of other possibilities. The potential range of surgeries is large and the determined aspirant may continue for years to undertake more and varied forms. In some cases these surgeries, too, have analogies in the non-medical, body modification arena. The description and illustrations of surgery on male-bodied transgenders presented in an issue of the *International Journal of Transgenderism*, the house magazine of the society of psychiatrists and surgeons specialising in this condition set up by the sexologist Harry Benjamin, suggest similarities with the way that body modification procedures, including castration, are demonstrated on the Internet for the sexual satisfaction of devotees (Perovic *et al.*, 2005). The Body Modification Ezine website, for instance, carries bloody and graphic photos of brutal cutting practices such as suspension, which can be downloaded by aficionados for a price just like any other pornography on the web (Jeffreys, 2008). The journal article includes seven pages of hand-drawn pictures illustrating how a particular group of surgeons cut up the penis and then eleven pages of full colour photos of the 'disassembled penis' that are extremely gruesome with bloody bits and pieces of the penis held up by medical instruments for appraisal. The authors explain that they invert the skin of the penis to form a vagina and insert this into a 'previously prepared cavity'. Then they form labia from 'the remaining penile and scrotal skin' (Perovic et al., 2005: 43). This public presentation of the mutilation of the penis is not obviously very different from the forms of disassembly of the penis engaged in by male body modifiers –particularly nullos and transgenders – on the Body Modification Ezine website and may offer similar satisfactions to those involved. But it is presented under the mantle of science, which offers more respectability.

This mutilating practice has been so normalised as a 'therapy' for the problem of psychological distress about 'gender' that the physical harms involved are seldom remarked upon. But problems, as the *Journal of Transgenderism* article explains, can occur. They include unsatisfactory levels of moisture, 'rectovaginal fistula due to intraoperative injury to the rectum', 'vaginal shrinking in two patients', 'stenosis of vaginal introitus', 'late stenosis of urethral meatus in one patient due to injury during sexual intercourse', 'urethral prolapse', and 'posterior vaginal wall rupture during intercourse' (Perovic et al., 2005: 57). Patients whose new orifices have been fashioned from sufficient penile skin need to place objects called 'stents' in the surgically constructed vagina at night to keep it open 'until sexual intercourse is regularly practiced' (Perovic et al., 2005: 64). Those who have 'insufficient penile skin' are advised to apply stents 'continuously day and night for one year in order to prevent contractures following secondary epithelializaiton of free penile skin grafts' (ibid.). The patients are advised to use their constructed vaginas for sexual intercourse as soon as possible 'even though bleeding may occur'. Pain is not mentioned and the problems presented by reassembly in the case of those who change their minds are not addressed. Electrolysis to remove pubic hair is needed if scrotal skin is used to line the constructed vagina. In one case discussed in an article in the *Guardian* (Batty, 2004), that of Claudia, the skin of the scrotum that had been used in the constructed vagina had not had electrolysis to remove the pubic hair and the hair grew inside the vagina: 'One day I was making love and something didn't feel right. There was this little ball of hair like a Brillo pad in my vagina.' A surgeon pulled the hair out for him but warned it would continually grow back (ibid.).

The new orifice is not a vagina in the biological sense. Vaginas are connected into the reproductive system of the female body rather than being simply an external cavity, and they are self-cleansing mechanisms. The newly carved out orifices of male-bodied transgenders do not resemble vaginas; rather they create new microbial habitats in which infections develop and cause serious smell issues for their owners. The problem of bad smell is a commonly occurring discussion thread on transgender advice websites. The medical evidence is that a bad smell exists and is associated with faecal bacteria common to those male-bodied transgenders who engage in 'heterosexual' coitus: 'Frequent episodes of malodorous discharge were reported by one in four women and malodour was even more frequently observed upon gynaecological examination, which in turn might relate to the presence of faecal bacterial vaginosis-like microflora' (Weyers, et al., 2009). The neovaginas lack the lactobacilli connected with vaginal health in females.

Facial feminisation surgery

Surgeries for male-bodied transgenders do not necessarily stop at amputation of genitals, surgically created fake vaginas and breast implants. In the last decade the transgender surgery industry has diversified considerably and now offers a wide variety of facial feminisation surgeries (FFS). This surgery supposedly solves the problem, for adult men who transgender, of having masculine features. Some of the 'most popular' facial surgeries, according to the industry website facialfeminizationsurgery.info, include: brow lift; temporal lift; scalp advancement; frontal bossing reduction osteotomy; reduction osteotomy of the supra-orbital rims; nasal tip refinement; osteotomy of the bony pyramid; lateral lower mandibular shave; mandibular angle shave; submandibular liposuction; necklift; face lift; and many more (Facialfeminizationsurgery. info, n.d.). The industry website describes FFS as 'very invasive' surgery and provides a compendious list of warnings and possible harmful effects from severe risks, which include: blood loss; blood clots; infection; pneumonia; necrosis – death of tissue; and paralysis, through to less serious risks such as scarring (Facialfeminization.info, n.d.). There are also, apparently, psychological risks, including depression, and the website warns that 'almost every patient can suffer some level of post-surgical depression' as well as anxiety and regret. The link to finding a facial surgeon goes straight to the website of well-known US cosmetic surgeon, Dr Jeffrey Spiegel, who has added FFS to his usual array of facial cosmetic surgeries aimed at women (drspiegel, n.d.). Spiegel defines facial feminisation surgery as 'procedures that provide patients with the face they should have been born with' and the goal is 'to provide you with all of the major and subtle features that support your true gender'. Cheaper access to FFS is offered in Thailand, where a thriving medical tourism industry offers all forms of surgery connected with transgenderism (ThaiMed, n.d.). The range of surgeries that male-bodied transgenders can embark upon is very extensive and provides scope for those addicted to the surgeries and their effects to pursue these dangerous and invasive procedures for many years, providing greater profits for the industry. The harms associated with the surgery are compounded for those who change their minds and are unable to recover their health and physical functions.

Transgender regrets

The inconvenient fact that persons who have been on hormone regimes or had sex-reassignment surgery, and even gained new legal status as members of the opposite sex, can change their minds and experience regret is fiercely denied by transgender activists, and ignored by the medical professionals involved in transgendering, because it undermines the credibility of the practice. It is avoided by lawmakers, too, who prefer the fiction that none of those who gain gender recognition certificates in the UK, for example, will change their minds (Jeffreys, 2008). Opponents of the 2004 legislation that enabled transgenders in the UK to officially change their sex sought to get amendments that would allow persons who changed their minds to go back before the panel and get recertificated. They also asked what would happen to persons who changed their minds more than once and whether the legislation would be able to accommodate them. The government rejected these arguments as not being serious, but, in fact, regret is a very harmful effect of transgender treatment. Persons who regret, if they have spent years on hormones or have gone so far as surgical treatment, will have experienced some irreversible physical harms such as sterilisation. They are also likely to have experienced social harms such as isolation from family and from relationships, factors commonly given as reasons for wanting to de-transition (return to live in original sex). The phenomenon of regret undermines the idea that there exists a particular kind of person who is genuinely and essentially transgender and can be identified accurately by psychiatrists. It is radically destabilising to the transgender project.

The survivors' movement

Nonetheless, in the last decade, as the volume of transgender surgeries has increased, there has been a concomitant increase in the cases of regret, in which persons who transitioned have argued that they were misdiagnosed and some have sought to have surgery to reverse their sex reassignment. Those who regret their transitioning might also be described as 'survivors' of the harmful practices directed at them by the medical profession, and the terms will be used interchangeably here. The phenomenon of transgender regrets has been recognised in sections of the therapeutic community. Az Hakeem runs a therapy group at London's Portman Clinic that includes both men who aspire to transition and those who regret having transitioned, categories of persons who were previously kept separate, but who have useful things to say to each other:

> The preoperative group was characterised by hope and optimism, at times extending to a gender euphoria, whereas the postoperative group was characterised by despair, hopelessness and regret, mainly because the group members were individuals who wished they had not had surgery.
>
> *(Hakeem, 2012: 20)*

There is presently some evidence that a survivors' movement is under way and is developing a political critique of the practice. It offers support to those who are considering transition but are not sure, and to those who have doubts about their choice. Until the last couple of years, there were only two websites dedicated to survivors. One is that of Walt Heyer, a postoperative male-bodied transgender in the United States, who has de-transitioned and now believes that his surgery and all SRS are mistaken (Heyer, n.d.). Dissatisfied post SRS male-bodied transgenders have told their stories on the website, and one states that he realised that 'what he needed was simple psychotherapy, not sex change surgery'. The other is the website Gendermenders, set up from Melbourne, Australia, which criticises the idea of transgenderism and all forms of treatment (Gender Menders, n.d.). More recently, however, the setting-up of resources for regretters has accelerated. Atlas Strawberries was established in 2012. Its founders, two people who say they have 'de-transitioned', explain that it is 'meant to be a place where de-transitioners can anonymously share day to day frustrations and moments of loneliness and heartbreak'. They set up the site to provide 'solidarity' to those seeking to de-transition as they 'know how emotionally, physically, and psychologically devastating it can be' (Atlas Strawberries, 2012). In 2013 a new online resource for regretters was opened up called NoGoingBack, which describes itself as 'a group for people who spent time transitioning medically, socially and/or physically to another gender ... And then chose to stop transitioning and/or stop ID'ing as transgender/transsexual' (NoGoingBack, 2013). The proliferation of these resources indicates a watershed in the development of the phenomenon of transgenderism. It is no longer possible to suggest with much credibility that physical treatments are a 'cure' and the practice is facing a considerable challenge to its validity from the incipient survivors' movement.

Two of those involved in the online regretters/survivors' movement were interviewed for this book, a man and a woman. They were chosen because they do not just consider that they were misdiagnosed but have developed a specific, critical politics that challenges the practice of transgenderism altogether. They both have an active online presence in which they voice their critique and speak out with the hope of enabling others to escape the harms associated with transition. They can be seen as emblematic of a new consciousness and a new politics that may form the germ of a movement of resistance by survivors. They are also very brave because the backlash against them from transgender activists can be extremely abusive. Walt Heyer is a member of an older generation of male-bodied transgenders and had quite a classic profile of a heterosexual male cross-dresser before he went on to hormones and SRS. He was influenced by publicity surrounding the Christine Jorgensen case in the 1950s to consider taking such a step, but has de-transitioned and now campaigns against the practice of SRS. Heyer says that the Harry Benjamin Standards of Care were not followed in his case, even though he was treated by one of the doctors who drew them up. This doctor approved him for surgery after a forty-five minute consultation, and presently in the United States, he says, persons seeking to transgender can just walk into 'some doctor's office and tell him, you know, I want some hormones and you pay him the money and the guy gives you hormones, you don't have to have counselling'. In his opinion it is all about the money; 'the question they ask is do you have the money? That's your counselling, do you have the money?' He explains that, years later, he consulted several psychiatrists who all told him that he has, in fact, a dissociative disorder. Heyer de-transitioned because he regretted not so much the surgery, but its consequences, including alienation of his children, loss of employment, homelessness. He now considers that 'it's impossible for someone to change genders … you can make it appear as though a change was made but there is actually no way to change someone's gender'. He says he 'enjoyed being a female' mainly because of the pleasures of shopping for and wearing clothing associated with women, but knew he 'wasn't a female'.

Heyer, like all those who go public about regretting their transition, finds himself the object of considerable abuse and harassment from transgender activists. He excoriates the transgender activist movement for the way in which they police other transgenders who de-transition and dare not go public for fear of reprisals: 'I hate the fact that they have gained so much power.' He says he hopes that 'someone will finally drive a nail in this big balloon and explode it', but presently there are too few persons prepared to stand up to the bullying that being critical entails, and he is 'probably one of the few that has a website and they send me nasty stuff all the time'. Heyer's ideas are available at length in his books *Paper Genders* (2011), and *Sex Change – It's Suicide* (2013).

The other interviewee is Heath Russell, a young US lesbian who was attracted to the idea of transitioning in her teens as a result of the considerable media publicity and general public promotion of female-bodied transgenderism in recent years. Heath developed the idea of transitioning as a result of being bullied for not fitting into gender stereotypes as a girl child, and from absorbing the idea that it was possible to change sex from television talk shows. At sixteen she 'came out' about her attraction to women and received very negative reactions from her mother in particular. Like Heyer, she describes a perfunctoriness about the consultation process with a psychiatrist that led to her being prescribed hormones. Her suggestion that she was transgender was 'simply accepted', and the fact that she was a lesbian not considered relevant. Members of the transgender community told her to stay away from any therapists who questioned her transition, on the grounds that they were 'transphobic'. The complete acceptance of the idea of transgenderism among medical professionals meant that she was given no opportunity for ambivalence about the decision. She says that she had doubts about whether she was really a 'man' throughout the two years that she was using hormones.

She thinks that the absence of 'lesbian role models' and a 'proud woman loving culture' made her susceptible to the idea that she should transgender. It was only when she came across Internet resources created by proud lesbian women, who sought to halt the movement of young lesbians towards transgenderism, that she gradually began to change her mind about the steps she was taking. She gained the confidence to be a lesbian who eschewed femininity, rather than thinking she must really be a man. Another reason for de-transitioning was that the hormones were causing havoc with her body's natural systems. She began to experience heart palpitations that she had never experienced before, and an elevated pulse rate. She became more interested in information about the harmful effects that hormones could have, such as increased cancer risks and polycystic ovary syndrome, and decided to de-transition by quitting hormones 'cold turkey', which is not a recommended course. Some of the effects of the hormones reversed and some remained. She still has facial hair, which creates problems for her when out in public, and her driver's licence continues to say that she is a man, which could cause her problems if intercepted, as she says, in the women's locker rooms.

Russell developed what she describes as a radical lesbian feminist analysis of transgenderism, which helped her in understanding her own experience and in continuing to challenge the practice in her online activism. Her position is that 'there is no such thing as the wrong body' and she considers that queer theory messed with the minds of many young lesbians, making them susceptible to this erroneous idea. She now agrees with social constructionist perspectives on homosexuality and on gender roles, which posit that people are not born to be homosexual but, rather, can choose to be so, and considers that the gender non-conformity regularly found among homosexuals is constructed from their rebellious impulses.

Like Walt Heyer, Russell has been subjected to attacks because of going public as a de-transitioner. Her 'coming out', as she calls it, has included a television interview in which she eloquently argues against the practice of transgenderism, using examples from her own experience (Russell, 2013).The worst insults came from male-bodied transgenders, and she was called 'a failed male', a 'jackass', and a 'dickrag' and received death threats and rape threats. Female-bodied transgenders, on the other hand, just told her she should take responsibility for her decisions and that she was undermining the medical understanding of transgenderism. Her mother and father are having difficulties changing their pronoun use once more and her mother has difficulty accepting that, rather than being a man, her daughter is actually a lesbian.

In response to this challenge to the legitimacy of the practice, some transgender activists and commentators have shown considerable anger and hostility towards those who have gone public with their regret. The acrimony has been quite fierce and may make those transgenders who have regrets fearful of being open about them. A form of policing is going on within the transgender community in an attempt to shore up the leaky structure of the practice. One Australian regretter, who has been the object of this policing, is Alan Finch. He questioned his identity during adolescence, wondering whether he was homosexual or had been born in the wrong body, and in his twenties went through full sex-reassignment treatment including surgery. By 2004 Finch had decided that he was a man living without a penis and that he would not attempt to have further genital surgery although at the time he was considering having the constructed vagina removed as the skin had become 'scuffed and crusty'. Finch concluded, 'I can't see much point in mutilating my body anymore' (Batty, 2004). Finch has campaigned against what he calls the 'sex change industry', and believes that all treatment should cease. He argues that

> transsexualism was invented by psychiatrists … Their language is illusory.You fundamentally can't change sex … the surgery doesn't alter you genetically. It's genital mutilation. My 'vagina' was just the bag of my scrotum. It's like a pouch, like a kangaroo. What's scary is you still feel like you have a penis when you're sexually aroused. It's like phantom limb syndrome. It's all been a terrible misadventure. I've never been a woman, just Alan … The analogy I use about giving surgery to someone desperate to change sex is it's a bit like offering liposuction to an anorexic.
>
> *(Batty, 2004)*

Finch sued the only Australian gender identity clinic, at Melbourne's Monash Medical Centre, for misdiagnosis. Commentators from the transgender community were verbally abusive towards Finch for his desertion of the cause on the Susan's.org discussion forum, where 'Dennis' comments on Finch's legal case against the Monash clinic, 'this is a joke! people like (him) shouldn't be entitled to anything', 'I hope he loses', and calls him a 'media whore' (Susan's.org, Dennis, 2007). Another commenter, 'Melissa', says, 'People like this make me sick … I'm sorry, people who regret transitioning should be shot. They are a waste of oxygen', and 'Helen W' says that Finch should be 'laughed out of the courtroom', and calls him an 'arch manipulator' (ibid.). They reject the idea that regretters really exist and say they do not know of any.

Considering the huge distress and social and personal disadvantage the regretters/survivors suffer, their online detractors can seem remarkably cruel. The case of seventy-five-year-old Gary Norton of the UK illustrates this. He had SRS twenty-three years ago, felt uncertain even while on the operating table and is now living as a man (Strange, 2012). He wants reparative surgery on the National Health Service, but has been told there is no funding for reversals. Norton knew the sex change was a mistake 'when she grew sick of doing her hair and makeup and continued to be attracted to straight women'. He has been particularly distressed that his children have wanted no contact with him since the SRS and he is lonely because women do not want relationships with him. He relates that he went to his doctor about depression after being made redundant, and, on saying that he was a cross-dresser, was advised to start taking hormones. After SRS he found being a woman too 'fussy and time consuming'; he realised that he 'hadn't wanted to be a woman – I just liked dressing up as one from time to time for a thrill and it should never have gone any further. It was devastating. I was a man trapped in a woman's body and I was stuck with it' (ibid.). Norton's story, like that of Alan Finch, was not treated with any sympathy in the transgender online community. 'Samantha Cool Beans', in a discussion of his case on the website, Angels: supporting the TG Community, commented, 'For every one of these type of people/stories it makes 1000s of us look like crazy nutjobs!' (Angelsforum, 2012). Among many critical posts, Shantel, in a discussion at Susan's.org, comments, 'What an insipid moron!' (Susan's.org, 2012).

The complaints of regretters have instigated investigations of clinics and medical personnel involved in the transgender industry in the UK as well as in Australia. In the UK they have centred upon the best known psychiatrist in the UK transgender industry, Dr Russell Reid and the female-bodied transgender who took over Reid's private gender clinic, Dr Richard Curtis, Reid became the subject of an inquiry by the General Medical Council (GMC) after complaints from four doctors at the public Charing Cross Gender Identity Clinic, on behalf of patients who said they had been rushed into hormone and surgical treatment against the best practice guidelines, the Harry Benjamin Standards of Care (Batty, 2007a). The standards recommend that patients should not be put on hormones within three months of attending a clinic, and that they should not be operated upon unless they had done the 'real life test' of living as if they were women for twelve months. Reid's previous notoriety stemmed from his involvement in a 2000 *Horizon* investigation of the phenomenon of Amputee Identity Disorder, now more usually called Body Identity Integrity Disorder (BIID) (*Horizon*, 2000). It transpired that Reid was involved in referring two men to a surgeon, Robert Smith, in a Scottish hospital to have unwanted, healthy legs amputated. Reid explained that he considered that BIID and gender identity disorder were similar, and that both could usefully be treated by surgery to remove the offending body parts.

In the 2007 case, the GMC found Reid guilty of serious professional misconduct (Batty, 2007b). Two patients who testified before the panel considered that they had been misdiagnosed. One, a woman who thought that she was transsexual because she was suffering from manic depression, narrowly avoided a mastectomy. She testified that during her illness she had believed that she was Jesus and that a sex change would help her to become him (Batty, 2007b). After treatment for her manic depression she had no desire to change sex. Another, a convicted paedophile, had a sex change but wanted surgery to allow him to return to living as a man. The remaining three patients remained in their reassigned sex but considered that they did not receive a sufficient standard of care from Reid.

Russell Reid's gender clinic was taken over by the female-bodied transgender, Dr Richard Curtis, who, like Reid, was being investigated for misconduct in 2013. A 2005 news item reported that Curtis was the first transgender person to become a general practitioner in the UK (Day, 2005). Curtis decided in adulthood that she was really a gay man after several relationships with men as a woman. Her understanding of gender was very constricting and traditional: 'I've never wanted children, or a white wedding like most women dream of, or a man to take care of me. Instead, you were more likely to find me fitting a kitchen or tiling the bathroom' (ibid.). Curtis was investigated in 2013 after three patient complaints (Batty, 2013). The allegations are similar to those in Reid's case, such as the commencement of hormone treatment without referring patients for a second opinion and before they had undergone counselling, administering hormone treatment at first appointments, and referring for surgery before the twelve months real life test was completed. One woman complains that she was inappropriately prescribed sex-changing hormones and underwent a double mastectomy before she changed her mind. Curtis is also accused of administering hormones to sixteen-year-old patients without an adequate assessment.

Conclusion

There is increasing evidence to suggest that treatment aimed at physically changing the bodies of men and women who seek to transgender is ineffective in improving physical and mental health and social functioning. Nonetheless, large tracts of the medical profession, including many psychiatrists and psychotherapists as well as endocrinologists and surgeons, collude with the mental health problems of those who come to them seeking to change their sex, and do them harm. This is despite the fact that diagnosing the 'real' transgender is becoming more and more fraught, and the very idea of diagnosis is being challenged by some transgender activists on the grounds that hormones and surgery should be seen as a matter of choice and cosmetic alteration.

The inability of many, if not most, of those in the medical profession to accept that physical treatments of transgenderism should be considered professional misconduct is likely to reflect several realities. One is the amount of money to be made, particularly by the pharmaceutical industry, which needs a replacement for the failed ambition of placing the majority of older women on HRT. Another is the antiquated belief by this most patriarchal of professions that essential gender does exist and that when a man says he is a woman this should be immediately respected. If gender exists, then it can mysteriously, they believe, be misplaced. Another is likely to be fear of being accused of transphobia and finding their reputations in tatters, as transgender activists go after anyone critical of the practice online. But critical voices do seem to be increasing in number and are likely, at length, to reach the critical mass needed to challenge this harmful practice. As more and more of those who have been transgendered seek help to de-transition and some have the courage to speak out, the quackery of the practice should become more apparent to those who treat them.

4

'A GRAVY STAIN ON THE TABLE'

Women in the lives of men who transgender

Written with Lorene Gottschalk

The phenomenon of transgenderism is generally written about as if those who transition are engaged in an individual heroic quest and the persons who surround them – partners, wives, girlfriends, mothers, children, workmates – are mentioned only to stress the importance of their giving unqualified support. In fact transgenderism inflicts serious harms on the family members of transgenders. Though both men and women engage in transgenderism, family members who suffer most are likely to be women in both cases: wives, partners and mothers. There is no mention of male partners in the literature, which suggests that they are very rare. There is very little research literature on this aspect of the transgender phenomenon and accounts written by wives, as well as an interview with a woman partner of a man who has transitioned, will be used to find out how the lives of these women are affected. The wives of men who transgender, the partners of lesbians who transgender, and the mothers in both cases, describe similar experiences. These include psychological distress, grief and loss, social exclusion, humiliation and financial problems. This chapter will focus on the wives, female partners and mothers of men who decide to change their sex.

Cross-dressing and transgenderism

The husbands who make the decision to change sex are likely to have a history of cross-dressing. Increasingly, as a result of the greater visibility of the possibilities of transgenderism online and in the media generally, men with female partners who would once simply have been occasional cross-dressers are transitioning (Lawrence, 2007). As a result, there is no longer any clear distinction between the two practices of cross-dressing and transsexualism, with both now usually being placed under the same umbrella term, transgenderism.

As Virginia Erhardt comments in the introduction to her collection of narratives by the wives of 'cross-dressers and transsexuals', these practices, which cannot be clearly distinguished 'dilemmas of gender identity, rather than forming discrete categories, fall on a continuum' (Erhardt, 2007: 13). The Erhardt collection begins with the stories of wives whose husbands have not gone further than occasional cross-dressing, and end with those of the wives of men who have gone on to transgender. The clear similarities between the harms to the wives and partners in all cases support the idea that a similar phenomenon is being described. The cruel problem for the wives of cross-dressers is that they have to live with the knowledge that at some point their partners may start to live as that which they imagine to be 'women' full-time, and this can put them into a state of hyperawareness and stress (Erhardt, 2007).

Cross-dressers who are exposed to transgender activism through the online transgender community are likely to develop the desire to go further than would once have been the case. Helen Boyd, who has written two books on cross-dressing and speaks on a lecture circuit with her husband, Betty, explains how this can happen. She says that after her book *My Husband Betty* was published, the couple were immediately taken up by the transgender movement and Betty started to move towards the possibility of transition: 'We've realized since that even her exploration of her female side was a bit like a Pandora's box, which once opened cannot be closed' (Boyd, 2007: 9). Boyd describes her situation thus: '[l]iving with someone who looks as if she's transitioning and seems to want to transition but isn't transitioning is a little like living with post-traumatic stress disorder, feeling as if every bit of you is hair-triggered, waiting for the announcement, waiting for the crisis' (Boyd, 2007: 251). Being in a marriage that 'poses that "fight or flight" question every day', she says, is not conducive to long-term happiness.

Heroes of their own lives

The majority of the literature on transgenderism represents the process of transition as an epic adventure in which individuals seek to find themselves (Lev, 2004). Unfortunately, the significant others, partners, wives and mothers of transgenders suffer the negative impact of these adventures. The transgenders may be the heroes of their own lives, but the women they leave behind may not feel so positive. Christine Benvenuto characterises the behaviour of her husband as resembling a heroic quest: 'he sees his life as an epic tale of liberation akin to the Passover story' (Benvenuto, 2012a: 22). Her memoir of life with her transgender husband, *Sex Changes*, was met by a campaign led by her ex-husband to traduce and silence her in 2012. To his 'admiring fans', she says he is a 'martyr, a patron saint, Our Lady of Gender Variance. In the Valley of the Politically Correct, he expected approval – and he got it' (Benvenuto, 2012a: 237). When he gave a talk at her synagogue, he 'told a hero's tale' (Benvenuto, 2012a: 259). The wife's role in relation to the hero is to be a handmaiden, not a critic or an obstacle.

There is a new clinical literature developing, however, in which there is recognition of the severely harmful effects of men's transitioning behaviour on their female partners. Until quite recently, the literature on transgenderism has excluded the experience of partners; it has been 'TI-centric', TI meaning transgender identified, according to the family and transgender therapists, Donna Chapman and Benjamin Caldwell (Chapman and Caldwell, 2012: 37). But the partners and family members of transgenders cannot avoid being affected, as 'TI people do not just come out to themselves. They cannot remain closeted if they wish to actualize their gendered sense of self' (Chapman and Caldwell, 2012: 39). The families have 'no option' but to 'cope with it whether they like it or not, and they have been considered extraneous to the process of evaluation and treatment of the TI partner. Their needs have been marginalised' (ibid.). In fact, the point of coming out as a transgender for a cross-dressing man would be entirely lost if there was not an audience, and family members are likely to be required to form the first audience, however unwilling they may be. The majority of therapists who work with transgenders, some of whom have created niche practices from such treatment, adopt the perspective of their transgender clients that they are heroes, ignoring the harms inflicted on partners which might undermine the script. As Lisa Chase puts it, physicians and insurance companies like to think that transition is curative for transgenders and '[t]he idea of partners speaking out by acknowledging a need for support was too much of a risk and may have jeopardized the trans' ability to transition', by undermining their health insurance claims perhaps (Chase, 2011: 430).

Arlene Lev is a therapist who takes the 'heroic quest' perspective, and has little sympathy for wives and women partners who might be suffering. Her book *Transgender Emergence* (2004) purports to provide a template for providing therapy to transgenders and their families. Lev is relentlessly positive about the way in which partners could gain by supporting transgenders. She explains that, traditionally, therapists expected the man to leave his wife, 'never looking at the situation from the opposite angle and asking whether the spouse is able to grow and change enough to support her husband's cross-gender "needs"' (Lev, 2004: 16). The 'needs' of the women partners are not recognised here. She encourages those treating the partners to see that 'having a partner who is transgendered might be fascinating, exciting, or desirable' (Lev, 2004: 17). The wives and partners who write about their experience, however, do not support this positive view at all (Benvenuto, 2012a; Erhardt, 2007), but struggle to survive the stress and the crumbling of everything they hold dear.

Virginia Erhardt, another therapist who specialises in therapy with trans-genders, is scarcely more sympathetic towards the wives than Lev. Erhardt created her collection of wives' stories because of her recognition that wives needed support: 'natal female partners are so groomed to pay attention to their husbands' needs in this situation ... that they often lose their own voices' (Erhardt, 2007: 2). But she is firmly wedded to the transgender ideology that the husbands simply cannot help themselves and she teaches that men's cross-dressing practices are nothing to do with choice or lifestyle: 'It is extremely important for a woman to remember that being a person of transgender experience is involuntary. I have heard women who leave insist on believing that their partner was frivolously choosing a "transgender lifestyle"' (Erhardt, 2007: 6). The wives in the collection are those who support and stay with their husbands, but their stories are a useful source material for this chapter because they detail the very serious stresses that they experience.

The small minority of therapists who are beginning to acknowledge the harm to wives, on the other hand, consider it to be very serious. Chapman and Caldwell call this harm 'attachment injury', which is a specific type of event that involves the 'violation of trust or betrayal coupled with the inaccessibil-ity of the partner' (Chapman and Caldwell, 2012: 44). They explain that the partner of someone who transgenders experiences a role and identity change that is 'unplanned and uncontrolled' (Chapman and Caldwell, 2012: 37), whereas their partner is embarking on a long planned and anticipated quest. In response to the transition, the partners left behind may suffer in ways that 'meet definitions of trauma' (Chapman and Caldwell, 2012: 43). Attachment injuries, they explain, 'behave much like PTSD injuries in that they re-emerge in the form of traumatic flashback, avoidance, hyper-vigilance, and numbing and are overwhelming' (Chapman and Caldwell, 2012: 45).

The self-centredness of transgenders

One significant source of harm to wives is the self-centredness of transgen-ders. Wives and partners suffer because the transgenders behave as if only their quest has importance, and do not take the distress they are causing seriously, or are puzzled by it. Chapman and Caldwell say that it is difficult for transgenders to hear about injury to partners because 'inherent in TI pro-cessing is a profound self-centredness' (Chapman and Caldwell, 2012: 47). Helen Boyd says that a friend calls this behaviour 'male autism' (Boyd, 2007: 255). A wife in the Erhardt collection makes a similar point about the self-centredness of transgender husbands: 'From the beginning of the transition, it was all about Bobbi's dreams, wants, and needs' (Erhardt, 2007: 120). The men's transgenderism is a masculine prerogative, and not to be trammelled with extraneous concerns. The literature on male abusers of female partners in other settings suggests that they demonstrate a similar lack of empathy (Harne, 2011).

The self-centredness of male-bodied transgenders and their lack of empathy are reflected in the way that they choose to 'come out' to their wives. The majority of women interviewed by Erhardt (2007) did not know about their partners' cross-dressing when they married. They found out after marriage, and, not uncommonly, twenty or more years into the marriage. In some cases, such as that of Christine Benvenuto, the husband may have mentioned the cross-dressing early in the marriage on a couple of occasions, but the wife was unlikely to take this seriously (Benvenuto, 2012a). As Benvenuto explains, she could not know that this might refer to an activity that would escalate and could result in transgenderism rather than being an occasional hobby. The transgender husbands did not necessarily consider their wives' feelings when they decided to reveal their proclivity.

The tactic of appearing 'dressed' before an unsuspecting and severely shocked partner seems, from numerous accounts by wives, to be common. It was the experience of the founder of a website set up specifically to support women who 'struggled' with having husbands who cross-dressed, and she expresses poignantly the distress she felt (Crossdresserswives.com, n.d.a). She was having a supposedly romantic New Year's Eve dinner, when her husband said he had something to tell her but needed to go upstairs first because it was easier to show rather than tell. After ten minutes he appeared 'dressed'.

> Finally, he came down the extravagant, sweeping staircase wearing his long, red, silk, otherwise unassuming robe. He sat next to me and silently opened his robe. Immediately I stopped breathing – no oxygen coming in or out. I was paralyzed. Something in his eyes made me realize this was no joke. He was dead-ass serious. While wearing what was supposed to be my black, silk stockings and matching black lace garter belt, items which he had emphatically insisted I needed, I tried so hard to compassionately understand as the man I loved disclosed his long time wish to try on lingerie. Then he wanted to make love.
>
> (*Crossdresserswives.com, n.d.a*)

She allowed what she called the 'sex game' to take place because she 'loved him enough to help him live out this bizarre fetish' but found the experience 'shocking, disturbing, poignant, joyless and dismal'. While he said it was the 'best sex he had ever had', for her it was 'by far the worst, exacerbated, frightening sexual experience for me' and reminded her of being date raped at the age of eighteen, 'the only other time I felt so powerless'. In both cases these 'unwelcomed sexualized acts' 'traumatized' her, because they were 'acts of abomination, betrayals that left me feeling permanently (though silently) horrified, violated and soiled' (Crossdresserswives.com, n.d.a).

The wives of transgenders typically progress through a range of emotions when they discover their husbands' cross-dressing. Initial reactions range from bewilderment and disbelief to shock and then embarrassment at the thought of others finding out (Erhardt, 2007). In Erhardt's collection, women experienced feelings of being violated, and of revulsion (ibid.). One wife was revolted by the fact that her husband had shaved his body hair and she could not relate to his hairlessness, and another said she felt physically sick. Other reactions included a deep sense of loneliness and feelings of not being good enough, sleeplessness and frequent crying, and a feeling of sexual rejection that led to feelings of sexual inadequacy (Buxton, 2006). One woman in Erhardt's study, after a sleepless night, decided that she would commit suicide, but in the end did not do so. The overwhelming and universal reaction from women who did not know at the time of their marriage that their husband was a cross-dresser, was betrayal at the deception and loss of trust (ibid.). The partner of a transgender who was interviewed for this chapter explained how dismissive her husband was of the pain he was causing her:

> It was as if I had fallen down the rabbit hole. He brushed off my questions with 'Hey, chill. You always make such a big deal of everything – nobody can predict the future'. I felt that my fear and distress was being minimised and dismissed. I felt totally alone.

Issues of trust

Some accounts suggest that the intensity of the distress experienced by wives and partners is exacerbated by the timing of the disclosure. Women who knew about their husbands' cross-dressing prior to marrying them, or very early in the marriage, could be more accepting of the behaviour, but shocked when it progressed to the stage where the men started to question their biological sex and identify as transgendered, rather than as cross-dressers (Erhardt, 2007). Other research, however, indicates that it did not matter at what stage husbands revealed their cross-dressing; the partners still felt deceived, unable to trust and unable to believe in their partner's word or their own judgement (Buxton, 2006). Wives who were not told before marriage refused to accept their husbands' explanation that they did not disclose their 'secret' for fear of rejection. They thought the marriage had been 'a joke based on dishonesty' (Erhardt, 2007: 34). One woman insisted that she had the right to decide whether or not she wanted to be married to a cross-dresser and 'that decision should not have been made for me' (Erhardt, 2007: 51). Christine Benvenuto describes the profound sense of loss she experienced. The decades she had been with her husband suddenly seemed to have been a lie and she lost the shared memories:

> You lose your partner and your access to his memories … He tells you that he has been posing as your partner, a fictitious character of his own and perhaps your invention throughout your relationship. Tells you every memory you've stored needs to be rewritten.
>
> *(Benvenuto, 2012a: 84)*

Effectively, she says, Tracey told her that the 'past twenty-odd years of my life had not actually happened' (Benvenuto, 2012a: 88). The betrayal of trust can extend to the husband's behaviour towards his children. Benvenuto explains that her husband used her young children as characters in his performance and sought to conceal this from her: 'My children's experience of Tracey's transformation and the break-up of our marriage is hands down the ugliest and most painful aspect of this story' (Benvenuto, 2012a: 119). He 'dressed' in front of his toddler child and when she made this known to her mother, he said he had not thought her capable of speaking about it (Benvenuto, 2012a: 80). When his eight-year-old daughter went to visit her father, he enrolled her in his practice as she explained to her mother, 'When I go to Daddy's he gives me his shoes and jewelry to try on. I do his hair. Sometimes we put on makeup' (Benvenuto, 2012a: 142). Eventually she refused to visit, refused to be alone with him and said she was afraid of him. He flew into rages, she said, if she refused to play dress-up: '"He told me I had to show him how to be a girl! … He said he'd never gotten to be a girl, so he wanted to experience what it was like through me!"' (Benvenuto, 2012a: 150). Benvenuto's husband, by her account, placed his children's interests second to his own pleasures.

Psychological violence

The behaviour of transgender husbands can go beyond a lack of empathy with their partners' suffering and become more abusive. In Christine Benvenuto's case, one form of abuse was the accusation that she was mentally unstable: '"You're sick," Tracey told me when I protested against any aspect of his behavior. "You're mentally ill. No one in the world thinks the way you do. Everyone else thinks what I'm doing is great"' (Benvenuto, 2012a: 85). He also engaged in other forms of bullying and threats and a new 'Tracey' emerged, she says, the one who 'intimidated and threatened, who laid down the law and expected me to abide by it. If Tracey was becoming a woman, he had never seemed so male – a tyrannical bully he had never been in our marriage' (Benvenuto, 2012a: 70). The threats issued to gain her compliance included the statement that he would take the three children from her if she left him. One wife in the Erhardt collection took her husband back to live with her after he had had an emotional breakdown and been hospitalised twice. He (called 'she' in this account) then proceeded to engage in psychological violence towards her through personal insults: 'In May, she began telling me all the things I do to hurt her. She also said that I smell bad, even right after a bath, and that it doesn't feel good when I touch her' (Erhardt, 2007: 120).

In some cases the husbands may not set out to cause hurt but their behaviour causes severe distress nonetheless. One problem experienced by the wives of cross-dressers, for instance, is that when their husbands come out as 'women' they are required to go into the closet. In the Erhardt collection several wives use precisely this metaphor with one wife saying about herself and her daughter, 'Mostly I resent his having put us into the closet' (Erhardt, 2007: 126). They find themselves unable to access support because they are expected to go out with their husband 'en femme', for instance, although not allowed to reveal what is happening, to their friends and family. Another problem that distresses wives is the feeling that their husbands want to be them in a parasitic way, to take over their persona. As one wife puts this, 'At times it seems as though Jane wants to merge with me, and I feel engulfed' (Erhardt, 2007: 165). Benvenuto explained this problem in a similar way: 'he didn't want to be *with* me, he wanted to *be* me' (Benvenuto, 2012a: 43). Another wife explained,

> There are 'turf' issues: sharing not only my clothes and 'my' kitchen but even my name and gender. It took me over a year to appreciate what a sweet gesture it was that Diane saw me as her model of a woman and even incorporated my name into hers: Dick + Anne + Diane.
>
> *(Erhardt, 2007: 197)*

Such parasitism may cause great distress.

The female partner that we interviewed for this chapter calls the way in which transgenders can accuse their wives of madness, when they notice and object to problematic behaviour, 'gaslighting'. She says, 'I think the constant online shenanigans, lying, secrets and gaslighting ("you are mad", "you are imagining stuff", "it's you that has a problem") is a form of psychological violence.' She says that after 'the fourth or fifth cycle of lies, being found out, more lies, more gaslighting and more lies, I snapped' and began to find him 'physically and emotionally repulsive', and had to build 'a shell around me to survive'. She says that 'in many ways' she identifies with 'women in "regular" abusive relationships' and believes that she has PTSD: 'I find social situations excruciating most days. I have very few friends now.' After suffering extreme

social isolation and anxiety it was feminism that gave her the tools to redis-
cover her strength:

> I have re-discovered feminism through the radical feminist blogs and
> books I have been encouraged to read by women I have met online,
> and now (in a few cases) in 'real life'. What a relief it is to know that I
> am not 'mad'.

She is pleased that there are now words for what she is going through, 'psychological violence', and that this form of 'oppression' has been named. In
this straightforward way, feminist understandings can comfort and support
women who have experienced such abuse. Those feminists who publicly
support the practice of transgenderism could be seen as guilty of abandoning
the wives, who are left high and dry. The feminist project should be to support women who are abused by men, rather than the men who are responsible for the abuse, otherwise men's transgender behaviour can split women
and feminists from each other.

The hijacking of women's lives

When men come out as cross-dressers or transgender the lives of their wives
are likely to be hijacked. However they had once thought they would spend
their lives, they will, if they seek to stay with these men, find that the priorities
created by the men's particular sexual interest will take over their time, energy
and financial resources. The wives of men who cross-dress, as well as those who
go on to transgender on a more permanent basis, become very much bound
up with their husbands' practice. One wife of a cross-dresser comments, 'I really
don't want this CDing (cross-dressing) to overtake my life and it seems like it
has – it's become much more central than I want it to be' (Erhardt, 2007: 55).
Another wife says she often just does not feel like playing dress-up games but
feels under pressure: 'Even today when I'm tired, hungry, or just emotionally
worn out and Lucy wants to emerge, my reaction is "no"' (Erhardt, 2007: 59).

The husbands frequently take their wives as their models and the wives
acquire a new form of housework in facilitating their husbands' 'womanhood'. It is their wives' clothes that the men often wear and they require their
wives to transform them into women. As one wife explains,

> I tried to teach Tommy to do his own makeup, but it was hopeless. He
> always made up his eyes too dark, so he looked French. I decided that I
> would just do all the makeup. I also tried teaching Tommy how to walk
> in a more feminine way, but it didn't work; he still walked like a guy.
> *(Erhardt, 2007: 74)*

Such work is particularly important if the husband is able to persuade his wife to go out in public with him, because it is more humiliating if his imitation of a woman is particularly woeful. Shopping is another chore: 'We shop together. I've helped him with makeup. He dresses in my presence. I accept, support, and even encourage' (Erhardt, 2007: 90).

If wives become involved with the transgender support organisations that their husbands join, then they acquire a whole new range of responsibilities and work. One wife explains that she and her husband 'became very involved with support groups. Diana went on to become a founder of a support group in our area, and I became an activist for significant others' (Erhardt, 2007: 66). She also says, 'There are times when I feel it impacts our lives too much; but Diana, being considerate, will back off a bit when I mention this' (Erhardt, 2007: 67).

Wives are expected to share their husbands' fascination with the practice. One wife talks of how her life became centred on her husband's interest in cross-dressing: 'We got the Internet and our lives revolved around cross-dressing. We spent hours in chat rooms and going from site to site looking for information' (Erhardt, 2007: 123). Another wife commented, 'The biggest stressor in our relationship is the amount of time and energy gender dysphoria and the transition process take from our relationship. I often run out of patience' (Erhardt, 2007: 144). She says she often feels as if her 'only role in this relationship is to be support for "the big decision"' (ibid.). Feminist research on the unpaid work of wives suggests that supporting men's hobbies and leisure activities, e.g. by washing the football outfit, is an under-recognised aspect of housework (Delphy and Leonard, 1992). In the case of transgenderism, the work required is rather more extensive. Wives may find that, rather than taking a more equal share of the housework in their new female persona, their husbands may engage in a form of learnt helplessness they think is suited to femininity and place even more burdens on their wives. Our interviewee explains that she was required to 'remember that he was "female" at all times, and treat him "like a woman"', which 'even extended to refusing to carry heavy bags when out shopping, even though he is a foot taller than me and had far greater upper body strength'. She explains that her husband 'has refused to do some things in case he breaks a nail – I kid you not. He has literally said that.' Helen Boyd reports similar behaviour and says that wives of cross-dressers find it infuriating that their husbands become helpless as they begin to imitate their idea of what a woman is, in a way which is insulting to women and creates extra work for them. This might include 'having your former husband tell you she can't put up bookshelves because she might break a nail while the unspoken assumption is that it's okay for the woman raised female to put them up' (Boyd, 2007: 255).

Financial exploitation

Wives commonly complain about the impact of their husbands' practice on the family finances. Family money is used to buy clothes and make-up, to pay for cross-dressing weekends, for hormones, and in the case of those who go further, a range of surgeries from amputation of genitals and the creation of a fake vagina, to voice box and facial feminisation surgery. One wife in the Erhardt collection remarks, acidly, of the financial burden of her husband's pursuit, 'Gwen feels compelled to devote most of her time to a career in activism that does not pay the bills' (Erhardt, 2007: 176). Another says, 'We have spent or saved an incredible amount of money for Theresa's new wardrobe, hair care, electrolysis, and hormones, not to mention SRS, and also possibly a hair transplant. This is a big financial burden' (Erhardt, 2007: 132). The wives of 'Stephanie' and 'Trish' and 'Mandy' complain about the difficulty in finding money for electrolysis, clothes and accessories, hormones and surgery (Erhardt, 2007: 139; 146). 'Trish's' wife remarks tellingly that 'I had never spent that kind of money on myself' (Erhardt, 2007: 152). But the husbands had a masculine sense of entitlement that trumped their wives' financial worries and careful husbanding of resources.

The loss of community and support

The distress of wives may be compounded by the fact that their husbands' behaviour may separate them from their support networks. Members of their communities may cleave to the transgender husband rather than the abandoned wife. As Christine Benvenuto expresses it, '[T]he political correctness quotient meant that much of what I had thought of as my community went to Tracey' (Benvenuto, 2012a: 81). She considers that this is because supporting a man who is transgendering is much more politically hip than being loyal to his wife. Benvenuto lives in a college area full of persons who like to think of themselves as politically progressive: 'In the Valley of the Politically Correct, it's easy to support a transgendered friend or acquaintance. Better than easy. It gives one a sort of panache, for some people a kind of frisson' (Benvenuto, 2012a: 170). Such people found it 'impossible ... to express even basic human sympathy for me or for my children' and their desire to be politically correct meant they had to be 'fully on board with his gender project' (ibid.). Women who supported her husband went so far as to tell her 'that my wifely role was to support my man's gender-bending and to get my children on board with the project. My responsibility was to Tracey. Tracey's responsibility was to Tracey' (Benvenuto, 2012a: 62).

Benvenuto found when she published her memoir that lack of community support was overtaken by actual persecution. Unlike other accounts by wives who support their husbands' proclivities, despite lamenting the disadvantages they suffer (Rudd, 1999; Boyd, 2004, 2007), Benvenuto's memoir is a cry of rage that reveals the cataclysmic effect upon herself and her children with great clarity. Perhaps because of this, she has experienced considerable backlash for her temerity in writing it. Her ex-husband, Joy Ladin, an academic, enlisted friends and members of the transgender community to campaign against Benvenuto's writing. In November 2012, Ladin's supporters appeared at a book reading by Benvenuto to raise their objections to the book, and their behaviour was so problematic that the police had to be called (Pfarrer, 2012).

Benvenuto also experienced backlash over an article she put into a Jewish online newspaper about what it was like to live in the same small town as your transgender ex-husband (Benvenuto, 2012b). She describes details such as attending a doctor's appointment about one of her children with her ex, during which they were seen as a lesbian couple and the child to be the offspring of a sperm donor. The article is no longer available online because her ex complained that she had referred to him with male pronouns. The journal, *Kveller*, gave the following reason for its act of censorship:

> When it comes to issues that impact a historically (and currently) persecuted community it is our responsibility as editors to be extra sensitive to the exact language being used. Kveller and its parent organization … are committed to honouring the identities and life experience of all people, including transgender people.
>
> *(Kveller, 2012)*

Interestingly, it is husbands who transgender who are seen as persecuted and in need of honour and protection here, and not the wives who have suffered psychological violence from their husbands. Benvenuto does not accept that her ex-husband is a woman on the grounds that she has had a lengthy sexual relationship with him and borne three children from his semen. But her perspective is not honoured. This might suggest that such behaviour by men is an expression of masculine privilege, which elicits the approbation of patriarchal communities and organisations, and the blaming of women.

Our interviewee turned to an online group for transgenders and partners when in severe need of support and found there was little to be had. It was supposed to be for 'trans' and 'significant others' but had few active female members. The regulars were, she said, 'privileged, white, late transitioners', many of them simply cross-dressers who wanted to 'get under the big umbrella and benefit from legal protections. They love "gender identity".' She attended some social events for 'trannies', which were the opposite of supportive for partners, and the socials served as places where the men 'could show up and get "dressed" on the premises. It felt very highly sexually charged. There were male "tranny chasers" there who were about the creepiest men I have ever encountered. Leering and staring from corners. Ugh.' These experiences accentuated her distress: 'The TVs there didn't seem much interested in me – they wanted to speak to my partner, and a particularly leery, predatory one kept feeling him up. I may as well have been a gravy stain on the table.'

Not accepting a change of sex

The wives and partners of transgenders are unlikely to accept that a change of sex has actually taken place. Christine Benvenuto, for instance, said she was unable to use the male pronouns her husband demanded: 'Pronouns, of course, became problematic around a person crossing gender lines. I still use the male variety to refer to Tracey because even now I can't think, speak, or write about this person any other way' (Benvenuto, 2012a: 92). She is quite sure that Tracey did not become a woman: 'He also wasn't, for me never will be, a woman' (Benvenuto, 2012a: 126). It is, perhaps, not surprising that this level of certainty should be common among the wives and partners. They had, after all, been attracted to their husbands as men, lived with and had sexual relationships with them for decades as men, had children with them as men, and the idea that they could become women had no validity. Pronouns are problematic for the wives of cross-dressers as well, as one wife explained, 'I still can't seem to call my husband a "she" very often' (Erhardt, 2007: 76). Another wife of a cross-dresser said, 'One of my pet peeves is cross-dressers who insist that the women in their lives call them she, girls, or ladies out of respect, or in order not to hurt their feelings' (Erhardt, 2007: 90). She explains that she was 'born a woman' and deserves 'the title of "she" and shouldn't have to share it ... I don't want to be expected to see cross-dressers as "real women"' (ibid.). Husbands can seek to enforce their pronouns of choice on their wives through emotional blackmail. Our interviewee explains how this can work, 'He was soooo hyper-sensitive about any male pronouns and I had to police my language to the extreme lest he burst into tears and dramatically flounce off, leaving me alone in some bar somewhere on the other side of town.'

Wives are often deeply discomforted by the ideas that their husbands have about 'femininity' and womanhood, which are sometimes in stark contrast to their own. Helen Boyd's account of living with her transgender husband, Betty, is most instructive regarding the profound disbelief female partners can feel at the extreme and fantastic versions of 'femininity' the men adopt and expect to have accepted as constituting an essence of womanhood (Boyd, 2007). Boyd explains that she had been a 'tomboy' in her youth, never knew exactly what feeling like a woman was supposed to mean and rejected femininity as socially constructed and constricting. She was surprised, therefore, when her husband told her he did know what it was to feel like a woman, and it was certainly not what she had ever felt. She explains,

> The more I encouraged him to find an identity that felt comfortable and natural to him, the more unnatural he seemed to me. His manner changed, as did the way he used his hands. He flipped his hair and started using a new voice.
>
> *(Boyd, 2007: 78)*

She hoped his behaviour was just a 'phase' because 'I felt as if I were living with Britney Spears. It was like sleeping with the enemy' (ibid.). Boyd objected very much to being lectured at by cross-dressers that she was not doing femininity correctly, 'for not living the glories that are the feminine' (Boyd, 2007: 79). She particularly disliked criticism by cross-dressers of her sensible shoes: 'Having men in size 12 sling-backs mock my "librarian shoes" is probably the worst kind of experience I've had in the MTF community' (ibid.). Our interviewee also found her husband's 'parody' of female behaviour through hair flipping hard to cope with:

> I can tell when he's been thinking about being a woman, or fantasising about it ... because his voice gets a bit higher and he does that limp wristed thing with the other hand on his waist and he flicks his hair a lot.

Her husband was not interested in his wife's clothes because they did not feed his fantasy: 'He doesn't wear my clothes – not "feminine" enough. He likes to wear short skirts, low cut tops, high boots. He calls it a "rock-chick" look.'

Several of the wives in the Erhardt collection express similar frustration at the creation by their husbands of a femininity they cannot relate to, since they were never much interested in such fripperies themselves. As one expresses it, 'I, who had never cared much about clothes and resented the "Barbie doll" image of women, had a husband who seemed obsessed with clothes and was helpless while his nail polish was drying', and resembled the 'teenage primping I have never wanted to do' (Erhardt, 2007: 193). Many women accepted their husband's or partner's transgenderism on the surface but few completely accepted the idea of a woman in a man's body. An extra difficulty for wives if they were to accept that their husbands had actually changed their sex is that they would then have to see themselves as 'lesbians', and many found this an impossible requirement (Buxton, 2006).

Our interviewee explains that she had been a 'do-gooding liberal' who just accepted what people said about themselves without 'examining the political or cultural context of their assertions', but no longer thought that way. Nonetheless, as she says, she had never 'been into "woo" or magic spirits or essences', and now realised that 'a lot of what gets printed about the "woman in a man's body" makes no scientific or rational sense' and is 'completely without any credible physiological or neurological basis'. Interestingly, she says that she 'witnessed' the way that the male-bodied transgenders 'developed and honed their narratives' as they changed from just being cross-dressers, who were open about their 'sexual fetish', to considering themselves trans, and saying, 'Oh my gawd, I must get hormones or I'm gonna kill myself – I am a WOMAN!' They gain respectability by identifying as transgender rather than just cross-dressers: 'Most men are ashamed of their fetish. Calling it "transgender" and developing elaborate theories about it is a means of making it "respectable" and gaining sympathy from the "born this way" advocates.' The narratives of wives can be more enlightening about the motives for this variety of male behaviour than the clinical and popular literature, which tends to accept transgender ideology as truth.

The role of wives in feminisation

The unpaid labour that wives and partners are required to perform in support of their husbands' impersonation of womanhood frequently has a sexual component, which may involve playing the dominatrix in sexual scenarios in which they are expected to 'feminise' their husbands. There is a very considerable industry online to service male-bodied transgenders, supplying equipment that includes not just clothes, breast and hip forms, padded pants, corsets, wigs, make-up, and high heels, but also training courses for voice and posture, and pornography. The main theme of both the training materials and of transgender pornography is 'feminisation', that is erotic humiliation, and in these rituals wives have a starring role. In the pornography men are forced to adopt clothing and behaviour that they associate with the subordinate sex caste, and 'Amber Goth's Forced Feminization' site demonstrates the enlistment of wives and female relatives. Goth explains the content of 'forced feminisation' pornography thus:

> Some of our stories feature mothers, aunts, grannies, wives etc. who feminise boys or young men and turn them into girls. This is a common theme in transgender fiction and is about wish-fulfilment on the part of transgendered folk, who really wish that this could happen to them!
>
> (Goth, 2012)

Another example is Cindel Sabante's book, *My Husband, My Panties*, in which the sexual fantasy involves the wife, and may help to explain why male-bodied transgenders like to surprise their wives while 'dressed', expecting an enthusiastic response in which the wife turns into a dominatrix, as here:

> Expecting the worst, Annie instead finds Mark in an embarrassing position on the bedroom floor. Mark had passed out wearing her clothes! Seeing an opportunity for a little fun, Annie decides to change Mark into her own little female friend, and tests the limits of how far Mark is willing to go.
>
> *(Sabante, 2013)*

The active role expected of wives is indicated in the fact that they are referred to as 'trainers' on websites devoted to that aspect of transgenderism that involves women's underwear. A search for 'My Husband, My Panties' brings up 6,010,000 hits and shows the popularity of this theme for cross-dressers (e.g. My Husband's Panties, 2005). Discussions on the sites include men saying they first wore their mothers' underwear at the age of twelve, or used to steal the underwear of the girl next door. Men also speak of specially buying underwear for their wives so that they can wear it themselves. Many of these themes come up in the accounts by wives featured earlier in this chapter. It is likely to prove quite disappointing for husbands trained to respond sexually to such fantasies through their pornography consumption, to find that their wives do not want to act as 'trainers', become distressed, and reject the sexual servicing opportunities that are being offered to them.

The most explicitly sexual version of feminisation is 'sissification', which is very clearly a form of masochistic satisfaction for the male devotees. Men are 'sissified', or humiliated, by being required to wear clothing they associate with women, and then being spanked or subjected to sadomasochist scenarios by dominatrixes, schoolmistresses and other female authority figures (Sissification, n.d.a). The practice is so enchanting for men that a search on the word brings up 744,000 hits. The use of the term 'sissy' is illuminating since it is very clearly a term of abuse based upon women's subordinate status. It does indicate that there is no positive association with women attached to this practice, only a degrading and demeaning one. The website entitled Sissy School offers, 'The Queendom of sissification. And it's very pink, very frilly, and very girlie.' It offers material on 'sissy phone sex, sissy domination, sissy cuckold training or sissy maid training' (Sissy School, n.d.). Much of the material, though, is in the form of video pornography, which was not examined in the research for this book (Sissification, n.d.b).

The advice and visual materials on 'female body language secrets' are useful indications of the transgender perspective on what 'essential' femininity consists of. The full 'feminisation kit' includes videos, expert interviews, 'special reports', 'cheat sheets', a 'worksheet', a 'resource guide', a 'hypnosis program', and advice on walking, make-up, clothes, hair, and voice feminisation. The idea of a 'feminine essence' is somewhat undermined by such an industry, however, since that which is 'natural' and biologically determined could not possibly require such detailed instruction. The hypnosis programme will teach a man how to be a woman on the 'inside' in only fifteen minutes: 'All you have to do is sit back, relax, and let your mind take you on a feminine journey. In time, you will find yourself effortlessly thinking, feeling, and acting like a real woman!' (Sorella, n.d.).

Transgenders and cross-dressers who gain sexual excitement from women's subordination can be quite knowledgeable about how such subordination works, as the following quote from advice to men on 'feminine posture' makes clear. The instruction is called 'Open vs. closed' and explains that women 'take up less space than men. This might seem obvious, but I'm amazed at how many girls forget to keep their legs together and their elbows in. (Genetic girls, too!)' (Sorella, n.d.). The men gain their satisfactions from thinking about and acting out precisely the restrictions of movement that those born and raised female have been tormented and trapped into by a lifetime of training in subordination, and they understand very well what they are doing: 'Open body positions are associated with the display of power. Besides making you look more passive and feminine, a closed body position makes you appear physically smaller' (Sorella, n.d.). In this example, the reality of women's subordination becomes a plaything for men's sexual excitement. Though many wives may be unaware of the transgender pornography empire that underlies their husbands' practice, they are likely to find the role expected of them as audience, helpmeet and dominatrix distasteful, and some are answering back.

The resistance movement of wives

Increasingly, wives are speaking out and the germs of a movement of resistance to what they are being subjected to are becoming visible. It is not a movement which comes close in size and influence to the transgender activist movement, through which their husbands can gain support, legal remedies and resources. Online sites that are offshoots of that movement purport to provide for wives but do not necessarily do so. Benvenuto sought support from an online message board for transsexuals and their family members, only to find that the message was to give unqualified support to their transitioning partners: 'Yes, they could be emotionally abusive. But didn't their husbands really have it much worse? Wasn't a wife's job to be supportive – no matter what?' (Benvenuto, 2012a; 128). One online support site for wives, however, crossdresserswives.com, takes a very different perspective (Crossdresserswives.com, n.d.a). It is specifically for wives who are finding it very difficult to survive their husbands' behaviour and does not allow 'stewarding' by husbands. The site provides a Bill of Rights that is illustrative of the aspects of men's cross-dressing practice that wives find most problematic. Though it applies ostensibly to the wives of cross-dressers rather than men who seek to live as women full-time, all of the 'rights' are about precisely those aspects of their husbands' behaviour that the wives of more committed personators find distressing (Benvenuto, 2012a). It begins with the right 'to know prior to marriage/cohabitation – not to be lied to at the altar', and goes on to encompass the right to tell other people about the problem, to have negative feelings about it, the right to reject the practice 'including sexual acts', the right to 'refuse to participate or be exposed to the practice of cross dressing', the right to leave the relationship, the right to 'insist on therapy', and the right to protect the children from 'psychological trauma' (Crossdresserswives.com, n.d.b). The material on the website is anonymous, which protects contributors from the sort of punishment Benvenuto received.

Most of the accounts by wives are explicit about the fact that their husbands' cross-dressing is a sexual practice that wives are now being expected to tolerate, or take part in, on the grounds that it is some kind of biological condition that the men cannot control. Sexologists and sex therapists have traditionally expected women to endure their husbands' expression of their masculine sexual prerogatives (Jeffreys, 1990; Tyler, 2011). Women have been guilt-tripped by sex writers such as Alex Comfort, author of *The Joy of Sex* (Comfort, 1972; Jeffreys, 1990), into accepting sadomasochist practice that disturbed them, for instance, and into chores such as swallowing semen though they found it distasteful, and many other practices aimed at men's satisfaction at the expense of their own. It continues to be a problem that as men's sexual interests change – often through their consumption of pornography and other elements of the sex industry – the demands upon wives escalate. Anal sex is now commonly demanded by male partners to the extent that sexologists have invented a new sexual problem 'anodyspareunia' to account for women's reluctance and pain and to justify creating therapies to enable women to overcome this (Stulhofer and Ajdukovic, 2011). In the case of transgenderism, it may be even harder for women to object because the practice is framed as inevitable and uncontrollable.

The mothers of transgenders

All of those who transgender have had mothers, and the mothers suffer many similar hurts to those experienced by wives and partners, but this group has not been studied at all. There is one book that covers their experience, called *Transitions of the Heart* (Pepper (ed.), 2012). It is composed of the stories of mothers, including those who identified their toddler children as transgender and those whose adult sons transitioned in middle age. The stories are presented with no analysis, the mothers are uncritical of transgenderism as a practice and all support their offspring wholeheartedly, but the extraordinary stresses they suffer are clearly expressed. The book appeals sentimentally to mother love, as mothers who accept that their children are transgender and support drugs and surgery for them are represented as particularly loving.

Mothers who identified their children at a young age as transgender – in one case as early as one year old – did so on account of their preferences for particular toys or clothes. Their criteria directly reflect those that comprise the definition of gender identity disorder in childhood and reflect traditional sex stereotypes that feminists have long critiqued. Mothers who are involved in imposing such rigid roles on their young children should not, perhaps, be seen as entirely blameless in the transgendering of children, as they play an active role. At the other extreme, some of the offspring are themselves already retirees and came out as transgendered to their mothers at an advanced age. The mothers generally express grief at the loss of the little girl or boy that they gave birth to. They express mourning and talk of endless crying as they tried to come to terms with their grief. The editor, Rachel Pepper, expresses the dilemma of mothers thus: 'For as children transition, so too must their families' (Pepper, 2012: xviii). The mothers suffered severe psychological distress, as one described: 'I whirled mentally and emotionally … Feelings of confusion, insecurity, fear, and sadness' (Pepper (ed.), 2012: 84). They express a strong sense of loss at the transgenderism of their offspring. They loved them as the biological sex to which they were born, and felt they lost those loved persons when they transitioned.

One woman describes her grief at seeing her adult son go through extreme body dysphoria as he embarks on many surgeries to remake his body in the image of his fantasy: 'Yet another operation for my child … My transgender daughter says she's still not right, still doesn't look a hundred per cent like a woman. She has gone through gender reassignment surgery, cosmetic shaving of the jaw line and nose, and two hair transplants. She now says that the bones of her eyebrows and the hairline are not right' (Pepper, 2012: 119). In describing her son she says he, 'still stares endlessly in the mirror, still sees things no one else sees, and I grieve for her'. Watching this self-mutilation caused great distress. Since the National Health Service in the UK would only pay for sex-reassignment surgery and not all the extras, the mother worried about the cost to her son's family finances: 'will it just be another 5,000 pounds down the drain?' (Pepper (ed.), 2012: 118).

Mothers, too, suffer from the self-centredness that the men who transgender can exhibit. This same mother describes the disturbing change in personality that took place in her son as he transitioned:

She was still operating as a man at this point. She was so full of hate and anger towards women. I wondered if it was jealousy ... she has become remarkably flat in personality. We find this apparent lack of emotion difficult to accept. She is highly intelligent, but the self-obsession, paranoia, and the avoidance of society which seems to go with her condition, has taken its toll. We are all hoping that she will now finally move on with her life.

(Pepper, 2012: 120)

The 'all' who were so adversely affected included his mother, wife and young children.

Some mothers have the misfortune to have to go through multiple experiences of losing their family members to transgenderism. In one case a woman lost both her twin daughters, who had come out as lesbians at high school but went on to transition (Pepper (ed.), 2012: 125). In another case a mother lost both her husband and her daughter to transgenderism. The mother explains that the husband was a cross-dresser who went on to transition, and influenced the girl child to follow his lead: 'My husband wanted our twelve-year-old daughter Heather to go through transition with him, including surgery' (Pepper (ed.), 2012: 155). Heather changed her name at sixteen and at eighteen had a hysterectomy. When parents enable their children to transition, the financial costs they bear are considerable. Puberty blockers for the children cost US$4,500–15,000 yearly, and therapy adds another cost (Pepper (ed.), 2012: 125). Whereas some mothers are clearly the victims of the practice of transgenderism, in some cases they can be seen to collude with patriarchal sex stereotyping and may even offer up their children as sacrifices upon the altar of 'gender'. Research is needed into the parents who actively seek to transgender their offspring.

Conclusion

It is time for a rethink in relation to the suffering that men who transgender inflict upon their wives. It may need to be understood as an under-recognised form of psychological violence towards women, a situation in which women need the serious support structures that are seen as appropriate when they are the victims of other forms of bullying from male partners. An understanding of the harms that male-bodied transgenders inflict upon their wives should cause all feminists, women concerned for the welfare of their sisters, to think seriously about the ethics of unconditional acceptance of the identities and pronouns of men whose wives are suffering. Feminists who accept a man as 'she' when his wife, children, mother cannot, and feel abused by the demand that they should, are abandoning an increasingly large section of womankind and expunging them from the community of women who deserve respect, in favour of supporting men in the exercise of their prerogatives.

Husbands transition as a result of their masculine prerogative, which is particularly forceful around matters that concern their sexual satisfaction. But wives are no longer as submissive and self-effacing as they were in the early days of transgenderism. Some are becoming very angry, and the beginnings of collective organisation are emerging. The voices of wives need to be heard because they have the capacity to break through the liberal fantasy of essential transgenderism. Wives say that their husbands are not, and cannot be women. It makes no sense to them that the men whose semen was essential to the creation of their children, and whose 'feminine' endeavours resemble Barbie dolls, should be called 'she' and given social kudos. Unfortunately, women's voices are not powerful in patriarchal societies where the voices of the fathers in the form of sexologists, psychiatrists and endocrinologists are taken seriously when women's lifetime experience is disdained.

5

WOMEN WHO TRANSGENDER

An antidote to feminism?

Written with Lorene Gottschalk

The transgendering of women and men need to be considered separately because they are very different phenomena. They are, however, usually run together in the literature as if they were but two faces of one single practice. The main difference stems from the fact that 'gender' is a political category that signifies caste status. Therefore, members of the superior caste, men, ostensibly lose status when they transgender, but for cross-dressers this can be precisely the reason for doing so as they can gain masochistic satisfaction. However, it should be recognised that, as we have seen in the last chapter, men who transgender do not surrender all their male privilege but carry it with them into different social contexts and are still able to wield authority over women. Members of the inferior caste, women, have quite a different experience when they transgender. They raise their status thereby, and in a society in which hatred and degradation of women has very harmful effects on women's sense of self, as well as a depressing effect on their lifetime earnings, this could be a powerful motivation to seek to enter the superior sex caste. The transgendering of women is an antidote to feminism because it is a way in which individual women can raise their status by joining the caste of men. In contrast feminism seeks to dismantle male superiority so that the status of all women is raised, and this task is in no way advantaged by the social mobility towards masculine status of a tiny minority of women.

Men who transgender find the existence of women who have transitioned useful because they can be seen, in the absence of any recognition of the differences, to confirm the authenticity of their own practice. Phyllis Frye, for instance, a US judge and one of the architects of the International Bill of Gender Rights 1995, specifically comments on how helpful the existence of such women has been:

> In my experience, nothing destroys the stereotypes of transgenders bet-
> ter than when a person unexpectedly meets a long-term FTM (female-
> to-male). FTMs completely obliterate the stereotype of the transgender.
> FTMs also provide a strong link to the feminist movement. Because
> many of them have backgrounds in lesbian and women's rights politics,
> they are able to bring training, insight and political connections.
> *(Frye, 2000: 141)*

The similarities consist of the fact that the idea of transgenderism is a construction of the medical profession in both cases, the fact that both practices
rely upon, and reinforce, harmful stereotypes of gender, and the fact that they
inflict severe harms to health and human functioning. In other respects, however, the differences are considerable. To begin with, men dominate the practice. There has historically been a considerable gap in the numbers, which
is still reflected in those who receive gender recognition certificates in the
UK today, with three in every four persons who transgender being male
(Ministry of Justice, 2012). There are differences in sexual orientation. The
majority of men who transgender are heterosexual and in relationships with
women at the time, and only a minority are men who have relationships
with men (Lawrence, 2004). They are attracted to women prior to transition,
and continue to be attracted to women after transition, at which point they
are likely to identify as lesbians. In the case of women who transgender, the
vast majority relate sexually to women and most identify as lesbians and have
been long-term members of the lesbian community before they transition
(Devor, 1999). They are straightened out by transition and mostly consider
themselves to be in heterosexual relationships after the event.

The very different contexts in which men and women transgender constitute another very considerable difference between these practices. The
heterosexual majority of male-bodied transgenders have no male culture of
femininity through which to understand themselves. The vast majority of
female-bodied transgenders, on the other hand, have inhabited a lesbian culture in which masculinity is valorised and many will have adopted aspects
of stereotypical masculinity in their appearance long before they decided to
transition. Within lesbian culture, the practice of butch/femme role playing,
in which the female partners in a relationship adopt the stereotyped roles that
provide the foundation for heterosexuality, was common in some sections of
the community before the advent of second wave feminism in the 1960s and
has experienced a rebirth since the 1980s (Jeffreys, 1989). It is in the role playing of butchness and the valorisation of masculinity that the phenomenon of
female-bodied transgenderism has its origins (Jeffreys, 2003). This very considerable difference between male and female aspirants affects, for instance,
the degree of support that they receive. The female partners of women who

transgender may see transition as simply an extension of the butchness they have already accepted as part of role playing practice. The lesbian communities in which female-bodied transgenders come out as 'men' may find this unsurprising to the extent that they have previously accepted extreme forms of masculine acting-out as an ordinary part of lesbianism. For male-bodied transgenders the situation is different. Though they may have gained satisfaction from thinking about themselves as 'feminine' for some time, they will usually have partners and communities for whom the idea of femininity in men is an unfamiliar and unpalatable concept.

Another singular difference, as the sexological literature makes plain, is the fact that transgender behaviour on the part of women is not a form of sexual fetishism as it commonly is for men (Bailey and Triea, 2007). While sexual fetishism – in the form of being excited by donning clothing stereotypically associated with women or seeking 'female' body parts – is increasingly being seen as explanatory of much male-bodied transgenderism, it offers no explanation for the female-bodied variety. Female-bodied transgenders do not have histories of cross-dressing in men's underpants for sexual excitement, and another form of explanation must be found.

There is, however, no literature that seeks an explanation for transgenderism on the part of women. The literature either takes transgenderism for granted, as though it was a natural phenomenon, or it is celebratory. Critical examination that seeks explanations would likely be viewed as hostile and 'transphobic' because it undermines the ideology that represents transgenderism as inevitable and essential. But if the phenomenon is not viewed as a work of nature, which just happens to be manifesting itself with remarkable frequency in the last three decades, then it is necessary to ask why it is taking place. Understanding female-bodied transgenderism from a feminist perspective provides a number of forms of explanation, all of which are related to the workings of male domination (Thompson, 2001).

One form of explanation to be considered here is that transgenderism is attractive because the societal hatred and subordination of women and of lesbians, and the valorisation of men, are forces that make it more attractive for some women to escape their relegation to subordinate womanhood and seek the advantages that the adoption of manhood will bring. There is little doubt that men in Western societies gain significant advantages from their sex caste status. These are economic, reflected in much higher lifetime earnings; physical, in terms of safety from male sexual violence and unwanted pregnancy; and psychological, in terms of self-regard and well-being. These advantages have been termed, by the male-bodied transgender sociologist, Raewyn Connell, the 'patriarchal dividend', which constitutes 'the advantage men gain in general from the overall subordination of women' (Connell, 2005: 79). Another form of explanation consists of the way in which female-bodied transgenderism emerges as an extension of butch role playing in lesbian communities. 'Gender' is the sorting system of male domination and constitutes the hierarchy in which men have power over women. Its ubiquity and importance make it hard to think outside the box of gender and traditionally, in lesbian communities, 'gender' has been reproduced as lesbians have sought to understand themselves within the norms of their society.

Butch/femme role playing and transgenderism by women

Butch/femme role playing was common in parts of some lesbian communities before the 1970s. It was challenged by lesbian feminism, which sought to create equal relationships between women, free from the constraints imposed by a patriarchal heterosexuality that framed eroticism as only imaginable between persons playing masculine/feminine roles. In the 1990s lesbian role playing was rehabilitated and created a foundation for the transgendering of lesbians. Some lesbians resented the feminist challenge to role playing because they considered that their sexuality was linked to butch/femme roles and that this eroticised inequality was indeed the very embodiment of essential lesbianism. Such a reaction is described by Arlene Lev, a lesbian psychotherapist who works with those who consider themselves transgender and wrote the book *Transgender Tapestry* (2004). Her perspective is important because her book has made her influential within transgender studies. She explains, in the *Journal of Lesbian Studies*, her despair at entering a lesbian event in the late 1980s and finding that all the lesbians who were there, who were having a great time, were ungendered in their appearance. She found she was not sexually attracted to any of them:

> I looked around at the room of androgynous lesbians – sweet women, laughing and enjoying themselves, comfortable in their bodies and the celebration of sexuality that dancing with your own can bring – and with the suddenness of an electric shock, I realized there was not one woman in the room who I could imagine dating. My community, a home in my heart, left me sexually cold, aloof.
>
> *(Lev, 2008: 134)*

They were not role playing power difference so they were simply not attractive to her.

Feminism wrought dramatic changes on the practices of lesbians in the 1970s (Jennings, 2006). In her fascinating account of the history of the iconic London lesbian club, the Gateways, from the 1940s to the 1980s, *From the Closet to the Screen*, Jill Gardiner uses material from her interviews to describe how feminism influenced the club clientele (Gardiner, 2003). Prior to the 1970s, lesbians who used the club were likely to engage in role playing and even call themselves by male names, as the novelist Mary Duffy describes in her novel, *The Microcosm* (Duffy, 1966). Recalling that time, lesbians explain that there was no option to identifying as butch or femme, and lesbians who were not identifiable were derided (Jennings, 2006: 218). Historian, Rebecca Jennings, explains that in role playing etiquette 'strict codes of behaviour structured who might dance with whom' and 'established boundaries, defining who was sexually available to whom'. This paralleled the rules of heterosexuality, 'a similar organizational function to that provided by notions of gender in mainstream society' (Jennings, 2006: 220, 221). The impact of feminism, Jennings explains, made adoption of 'the extremes of masculine and feminine which were central to butch/femme clothing' unnecessary, because lesbians could 'wear trousers and … follow their personal preferences in dress' without question. Also feminism caused many to feel 'uncomfortable with the notion of asking a butch's permission to dance with a femme and refused to comply with accepted conventions' (Jennings, 2006: 223). Lesbians who embraced feminism abandoned role playing and were able to engage enthusiastically in sexual relationships without any resort to the trappings of gendered power difference. But some, like Lev, clearly found this difficult.

According to the anti-feminist narrative of transpolitics and sexual libertarian/queer lesbianism, it was precisely lesbian feminism that oppressed butches and femmes and drove them out of the lesbian community, and the resurgence of role playing practice from the 1980s onwards is seen as the return of the repressed. Arlene Lev writes, 'The rise of lesbian-feminist politics in the 1970s effectively drove butch-femme identities, communities, and expression underground, silencing, and therefore historically distorting, discussions of gender expression in lesbian relationships' (Lev, 2008). The great mistake of lesbian feminists, she says, was that 'gender expression itself became seen as a tool of the patriarchy' (Lev, 2008: 131). She is correct in that 'gender' roles are understood in feminist theory not as harmless tools of sexual excitement and fashion, but the stratification system of male domination. They show who is up and who is down, and regulate behaviour accordingly. In transgender mythmaking, it was lesbian feminists who should bear some responsibility for constructing female-to-male transgenderism through this process of expulsion. Butches, unable to find a valorised place in lesbian community, were forced out into transgenderism.

In fact, though she represents role playing as simply the natural form of lesbian interaction, Lev makes it clear that she does indeed understand role playing as representing the traditional roles of patriarchal heterosexuality. She explains,

Butch and femme are, at their root, gendered erotic identities. Butches, assigned and identified as females, experience their sexuality as mediated through masculinity. Femmes, by reclaiming a socially scorned femininity, broadcast their sexuality – a lesbian-specific sexuality – by publicizing their attraction to masculine females.

(Lev, 2008: 133)

The biggest problem, and it is one that the femmes complain about a great deal, is that this does not work for them since their lesbianism is invisible. Both in the malestream world and in lesbian communities, they may not be recognised as lesbians and find they are assumed to be heterosexual (Jeffreys, 1989). They suffer the marginalisation and exclusion that are commonly women's lot in a heteropatriarchal society that valorises masculinity. Similarly, as we shall see in this chapter, the partners of lesbians who transgender can find they have no role in parts of the lesbian community and are not recognised as lesbians, while their transgender partners do have a place.

Lev explains the role of the femme as being the responsibility to support the butch, as the 'butch/femme dance' celebrates 'the masculinity of butch lesbians, and in that act heals some of the disembodiment butches can experience' (Lev, 2008: 136). Femmes are required to sustain the masculinity of their lovers and this role, too, is common to the dynamics of relationships in which one partner transgenders. Butches are heroised as the true lesbians, those who bear the slings and arrows of anti-lesbianism and deserve acclaim for their political resistance. There is an analogue of this in the problems of non-transgender partners of female-bodied transgenders, who must put effort into creating the illusion of their trans partner's manhood, even to the extent of pretending that she did not have a 'girlhood' and was always somehow male. The partners are required to enter into a *folie à deux* to maintain the precarious, and ultimately implausible, idea that one partner has changed their sex.

Within lesbian role playing, butch/femme couples, Lev explains, recreate heteropatriarchal roles very precisely and 'according to emerging reports' they 'enact family roles in sexualized and erotic ways … meaning that roles of Mommy, Daddy, Son and Daughter, are enacted – sexually and romantically – within the intimate narratives of the couple' (Lev, 2008: 138). Femmes, she says, act just like the traditional wives of male domination by creating safe homes for their butch and family, 'I would like to suggest that one of the most subversive acts that femmes have accomplished is the establishment of a safe haven for their families in often hostile environments, through the creation of homes and through the process of homemaking' (ibid.). Femmes, it transpires, do 'Women's domestic work – the work of cooking, cleaning, mending, and kissing "owies" – work that I suspect originated from and was sustained by the hands of femmes in femme/butch relationships, has mostly gone unnoticed or judged irrelevant or apolitical' (Lev, 2008: 139). As feminist economists have pointed out, housework is still viewed as 'women's work' and those sporting masculinity are exempt (Jeffreys, 2012; Waring, 1989). That which Lev seeks to romanticise is fundamental to women's inequality.

It is this normalisation of butch/femme role playing that created the foundation for the development of the practice of female-bodied transgenderism in the 1990s. Lesbians who transition, like Chaz Bono, often understood themselves to be butch lesbians beforehand (Bono, 2011). The issue of whether lesbians who transgender are simply going a bit further than those who remain identified as butches and eschew the opportunity to transition has been much debated in the lesbian community. Indeed a phrase has been developed to discuss this issue, the 'border wars', meaning the border between butchness and transgenderism (Halberstam and Hale, 1998). Some lesbian writers have argued there is scarcely any difference, while others have sought to establish that there is a considerable difference, not just one of degree of masculinity adopted, but in the essence of the practice, meaning that the lesbians who transgender really are 'men' whereas butches remain female however they behave. Butch/femme role playing recreates the roles of the heteropatriachy, while transgenderism goes further by attempting to recreate the bodies thereof. Butches are often proud of their lesbianism, but those who transition extirpate their lesbianism and engage, through the use of hormones and surgery, in the medical creation of heterosexuality. It is an archetypically heteronormative practice.

The transgendering of lesbians can be characterised as another example of the ways in which the medical profession has sought to straighten out lesbians, since the majority of those women who 'trans' relate to women afterwards, creating a heterosexual couple (Jeffreys, 2003). This could be understood as a human rights violation, just one more way in which the socially despised status of 'lesbian' can be expunged through the connivance of the medical profession and the state. Only if they are recognised as 'men', in most states, are lesbians permitted to marry each other or access other rights (McConville and Mills, 2003).

The harmful effects of female-bodied transgenderism on lesbians and on feminism

Within lesbian communities dominated by queer politics, an increasing number of women are transitioning to a simulacrum of maleness (Bauer, 2008; Weiss, 2007). The harmful effects of transgendering on the bodies of those women who transition are dealt with elsewhere in this volume. This chapter examines the harmful effects on the lesbian community, on lesbian relationships, and on feminism. During the wave of transgendering of males that began in the last decades of the twentieth century, lesbians were slow to join in. The practice was unknown in the lesbian community of the 1970s and remained very rare well into the 1990s. The phenomenon does not figure in important collections of lesbian essays in the 1970s such as *Our Right to Love* (Vida (ed.), 1978), or even in Julia Penelope's edited collection *Lesbian Culture* from 1993. The latter included a piece on butch and femme in the 1950s from Joan Nestle, but nothing about transgenderism.

One clear effect of the transgendering of lesbians is that it disappears their lesbianism in a literal way, by so changing their bodies and presentation that they no longer resemble women or lesbians, though they generally seek relationships with women and lesbians and remain within lesbian communities. The history of lesbianism has been shown by lesbian historians and commentators to be one of persecution, and elimination from the public record (Klaich, 1974). Transgenderism fits into this grim history by once more making lesbians invisible. For many of those who would once have been lesbians, transgenderism is the newly fashionable style. All of the city groups and services that were once set up by lesbians and feminists in the 1970s to provide for lesbian communities have now been replicated for lesbians who transgender. There are social groups, political groups, financial planning groups (to pay for surgeries), lists of transfriendly venues, lists of potential trans roommates (Hudson, n.d.).

There is one significant difference, however; the existence of groups for the partners of lesbians who transgender. Before the phenomenon of transgenderism, both partners in a relationship were lesbians and could attend all the same groups and neither required special services. Female-bodied transgenderism shuts the partners of these women out of the lesbian communities that have shaped and supported their lives because they are now seen as really heterosexual. This disappearance of lesbians has a negative effect upon feminism too, because lesbians were the founders of so many important institutions for women, refuges and rape crisis centres, publishers, bookshops, theatre groups and bands. Lesbian feminists in second wave feminism worked with huge energy for the benefit of all women, including other lesbians. To the extent that pride in being women and lesbians has been the basis of lesbian feminism, and therefore crucial to the feminist movement, this disappearance of lesbians constitutes a severe harm to this politics.

Presently female-bodied transgenderism has progressed as a practice to the point where it is plentifully justified, described and celebrated, even in the feminist academy. In the last few years there have been special issues on transgenderism of *Women's Studies Quarterly* (Volume 36, 3 and 4, 2008), and, on transgenderism and intersexuality, of the *Journal of Lesbian Studies* (Volume 10, 1 and 2, 2006). There is little or no critical comment about transgenderism in the journal articles. This level of coverage is indicative of the burgeoning of the practice. In 2013, the peak body for women's studies in the United States, the National Women's Studies Association (NWSA), has an 'interest group' for 'feminist masculinities' (NWSA, 2013). Whereas once those involved in women's studies, like other feminists, would have seen masculinity as the problem that feminism needed to dismantle, now it is being vaunted as a lifestyle choice that is consistent with, if not exemplary of, academic feminism. This is a good indication of the extent to which some branches of academic feminism have drifted away from feminist activism and the feminist movement, and become at best irrelevant and at worst toxic to the possibility of the liberation of women.

The physical harms that women experience from hormones and surgery are considerable and are covered in detail in a previous chapter, but multiple harms are inflicted upon women's and lesbian communities, too, from this practice. The women partners of those lesbians who transition suffer grief, loss and distress that is similar to the suffering of the partners of male-bodied transgenders, but there are some significant differences that result from the fact that the transition takes place in a lesbian couple and takes the form of emulating masculinity, which is the behaviour of the superior sex caste of men.

Accessing the patriarchal dividend

Women who transgender have access to the patriarchal dividend, the privileges and advantages that appertain to men in systems of male domination. For lesbians, in particular, this may be an attractive option, because as 'butches' they suffer anti-lesbian discrimination and harassment that can be alleviated if their persecutors consider that they are actually 'men'. One important and very material aspect of the patriarchal dividend is economic. The economic dividend is clearly revealed, for instance, in the very great differences between the average amounts of money that women and men will earn in their lifetimes and the amount of money on which they can hope to retire. Female business executives in the UK will earn only two-thirds that which male executives, who are similarly situated and start and finish working at the same age, earn in their lifetimes (Barrow, 2012). This is a very substantial advantage for men and it has been poorly explained by economists. Very interesting research by Kristen Schilt, however, has demonstrated precisely how the patriarchal dividend works for female-bodied transgenders in the workplace (Schilt, 2006). Schilt interviewed twenty-nine women who had transgendered about their experience while working as women, and after their transition. Some of the women remained in their original places of work during and after transition, and some changed their place of work, but in both cases they received considerable advantages compared with their previous experience. Schilt explains that though the women had exactly the same skills, education and abilities after transition, how 'this 'human capital' is perceived often varies drastically once they become men at work' (Schilt, 2006: 466).

Female-bodied transgenders gained a 'reward' in the form of 'a type of bodily respect', which meant 'being freed from unwanted sexual advances or inquiries about sexuality' (Schilt, 2006: 479). The behaviour from male co-workers that ceased after transition included grabbing breasts and being called 'honey' and 'babe'. According to two respondents, being transgender was greatly preferable to being 'obvious' lesbians in the workplace as they could escape 'sexualized comments' and 'invasive personal questions about sexuality'. Such privilege was only available to 'stealth' transgenders, that is those who were not open about their transitions. Stealth transgenders gained 'physical autonomy and respect' and 'less touching, groping' (Schilt, 2006: 479).

There were other very substantial gains, as female-bodied transgenders found that they acquired greater respect and authority in their work, and were given more staff and resources to do their jobs. When seen as 'men' they had to work less hard, received more positive reviews for that work, and were more rewarded. One of Schilt's interviewees explained how these advantages accrued not just to employees, but to those who set up their own businesses: 'I have this company that I built, and I have people following me; they trust me, they believe in me, they respect me. There is no way I could have done that as a woman' (Schilt, 2006: 482). This female-bodied transgender explained that though some women achieved success as entrepreneurs, it would have been particularly difficult for an obvious lesbian to do that. Transitioning eliminated that disadvantage. Several other interviewees explained that as lesbians who were butch or 'gender ambiguous', they received cruel humiliations such as not being allowed to walk in the front door of the restaurant in which they worked lest they project the wrong image for the establishment. As 'men' they were able to wear clothing that they would otherwise have been pilloried for and achieve the professional success that would otherwise have eluded them.

One-third of the participants said they did not gain an advantage, but this was usually because they were in the early stages of transition or not seen as men. Height could make a big difference, since small women would, after transition, be smaller than average men and might not garner the same respect as a taller male would. Some felt they looked extremely young after transition and this affected the way in which they were treated. Black and Asian women who transitioned reported that though relieved of the structural disadvantage of being seen as 'women', they still suffered disadvantage as a result of racism. As Schilt comments, the advantages that women gain when they transition bring into focus the effect that cultural beliefs about gender, which are embedded in workplace structures, have on women's inequality. The research illuminates the invisible but very important and pervasive everyday discrimination that women experience, but may not, in the absence of anything to compare it with, be able to identify. It also shows, Schilt argues, that women are not impeded in their advancement in the workplace by socialisation as female, which affects their decisions and behaviour, since women with the same socialisation who transitioned were able to advance perfectly well. Women, this shows, are structurally disadvantaged by the way that others see and treat them, rather than any qualities they may display.

In later research, Kristen Schilt and a colleague examined the workplace experience of male-bodied transgenders (Schilt and Wiswall, 2008). They found that men who transition lose money, through 'significant losses in hourly earnings' (Schilt and Wiswall, 2008: 4). They conclude that the later average age at which men transition, forty years, compared with women, thirty years, is related to these losses. They suggest that men intending to transition strategically 'change their gender later to preserve their male advantage as long as possible', whereas female-bodied transgenders 'on the other hand ... maximize their expected gains from becoming men by changing their gender earlier' (Schilt and Wiswall, 2008: 19). Schilt's work is important as an excellent example of a feminist understanding of gender as a hierarchy and a way of organising power difference, rather than as an essence, as it is commonly said to be in transgender theory. Her 2006 article is titled, 'Just One of the Boys: Making Gender Visible in the Workplace'. It does not use the word 'gender' to refer just to clothing preferences or ways of behaving, as is commonly the case in transgender ideology. What is made visible is the way in which 'gender', as a caste system, creates advantage for men and disadvantage for women.

Another significant gain from transitioning consists of greater physical security and freedom from fear. Women who transgender escape the abuse, harassment and violence from men that those women who remain on the gender frontlines continue to experience. In the workplace, as Schilt shows (2006), sexual harassment in the form of grabbing body parts and sexualised comments and questions are all part of the disadvantage that female-bodied transgenders leave behind when they transition. Moreover, transitioning out of womanhood may offer a vision of safety to some women who have suffered severe violence from men. Though there is a dearth of research examining the experiences that female-bodied transgenders have of violence, there is some work that suggests a connection. Holly (now Aaron) Devor, for instance, found in research she carried out before she herself transgendered that female-bodied transgenders had experienced a high occurrence of violence in childhood (Devor, 1994). Seventeen of her forty-five respondents (38 per cent), reported significant physical abuse in their childhood homes, and fourteen (31 per cent), reported sexual abuse. Altogether, 60 per cent of her total had experienced physical, sexual or emotional abuse, and in most cases, she explains, these forms of abuse were those likely to lead to the most significant psychological harms in later life. She takes pains to point out that these figures reflect only those who chose to bring up abuse while telling their stories, since she asked no questions about it. She adds that the fact that trangenders are keen to represent themselves as psychologically robust, lest they be denied medical treatment or suffer greater discrimination, may further reduce the percentage of those mentioning abuse. Nonetheless the figures are significant. She suggests that 'in some cases transsexualism may be an extreme adaptive dissociative response to severe child abuse' (Devor, 1994: 66). In these cases, she hypothesises,

> a male protector/survivor personality, which functions co-consciously … with the original female personality, might act first as a defense, and later, after many years of reinforcing psychological and socialization experiences, as an escape route from otherwise intolerable psychic pain.
>
> *(ibid.)*

These women had created a male 'avatar' to give themselves a shield against violence in their youth and this formed the template for the male they then sought to become. This research was conducted two decades ago, and there has, unfortunately, been nothing similar. It raises the question of how little investigation takes place by the medical profession into the backgrounds of the women whom they transgender.

There are other disadvantages of womanhood that women who transgender are able to escape from, such as the onslaught of 'beauty practices' that girls and women are required to carry out upon their bodies in order to be acceptably feminine and sexually attractive to men. These include depilation, diets, cosmetic surgery, make-up, high heeled shoes, tight and revealing clothing (Jeffreys, 2005). Male domination, and the low and stigmatised status of women, cause teenage girls to engage in punishment of their bodies through eating disorders and self-mutilation (Jeffreys, 2000, 2008). There is increasing evidence that woman-hating Western cultures are toxic to girls and very harmful to their mental health (APA Task Force, 2007). It is, perhaps, not surprising, therefore, that there seem to be some girls baling out and seeking to upgrade their status. Medical developments in surgery and drugs, and an increasingly entrenched medical ideology of essential gender that can accidentally reside in the wrong body, could appear to provide forms of escape for some girls and women. Lesbians may seek to escape anti-lesbian discrimination and the abuse that stems from the social hatred of lesbianism, which is a subset of the hatred of women. Becoming self-confident lesbians or feminists can protect women from the worst effects of this misogyny, but at present most women are likely to see no way out but to comply with the demands of femininity or suffer the ignominy of social exclusion for their refusal. In the absence of feminist revolution, transgenderism may appear to offer a solution to some, but one that entails severe punishment of the body. It wreaks havoc on the potential equality that can exist in lesbian relationships too.

Female-bodied transgenderism in relationships

In the last few years feminist researchers have studied the relationships that female-bodied transgenders have with other women. This work is fascinating on several fronts. It enables an evaluation of the claim that transgenderism is transgressive, and shows the heteronormative architecture on which the relationships are often built. Also, this research shows quite clearly that transgenderism is not just an individual pursuit, as the masculinity of the trans partner has to be constantly reproduced in relationship with others. Masculinity is part of a binary and requires its opposite, since, in the absence of femininity, masculinity would have no meaning. Much of the hard work of the non-trans partners is directed to the construction of their partners' masculinity, physically, through doing the hormone injections and, symbolically, by femming up to emphasise the gender difference.

Exponents of queer and transgender studies commonly argue that transgenders challenge and transgress gender norms and the rules of heteronormative relationships. In an article on how challenging transgender lifestyles are, the authors argue, 'The experiences and perceptions of transgender individuals fundamentally challenge society's normative beliefs and theoretical ideas about the nature of gender roles, gender identity, and sexual orientation' (Nagoshi et al., 2012: 406). Such research is usually short on details of exactly how this occurs. Research that studies the relationships that transgenders actually have, does not bear out the much vaunted transgressiveness of the practice at all, with one study of the relationships of transgenders finding that 'participants were strongly influenced by heteronormative discourses' (Iantaffi and Bockting, 2011). This has been found to be the case in the relationships that female-bodied transgenders have with women, too, and this is perplexing, since research on housekeeping in lesbian relationships where neither partner has transitioned, for instance, shows something rather different, a quite equal division of labour (Dunne, 2000; Kurdek, 2007; Solomon et al. 2005). When lesbians transgender this equality drops away, and a common theme of research on their relationships is that they seek to mirror heterosexual ones in many ways (Brown, 2009). Transgenderism re-establishes inequality in relationships between women. As we have seen in the previous chapter, the wives of men who transgender also find themselves burdened with new forms of housework and with the creation and maintenance of their partners' new 'gender'. In both cases it is female partners who are expected to shoulder these burdens.

One of the heteronormative dimensions is the onus of relationship building and maintenance, which in heterosexual relationships rests on the female partner (Kamo, 2000). Pfeffer's research, in which she interviewed the non-trans partners, has found this pattern also appertains for women in relationships with female-bodied transgenders (2010). She found that the stories of the non-transitioning partners 'resonate' with heterosexual couples in that they perform the traditional household duties as well as the emotional labour, just as heterosexual housewives have been expected to do. Importantly, the non-transitioning partner takes on the burden of supporting and enabling the aspirant partner as she goes through the transition process. The participants commonly reported 'inegalitarian, gender-stereotyped divisions of household labor between themselves and their trans men partners' (Pfeffer, 2010: 173). One woman, when asked how much of her life comprised 'taking care of her partner and issues related to transition' said, 'about 70% of my life. That's scaled back from what it was' (Pfeffer, 2010: 174). She maintains the household, does 'massive' amounts of her partner's 'own work – school work', as well as 'a huge amount of emotional time spent in processing transitioning, family, frustrations around the transition process'; meanwhile her own thesis was neglected.

The partners of female-bodied transgenders found themselves engaged in exhausting emotional work, not only in terms of supporting their partner through transition, but also dealing with communication within the relationship and managing family and community issues. A problem that was common among the partners was one that features strongly in heterosexual women's dissatisfactions with their male partners, the inability of the transgendered partners to communicate. The trans partners just did not speak, particularly about the problems of transition, and they were, as one woman expresses it, 'clumsy' about feelings. One woman in Pfeffer's study described her partner as forgetful and messy and not being able to take care of 'himself', and said that was why she fulfilled this role. As Pfeffer comments, 'These narratives were strikingly similar to those offered by women partners of non-trans men' (Pfeffer, 2010: 175).

One arduous task that the women undertook was the medical care of their partners as they transitioned. This included 'emotional support, advocacy, bimonthly testosterone administration' (ibid.). Moreover, Pfeffer points out, this work is likely to be endless since 'transition should be considered an iterative, relational, and lifelong process' (ibid.). The non-trans partners were expected to find sympathetic doctors, make appointments, monitor treatment. In relation to the very brutal surgeries involved in transition, personal care of the transgender partners could be very disturbing. It involved not just twenty-four hour care for the patient after surgery, but care of serious wounds after 'top' surgery, for instance. As one partner remarked, 'I get kind of queasy and stuff and I remember the smell being really intense' (Pfeffer, 2010: 177). As Pfeffer puts it, the partners served as 'unpaid and untrained personal medical and health care advocate, therapist, assistant, and nurse' (Pfeffer, 2010: 179). They also had to arrange finances for the surgeries, 'saving, raising, and contributing funds for transition-related procedures' (ibid.).

Abusive relationships

Another way in which relationships that include a female-bodied transgender can replicate heteronormative patterns is the psychological abuse and physical violence that are exercised by some of the transitioning partners. No research has specifically examined this problem, but Nicola Brown, while carrying out interviews with partners of transgenders that did not ask questions about violence or abuse, found that five of her twenty participants spontaneously brought up the problem (Brown, 2007). The types of abuse the partners reported included manipulation, emotional and verbal abuse, name calling and demeaning put-downs. More aggravated abuse included one trans partner who frequently kept her partner in a state of sleep deprivation, punching walls, destroying her possessions and throwing objects. Controlling behaviour included repeated violations of agreed rules in a non-monogamous relationship and not being allowed to initiate sex. Two of the five were manipulated into financially supporting their transgender partner. Similar forms of abuse were perpetrated against participants in Joslin-Roher and Wheeler's (2009) study, where one partner in particular had to take on full financial responsibility for both of them, when her transgender partner could not find work.

One form of coercion is quite specific to relationships in which there are trans partners, and consists of the use of the victim status of transgenders to establish control. In such relationships the abusive trans partners utilise a form of blackmail, involving threats of exposing a non-compliant partner as 'transphobic' in a similar way to the male-bodied trans partners in the previous chapter. Brown found that transgender abusers used 'trans status and/ or political discourses' against partners. Non-trans partners could be controlled by accusations of transphobia if they failed to behave in supportive ways, including being financially supportive: 'I spent so much time paying for his blood work and his testosterone, which he needed and if I didn't pay … I was a bad girlfriend, I wasn't supportive of him, and then I became "anti-trans"' (Brown, 2007: 380). There is increasing evidence that accusations of 'transphobia' can be used by female-bodied transgenders in order to discredit their partners' legitimate concerns and guilt-trip them into obedience. A quotation on Elspeth Brown's blog about her research into relationships in which one woman is trans indicates the ubiquity of the accusations.

She explains that she was going through her interviews and the problem of a partner being called transphobic came up 'yet again'. Her interviewee states, 'I've been called transphobic so many times I can't even count' (Brown, Elspeth, 2011).

Women suffered particular difficulties in recognising or protesting abuse when in relationships with trans partners. This was because the ideology of transgenderism had trained them to see their partners as victims so they could not also be seen as abusive or, if they were, this could be justified as an understandable result of their oppressed condition (Brown, 2007: 377). As Nicola Brown explains,

> The view that transsexual partners were 'more oppressed' as a consequence of their transsexual ... status ... seemed to prevent participants from thinking they could be abusive because it contradicted the dominant model of violence where the abusive partner is the person with more social power.
>
> *(ibid.)*

One interviewee explained that she took emotional abuse that she would not have tolerated from a man or a woman and spent a lot of time,

> educating myself on *his* 'oppression' and thinking of 'him' [as] so powerless in a societal sense that there would be no way he could have enough power to be abusive [and her partner] used his various identities – trans included – to reinforce that myth for me.
>
> *(ibid.)*

Another interviewee said that though she thought some behaviour was 'unfair' 'there was something about the fact that he was trans that let me think, "Okay, maybe that's okay"' (Brown, 2007: 378).

The abusive transgenders used their transgenderism as an excuse for their violence, for example an apology for violence might include a reason given such as 'well, it's because someone called me "she" today' (Brown, 2007: 379) as though that excused their violence or abusive behaviour towards their partner. The abusers put the blame on the victims, citing their faults such as not being loving enough, not being supportive enough, not being femme enough, and other solecisms. So, like heterosexual women in abusive relationships, the abused partners in Brown's study felt as if they were 'walking on egg shells' (Brown, 2007: 377) and were in a constant state of awareness. None of them reported the abuse to police, nor did they tell families or friends; moreover, they blamed themselves for the abuse and it was not until their relationships ended that they spoke of it.

Another form of abuse was the denigrating of lesbians and women that some female-bodied transgenders engaged in. Non-trans partners were the victims of hostile invective simply because they remained members of the despised, subordinate female sex caste. One of Brown's interviewees explained, 'Li also was prone to making fun of stereotypical female behaviour. He would call girls flippant or stupid or make remarks about women's bodies. He was suspicious of women: women were definitely something other than what he was. He constantly made distinctions between the "way women act" and the way he acts' (Brown, 2007: 382). This behaviour, though distressing for partners, is foreseeable, since the idea of 'masculine' gender relies on the differentiation and denigration of its opposite, 'femininity'. As Brown observes, such behaviour may reflect sexism in the sense of 'an identification with dominant, misogynist masculinity' or a 'disidentification process' through 'devaluation' of that which is female. Similarly, the trans partner is likely to want to dissociate as much as possible from a previous lesbian identity that undermines the authenticity of her transition. Invective that denigrates lesbians can be particularly hurtful to partners who saw themselves as lesbians in a lesbian relationship before their partner chose to change the goalposts. Elspeth Brown's informant describes a context in which this anti-lesbian abuse occurred and how disturbing it was:

> I got in a giant fight with my ex, who's a trans guy ... and I said something like, 'Don't you ever miss being a lesbian.' He was so offended, he was like 'I was never a lesbian'. But he said lesbian like it was just the vilest thing ... I don't accept it. And that doesn't make me transphobic.
>
> *(Brown, Elspeth, 2011)*

Straightening out

Non-trans partners who understood themselves to be in lesbian relationships before their partners transitioned are harmed by being required to relinquish their sometimes hard-won, lesbian identities and the lesbian communities that have been their support, in order to identify as heterosexual at the behest of their lovers. Brown's research (Brown, 2009; 2010) shows non-trans partners reflecting on and renegotiating their identities. Of the twenty participants in her study, twelve identified as lesbians prior to the transition of their partner, five as queer and three as bisexual. After the transition of their partners, only four identified as lesbians, twelve had changed their self-identification to queer, two identified as bisexual and two did not nominate an identity, referring to themselves as 'open or fluid' (Brown, 2009). Out of twenty participants in Pfeffer's (2008) study of the body image of female-bodied transgenders' partners, only seven identified as either a lesbian or dyke.

None of the participants in Pfeffer's (2010) work on fifty couples, of which 30 per cent were in a lesbian relationship prior to FTM transition, identified their relationship as lesbian thereafter.

One of Brown's respondents explained that she thought of herself as a lesbian but that she was aware that publicly she is seen as a heterosexual or bisexual woman (Brown, 2009). She considers herself to be in a 'strange and uncomfortable place' because if she objected to the way she is seen and called herself a lesbian, she would effectively out her partner as transgender (Brown, 2009: 67). She concluded that she was living in a 'kind of no man's land in terms of identity' (Brown, 2009: 70). One of Pfeffer's participants spoke of being unsure about how to identify to others (Pfeffer, 2010). She had previously identified as a lesbian, but now does not know whether to identify as a lesbian or a heterosexual woman, and feels she is compromising her trans partner if she calls herself a lesbian. Identifying as a lesbian was unthinkable to some non-trans partners as their transgender partners had started identifying as men. Retaining their previous lesbian identities would disrupt the carefully constructed myth that their partners had really become 'men'. As non-trans partners adapted to being heterosexualised by their partners' actions they lost their communities too, feeling that they must leave the lesbian group in which they had found support, for instance. The conflict between attachment to community and attachment to their partners caused them and their relationships a great deal of distress (Brown, 2009). Identification with the lesbian community was important for the non-trans partners in Joslin-Roher and Wheeler's (2009) study, too. Being part of a community was a way for them to understand themselves and to be understood by others; it gave them a political ideal and interaction within the community was a way to meet others like themselves. But, ironically, while the female-bodied transgenders often stayed within and had a home in the lesbian community, the non-trans partners found that they had no place.

Transgenderism creates a barrier between women who were once both part of the same lesbian community. The achievement of 'gender' difference means that couples may end up with no community that accepts them both, as the female-bodied transgenders create their own community, which does not accept non-trans partners, and the lesbian community may not accept either party, since they have either abandoned lesbianism or changed their identity to straight (Cook-Daniels, 1998b: 7). A great displacement takes over from the sense of sisterhood and community that feminism and lesbian feminism seeks to create.

The trauma of having to change their sexual identity from lesbian to heterosexual can be particularly distressing for those, such as Loree Cook-Daniels, who have been very involved in lesbian activism, fighting for recognition and provision specifically for lesbians (Cook-Daniels, 1998b).

Cook-Daniels was a lesbian activist from age eighteen, when she set up a gay youth group and continued to organise marches and actions after having met a partner, Marcelle, who announced that she wanted to transgender. Cook-Daniels says she prevented her partner from transitioning because she wanted to preserve the lesbian identity that was so important to her. After her 'eventual decision to stop blocking Marcelle's dream', she abandoned her lesbian activism in favour of becoming one of the first to campaign around the issues of 'Lesbian-partners-of-FTMs', and said she was 'fired' by 'repentance for my sin against Marcelle' in delaying her transition (1998b: 2). Marcelle later committed suicide (1998b). The change in Cook-Daniels' priorities is a good example of the way in which transgenderism can derail lesbian and feminist politics. She is remarkably frank about the exclusion and denigration that non-trans partners received at the hands of the developing community of female-bodied transgenders in the 1990s. When she attended the second FTM of the Americas conference, she says, she was 'appalled at the way the partners were treated' (1998: 2). They were excluded, talked down to or ignored and seen as 'tag-alongs' (1998b: 3). She found that, despite her long record of activist achievement, Marcelle's transition 'relegated me to a sort of "Ladies' Auxiliary"' (ibid.). She was accused of a number of transgressions and attacked as a lesbian: 'I was unprepared for the anger and hatred many voiced about Lesbians, a category of people that I apparently personified' (1998b: 4). She had to fight for a place within the transgender community without being, as she put it, 'shot at' (1998b: 8).

In an article on the plight of lesbians with trans partners, Cook-Daniels quotes women speaking of their grief at losing the lesbian community, which, in some cases, they had played a key role in building (Cook-Daniels, 1998a). One explains that she sorely misses being able to go to lesbian clubs and events but does not feel able to, 'if the event is for lesbians only, I don't go … I worked for many years to create a space for lesbians to feel safe and free to express themselves' (1998a: 4). This woman, like Cook-Daniels herself, strove as an activist to put in place resources to alleviate discrimination and violence against lesbians, only to find herself upstaged in the oppression stakes. The transgender partners now required the limelight, claiming to be a more oppressed group than lesbians, and the lesbian partners were straightened out.

Body image

When a lesbian transgenders, it creates problems both for her own body image and for that of her partner. The female body and biology of the trans partner constitute profound hazards to negotiate if the idea that she has ascended to manhood is to be believed in against all the odds. The trans partners may menstruate, for instance, which is rather the antithesis of manhood as ordinarily understood. One of the lesbians speaking in Cook-Daniels' article on lesbian partners explains that, in her relationship, new language had to be created to explain this anomaly, which was described as, 'Cognitive dissonance week (his term for that time of the month when he has to use "masculine protection")' (1998a: 5). Other partners explain that to avoid any association with their previous lesbianism, the trans partners forbid particular sexual practices, different in each case, that they see as specifically 'lesbian'. One describes this in the following way: 'some FTMs feel using their hands is too lesbian coded, as are certain aspects of oral sex' (1998a: 5).

The severe body image problems of female-bodied transgenders are a common theme in accounts by both trans and non-trans partners and are characterised by a strong loathing of any parts of their bodies that reminded them they were women, such as breasts, hips and body fat (Brown, 2010; Pfeffer, 2008). For example, one transgender referred to her breasts as a deformity, which she struck repeatedly in anger and frustration, and another used words such as torture and plague when referring to breasts. Menstruation was referred to as horrifying and disgusting (Pfeffer, 2008: 329). These problems have a harmful effect on non-trans partners too, and one participant in Pfeffer's study said that she felt less proud of her own feminine curves as a result of her trans partner's denigration of the female body, and she felt that if she gained weight it was not pleasing to her partner (Pfeffer, 2008: 342).

Another problem for non-trans partners was that they might be required to feminise themselves in order to create a contrast to, and therefore bolster, the masculinity of their trans partner. Partners in Pfeffer's (2008) study reported making extra efforts to appear feminine, for example shaving legs and armpits, growing hair longer, dressing in more feminine clothing and in pink, and acting 'girly' (Pfeffer, 2008: 338). One female-bodied transgender, when recognised as a woman in public, turned on her partner and blamed her for not being feminine enough, for looking too much like a lesbian and therefore causing suspicion that the trans partner was not really a man but a lesbian after all (Pfeffer, 2008: 340). In this case the non-trans partner felt resentful: 'I was really upset about it ... like this was *his* transition and why would *I* have to change who *I* am just so he could be happy with who *he* is' (ibid.). However, she said that she came to the realisation that she needed to do this for 'him'.

The transitioning caused problems for the sexual side of relationships. Some partners found that they were affected by the dissatisfaction that their trans partners felt with their own female bodies, and started to question their own attractiveness. One woman said, 'I felt totally undesirable – utterly vacated of any kind of ability to generate any sexual desire in my partner' (Pfeffer, 2008: 336). Her feeling was not helped by her trans partner's accusation that she was not making herself desirable, without being able to tell her what she was supposed to do. Trans partners could go to such lengths to alleviate their own body dysphoria that this had a very negative impact on sexual practice. One female-bodied transgender, for instance, would not fully undress during lovemaking, in particular keeping her breasts covered, and did not allow reciprocal touching, which her partner said was 'crazy-making for me. I still wanted to touch him [*sic*] all the time' (Brown, 2010: 567).

Non-trans partners have to negotiate the problem of decreasing attraction to their partners as their bodies undergo profound changes – often involving the extirpation of characteristics – such as breasts, curves and softness – that had been the very foundation of eroticism and desire. Five of the twelve lesbian-identified partners in Brown's (2010) study were afraid that their FTM partner's physical changes would lessen their sexual desire for their partners after transition. They experienced distress as their partners developed a hatred for parts of their bodies they associated with womanhood. One woman in Brown's study said that she loved her partner's breasts, but 'he' hated them, another was opposed to her lover undergoing phalloplasty and another said she felt it hard to be attracted to 'him' as he began to look more and more like a man (Brown 2010). One respondent found non-monogamy to be a solution as she could continue to have sexual relations with women other than her transitioning partner.

One quite distinct problem for sexual relations was that as the trans partner became more masculine this could trigger memories of sexual abuse in the non-trans partner. Four of the partners in Brown's (2010) study reported histories of sexual abuse by men. Experiencing their partner's masculinisation brought traumatic memories to the fore and they felt increasingly unsafe as their partners gradually took on the appearance of the perpetrators. They found that feeling facial and body hair and the smell of their partner's sweat aroused fear in them, so that they had to create signals that meant slow down or stop sexual activities in order to cope with this.

Conclusion

Although there are some apparent benefits for individual women who transgender, the harms are considerable, in terms of not only their physical long-term health, but also what it does to their partners, to lesbian communities and to feminism. The tolerance and even celebration of the practice within lesbian communities, and even within the feminist academy, is hard to understand. The least well-recognised harm is to feminism itself. Women's status is adversely affected by the existence of transgenderism, because where once feminists were simply accused of wanting to be men if they expressed their outrage at inequality, they may now be adjured to actually become 'men'.

Transgenderism can act as a safety valve for women's indignation. Instead of working collectively to create social change, they can choose to change only themselves, though with considerable consequences for others, and can seek to escape one by one. Meanwhile, the attraction of this form of escape depends upon women's status remaining low, otherwise there would be no incentive for social climbing. It is important that feminists and lesbians oppose the normalisation of the transgendering of women in order to staunch the wounds that the practice is inflicting on the individual bodies of lesbians and on the lesbian body politic.

6

GENDER EUGENICS

The transgendering of children

The transgendering of children is one of the most troubling social harms that has resulted from the malestreaming of transgenderism. Though this practice is increasingly normalised through clinics devoted to transgendering children in major cities such as Melbourne and Toronto, there is an absence of media or academic criticism. I argue that its problematic nature can best be grasped through making links with eugenics practice. Eugenics practice employed sexual surgeries (Largent, 2008) and drug treatments to modify the behaviour of the 'unfit' in the early twentieth century, and family counselling in the mid-century (Stern, 2005), to regulate sex and gender. Presently, children as young as ten years in Australia, with the connivance of the Family Court, are being put on puberty delaying drugs as a result of being diagnosed with 'gender identity disorder', with the expectation that they will be moved onto cross-sex hormones at sixteen and receive surgery to amputate their sexual characteristics at eighteen (Jeffreys, 2006; Owens, 2011). Though Australia is in the forefront of this practice, other countries are catching up. In Germany in 2009, a sixteen-year-old boy had his genitals removed to become a 'girl' (*The Telegraph*, 2009), and in April 2011, the UK government agreed to enable an experiment administering puberty delaying drugs to children from the age of twelve years (Alleyne, 2011). This practice sterilises the children. There has been a surprising absence of critical feminist literature on the transgendering of children, which this chapter seeks to remedy.

The eugenic sexual surgeries and drug treatments of the past and the transgendering of children in the present share a number of similarities, which will be examined here. The most significant similarity lies in the fact that a project of social engineering lies behind both forms of practice. Both practices are based upon the idea that certain problematic behaviours have a biological basis and can be 'cured' by treatments that alter and affect sexual characteristics. In the first half of the last century, a project of social engineering took place in Europe and North America that was directed at the control or elimination of the economic underclass, 'morons' – prostituted women, criminals, those deemed to be 'gypsies', those seen as morally deficient, lesbians and gays, all considered to be the 'unfit' – through sterilisation (Dowbiggin, 1997; Lucassen, 2010). Presently a regime of transgendering children as well as adults has the effect of eliminating gender non-conformity through shoring up a correctly gendered and heterosexual state and citizenry. A similarity between these practices lies in the origin of the ideas for these treatments, which come in both cases from sexologists or scientists of sex, biologists, endocrinologists and psychiatrists. Another similarity lies in the targets of the sexual surgeries, as lesbians and gays were targeted by eugenicists, and those with same sex sexual orientations are, in practice, a principal target of the sexual surgeries of transgenderism today. The practices are connected too in that they were both supported by persons who had an otherwise progressive agenda, such as sexologists who were often socialists, and some feminists. This is certainly true of the practice of transgenderism today, which has been supported by many on the Left and many feminists, though the issue of transgendering children has not been much remarked upon by these constituencies as yet.

In this chapter I will first describe the way in which the practice of transgendering children has developed in the present, giving examples of how this is taking place from Australian Family Court cases. This is followed by a comparison between traditional eugenics and the new variety in evidence in the transgendering of children.

The transgendering of children

The practice of transgendering children is a consequence of the increasing normalisation of the practice of transgendering adults. There has been a campaign to transgender children from two constituencies, adult men who have been transgendered, and some sexual scientists, particularly endocrinologists. The demand for early intervention and treatment of children identified as 'transgender' has been spearheaded by organisations dedicated to the rights of those who have been transgendered, such as the Gender Identity Research and Education Society (GIRES) in the UK, and influential individual transgender blog activists such as Laura from Laura's Playground (Laura, n.d.). These male-bodied transgender activists generally transitioned later in life, from their forties onwards. This meant that passing as women was difficult for them due to their male bone structure and height. They argue that early intervention is vital to prevent what they see as 'transgender' children from experiencing puberty and the entailed physical changes that will make transition harder later on, and require expensive and more complex surgeries to achieve a convincing simulacrum of the desired sex. An example of this campaigning work is the 'international symposium' that GIRES, together with Mermaids, the support group for the transgendered, ran in 2005 to counter the significant resistance from within the medical profession to the idea of treating children. The symposium was for 'doctors … who care for children and young people experiencing gender variance', and GIRES and Mermaids 'remain in close contact with these professionals' (Department of Health, 2008). A precisely similar form of campaigning to enlist the services of the medical profession was employed by the Erikson Foundation on behalf of adult transsexuals 30 years before (Billings and Urban, 1982). The international campaign spearheaded by GIRES achieved a major success with the publication in 2009 of draft guidelines from the Endocrine Society that recommend that children identified as 'transgender' as young as twelve should be given medication to delay puberty (Endocrine Society, 2009). The recommendations are largely based upon the experience of a clinic in the Netherlands that has been prescribing puberty blockers for some time to those under sixteen years. The guidelines recommend that 'adolescents who fulfil eligibility and readiness criteria for gender reassignment initially undergo treatment to suppress pubertal development'. They 'suggest' that 'pubertal development of the desired, opposite sex be initiated at about the age of 16 years, using a gradually increasing dose schedule of cross-sex steroids' (Endocrine Society, 2009: 4). They recommend referring the children for surgery when they have completed a 'real life experience' of living as the desired sex, but 'suggest' that surgery should be deferred until the child is 'at least 18 years old'.

Pressure to treat children with drugs to delay puberty is also coming from some of the professionals at gender identity clinics. Norman Spack, for example, endocrinologist and co-director of the DSD (Disorders of Sexual Differentiation) Clinic at the Boston Children's Hospital, expresses a rather unseemly enthusiasm for being able to perform such treatment:

> Yes, we remain at a crossroads, salivating at the prospect of applying the Dutch protocol for pubertal suppression, yet without permission from health insurers to pay for the expensive drugs or pressure from the medical and mental health communities to demand it. The frustration level of parents is rising, fueled by knowledge of what could be done.
>
> *(Spack, 2008: xi)*

Spack knows what can be done and wants more freedom to treat children in the way he thinks appropriate. He is one of the authors of the 2009 Endocrine Society Guidelines that recommend puberty delaying drug treatment for children. Another specialist at Spack's clinic, a 'pediatric endocrinologist', was charged in September 2012 with receipt of a large amount of child pornography (Herald Staff, 2012). The prosecutor said the government plans to show that this man 'appeared to have a dedicated sexual interest in children, going back several decades. Based on those factors, we do believe the defendant is a danger to the community.' Those who engage in transgendering children may require greater oversight as to their motivations and competence.

As the campaign by lobbyists and sex scientists to transgender children has achieved increasing success, there has been an emergence of online NGOs to support the parents of 'transgender' children, and the publication of advice books. The practice of transgendering children is being normalised by books from psychologists who make a living from identifying and treating children as 'transgender'. One of these from the United States is a 'handbook', *The Transgender Child*, written by Stephanie Brill and Rachel Pepper, which advises parents on how to recognise that a child is 'transgender' so that they can receive professional help (Brill and Pepper, 2008). Stephanie Brill, who describes herself as a member of the 'butch/trans community' (St. John, 2010), is a 'gender educator' and founder of Gender Spectrum Education and Training (Gender Spectrum, n.d.), which offers support to parents of 'gender variant' children and offers gender training programmes for schools. Rachel Pepper is described on the book jacket as a therapist who specialises in 'transgender and gender variant clients'. A number of organisations set up to service the families of 'transgender' children dispense similar advice on their websites, such as TransYouth Family Allies (TYFA, n.d.) in the United States. A board member of TYFA, Andrea James, is the man who posted photos of the children of the sexologist Michael Bailey on the Internet with pornographic captions (Dreger, 2008). There should, perhaps, be a question mark over the suitability of such men to advise on how to treat children over such an important issue as their future health and fertility.

Parents are invited to identify their children as 'transgender', often at very young ages. Brill and Pepper tell parents that their first insight into their child's transgenderism will be at eighteen months:

> When your 18-month-old girl's first words are 'me boy,' or your 2-year-old son insists that he is a girl, and these responses don't waver or change over the next few years, you can be pretty sure that you have a transgender child.
>
> *(Brill and Pepper, 2008: 2)*

Parents are advised to be watchful for such matters as whether their young children select sex-appropriate 'underpants', i.e. the boy should not choose those with flowers on. The tone of these published and online resources is coercive, as parents and professionals are told that the treatment of transgendering children is the only responsible way forward, that it is just, and that it may be the only way to protect the children from self-harm and suicide.

One of the authors of the handbook, Rachel Pepper, subsequently edited a collection of stories from the mothers of transgender children (Pepper (ed.), 2012), which represents the mothers who identify their children as transgender at extremely young ages as brave and progressive. In one case a mother reports that she identified her boy child as a girl because, 'by the time he was two, he refused to play with boys' toys' (Pepper, 2012: 87). She took him to the Tavistock Clinic at six years old in order to be told that he had 'gender identity disorder'. This mother calls the endocrinologist, Norman Spack, her 'saviour'. Another mother noticed something 'different' about Alic 'when he was around age three or four. He saw me sewing and literally cried out, "No more pinafores, Mom, please!"' (Pepper, 2012: 109). Another mother identified her daughter as transgender on her first birthday when she cut up her party dress with a pair of scissors (Pepper, 2012: 61). This represents a remarkably pious, and callous, application of sex role restrictions by mothers, all under the guise of allowing the children to be the 'gender' they really are.

GIRES has been so successful in securing the support of the medical profession for its preferred treatment options that it was able to play a major role in developing the guidelines on medical care for persons seeking to be transgendered, which were published in a series of pamphlets by the UK NHS in 2008. The series includes one on medical care for 'gender variant children and young people' (Department of Health, 2008). This provides a useful insight into the ideas that medical practitioners are now advised to adopt. The NHS pamphlet explains that gender variance in children can be identified by boys saying 'they want to be girls, or that they actually are girls' and girls wishing themselves to be or believing themselves to be boys (Department of Health, 2008: 4). The pamphlet asserts that 'gender variance' in its 'severe' form is 'biologically triggered', 'small parts of the baby's brain progress along a different pathway from the sex of the rest of its body' (Department of Health, 2008: 5). In fact research to suggest that behaviours commonly associated with 'gender' difference are biological is very thin on the ground and likely to be as flawed as all forms of brain research are in proving that gender differences are inscribed in nature and not nurture (Fine, 2010).

Like the handbooks and online resources emerging from the United States on the need to transgender children for their own good, the NHS pamphlet uses strong persuasion to pressure health practitioners to accept the practice, stressing the extreme distress that children they consider to be 'transgender' experience at puberty. Treatment is justified as a way to avoid difficulties with 'passing' in adulthood: 'The irreversible effects cause lifelong disadvantage because they often make it difficult, or even impossible to 'pass', that is, to look and sound completely like a person of the opposite sex' (Department of Health, 2008: 13). The anxieties of adult men who are transgendered are clearly revealed here, as the pamphlet states that those who are not transgendered as children 'may be "read" on the street and consequently may suffer prejudice, harassment, humiliation and even violence' (Department of Health, 2008: 13). The language of being 'read' is common to the argot of men who cross-dress, and its use suggests that the concerns of adult males who may have quite different experiences and interests are being transferred onto children, for whom they may be entirely inappropriate.

Identifying 'transgender' children

Children are diagnosed with 'gender identity' disorder as a result of engaging in socially unacceptable behaviour, specifically behaviour considered unsuited to the child's biological sex. As such, I argue, the transgendering of children should be understood as a project of social engineering that has similarities to the practice of sexual surgeries that were carried out on persons seen as engaging in socially unacceptable behaviour in the previous era of eugenics. In the earlier period the problematic behaviours included chronic poverty, homosexuality and criminality. In this section I will illustrate the socially unacceptable 'gender' practices that lead to the diagnosis of a child as having gender identity disorder. Physicians are faced with the difficulty of distinguishing children whom they consider to be 'genuinely' in need of being transgendered from those many who, as they readily admit, are likely to have worries about gender but do not wish to be transgendered when they are adults (Department of Health, 2008). The NHS pamphlet does not create confidence in the process by which this is accomplished:

> As puberty approaches, the leading clinics will make a careful assessment of which children are almost certain to develop as transsexual adults and which are unlikely to do so. No physical test is available for detecting and measuring gender variance that may develop into adult dysphoria and transsexualism. Hence, clinicians must rely on the young person's own account of his, or her feelings, or information from the parents about the way the child talks and behaves and on psychological tests.
>
> *(Department of Health, 2008: 17)*

The main indicator that they use, though, is likely to be the response of the child to the physical changes of early puberty. Unfortunately, these days, puberty is arriving earlier and earlier for children. Precocious puberty is identified by the Boston Children's Hospital, which treats 'transgender' children, as before age eight for girls and as before age nine for boys (Stafford, 2011). If the logic underlying the transgendering of children is accepted, then children might have to be identified and treated with drugs even before these ages, as the pamphlet advises intervention early enough to suspend physical changes before they begin.

The diagnostic criteria for 'gender dysphoria' in children, previously known as 'gender identity disorder in childhood', appear in the new edition, number 5, of the *US Diagnostic and Statistical Manual* (DSM) in 2013. The criteria are based upon traditional gender stereotypes that have been constructed to confine and limit the behaviour of girls and justify their inferior status in different societies. Boys' behaviour, on the other hand, is constructed to justify their superior status. Children with gender dysphoria must have 'a strong desire to be of the other gender or an insistence that he or she is the other gender'. The indicators that they are of the 'other gender' are:

> in boys, a strong preference for cross-dressing or simulating female attire; in girls, a strong preference for wearing only typical masculine clothing and a strong resistance to the wearing of typical feminine clothing; a strong preference for cross-gender roles in make-believe or fantasy play; a strong preference for the toys, games, or activities typical of the other gender; a strong preference for playmates of the other gender; in boys, a strong rejection of typically masculine toys, games, and activities and a strong avoidance of rough-and-tumble play; in girls, a strong rejection of typically feminine toys, games, and activities.
>
> *(Winters, 2011)*

The children should also have 'clinically significant distress or impairment in social, occupational, or other areas of functioning'. The way in which these diagnostic criteria are applied in practice can be ascertained from the transcripts of the judgements made by the Family Court of Australia in cases where puberty delaying drugs for children were approved.

Examples from Australia

Australia is in the forefront of transgendering children, which is carried out by order of the Family Court and is usually requested by the parents or guardians of the children. When the thirteen-year-old girl called 'Alex' was transgendered through the Family Court in 2004, it was five years before the Endocrine Society issued their guidelines on the practice (Family Court of Australia, 2004; Jeffreys, 2006). The age at which the court was prepared to authorise the practice then started to go down. In 2008 a twelve-year-old girl, 'Brodie', was trangendered (Family Court, 2008). The youngest child in relation to whom such an order was made, in April 2011, was 'Jamie', who was a ten-year-old boy, and was said to have been living as a girl for three years (Family Court of Australia, 2011). In the court cases the evidence of psychiatrists, endocrinologists, social workers and parents is used to diagnose the child as having the disorder in order to begin treatment. The case of 'Jamie' provides a useful example of how this works. Jamie was one of twin boys of ten years and ten months of age. Agreement in the court to the transgendering of Jamie was straightforward because he was identified as 'a very attractive young girl with long blonde hair', that is he conformed really well with cultural stereotypes of what a girl should look like (Family Court of Australia, 2011, Reasons for Judgement, 2). Jamie's parents gave the necessary evidence to prove that Jamie had the disorder, saying that he

> first began identifying with the female gender when she (the transcript uses female pronouns) was about 2 ½ to 3 ½ years old. She chose female orientated toys, began to identity with female characters on television or in movies, and told her mother: 'Mummy, I don't want a willy, I want a vagina.'
>
> *(Family Court of Australia, 2011, Reasons for Judgement, 12)*

He also 'sought the friendship of girls' (Family Court of Australia, 2011, Reasons for Judgement, 14). According to his mother the 'turning point' was when Jamie wanted to wear a 'ball gown' on an outing to see *Phantom of the Opera* (Family Court of Australia, 2011, Reasons for Judgement, 17). Jamie was taken to see a psychiatrist in October, 2007 when he was seven years old, and was diagnosed as having gender identity disorder in December of that year.

The court experts adjudicate as to whether the child in the case before them is performing gender in an appropriate way. Thus evidence for Jamie's feminine gender was gleaned from the fact that he 'had the ambition to be a "female pop singing star" and performed for her male psychiatrist in a "very feminine and creative way"' (Family Court of Australia, 2011: 42). One expert explained that Jamie looked 'convincingly female in every way', despite the fact that he 'had typical male genitalia with a normal penis and testes. Her chromosomes were those of a typical male' (Family Court of Australia, 2011: 50). The arguments used as moral pressure to promote the transgendering of children that we have seen from GIRES are produced in the court. Dr C says that there was no time to lose in delaying Jamie's puberty in order to 'prevent the psychological distress that Jamie would experience if male puberty were to progress' (Family Court of Australia, 2011: 54). Jamie was in danger, Dr C said, of 'an increased likelihood of major mental disorder and behavioural difficulties, including severe depression and anxiety disorders and risk of self-harm' (Family Court of Australia, 2011: 63).

When cases involving the transgendering of girls are heard at the Family Court the diagnostic criteria change to reflect stereotypes of how boys should behave. In the case of twelve-year-old 'Brodie', she is described by her mother as always behaving in

> a way that I would describe as like a boy and she likes to dress like a boy and when we go shopping for clothes, (Brodie) will always look to purchase clothes from the body [*sic*] section of the particular store ... She has worn boy's underwear since she was about six years' old.
>
> *(Family Court of Australia, 2008: 55)*

Choice of underwear seems to be important as it is mentioned in a number of sources that provide advice on identifying children who should be transgendered. In the case of Brodie, as in that of 'Alex' who was transgendered in 2004, a main reason given for hastening treatment was the fact that these girls were very angry (Jeffreys, 2006). In Brodie's case she was very aggressive and bullied her younger sister. The reason for the anger of the children in the Family Court cases was not pursued, though it was commonly suggested that treatment for transgenderism would alleviate its worst excesses. Transgendering children, then, can function as a form of behaviour management.

The only clinic that treats 'transgender' children in Australia is at the Royal Children's Hospital in Melbourne, so it does seem likely that the children in the above cases were processed there. In a study of the effectiveness of its treatment, the clinic has announced that the numbers approaching it have increased 'eightfold' between 2003 when it was set up and 2011, meaning from one child per year to eight children per year (Hewitt *et al.*, 2012). The increase is explained as arising from a greater awareness of the treatment possibilities – 'improved awareness of a medical service for children with GID' – rather than to a real increase in the incidence of the problem. The increase is indeed likely to be a result of greater publicity about the phenomenon and its treatment. But rather than this enabling more children possessed of some essential and always existing problem to come forward, the publicity could create 'transgender' children by enabling parents to identify quite ordinary behaviour in young children as disordered, and create this understanding in their offspring. The clinic noted that in all its patients gender dysphoria was seen at about three years of age, though the children did not present for treatment until a 'mean age' of ten years old.

Perhaps surprisingly, considering the quite extreme forms of hormonal and surgical treatment of children and teenagers taking place in the present, there is an absence of criticism of the transgendering of children in social science literature and from feminist scholars. This is likely to be the result of the fact that critical analysis of the practice of transgenderism in general has declined to the point of invisibility in the last two decades.

Absence of critical literature on transgenderism

Though there are important connections between the early twentieth-century eugenics practice of carrying out sexual surgeries and sterilisation of the unfit for purposes of social control and social engineering, and the transgendering of adults and children in the late twentieth and early twenty-first centuries, these practices have not been linked together in scholarly literature. Indeed there is an absence of critical literature in politics and the social sciences today on transgenderism. In relation to the transgendering of children, critical work in the social sciences, with a few exceptions (Gottschalk, 2003; Jeffreys, 2006), is remarkably absent. The increasing quantity of social science literature on the 'transgender' child is not critical, or analytical. It consists of handbooks for social workers, for parents (Brill and Pepper, 2008; Mallon, 2009) and for teachers. All of this literature speaks of 'affirming' the 'transgender' child and the positive tone of the materials can be adduced from the titles of two examples, 'Working with Transgender Children and Their Classmates in Pre-Adolescence: Just Be Supportive' (Luecke, 2011), and 'Trans-Friendly Pre-School' (Dykstra, 2005). Unfortunately, parents and professionals working with children these days are likely to believe that gender difference is biological rather than socially constructed.

Despite the absence of critical work in relation to the practice of transgenderism in the social sciences literature, there is an emerging critique in the clinical literature. The psychologists Susan Langer and James Martin, for instance, argue that the diagnosis of gender identity disorder in childhood 'serves primarily to advance a political or social agenda' (Langer and Martin, 2004: 15), and the 'mental health community' should take a 'strong stand against the continuation of GIDC as a sanctioned diagnostic category' (Langer and Martin, 2004: 19). There are other mental health professionals criticising the diagnosis of gender identity disorder in childhood and adulthood, particularly for the way that it facilitates the social control of homosexuality (Bower, 2001; Wilson et al., 2002). However, neither the earlier critical literature, nor that which is beginning to emerge from mental health professionals in the present, connects transgenderism in any form to the history of eugenics. In the next section I will identify some connections between the transgendering of children and eugenics practice that may help inform the development of a more critical social science literature.

Connections between transgenderism and eugenics practice

There is a burgeoning literature on eugenics campaigns and practices from social historians and historians of science, which provides evidence of ideas and practices that are echoed in the contemporary practice of transgenderism. This literature describes how the eugenics movement developed in the United States (Largent, 2008; Reilly, 1991) and in Europe (Lucassen, 2010) and became centred on the practice of sterilisation. Some point out that this practice, though it was mostly brought to an end in the 1970s, lingers on, particularly in relation to teenage girls who are considered at risk of pregnancy because they are vulnerable to sexual predation (Largent, 2008). This literature makes few connections with the contemporary practice of transgendering children despite the fact that this, like the sterilisation of the unfit, is carried out by sexual scientists for the purpose of social engineering.

The ideological foundations of eugenics emerged from the work of Francis Galton, cousin of Charles Darwin (Largent, 2008). They were adopted and promoted by biologists, sexologists and psychiatrists who were politically leftwing such as J.B.S. Haldane and Henry Havelock Ellis in the UK, and Auguste Forel in Switzerland (Lucassen, 2010). It is relevant that all of these men saw themselves as socialists because, in the twenty-first century, the practice of transgendering men, women and children has been adopted as an issue of positive human rights by progressive people such as the Left theorist Judith Butler, rather than as a practice that violates rights (Butler, 2004). The Left of the late nineteenth and early twentieth century was generally supportive of eugenic ideas, as exemplified by Sydney and Beatrice Webb of the Fabian Society in the UK (Lucassen, 2010). In Sweden social engineering through the sterilisation of the unfit was adopted enthusiastically by the Myrdals, sociologists associated with the founding of the Swedish welfare state. Legislation to enable the sterilisation of the unfit was adopted in Sweden in the 1920s and from then until the 1970s, 63,000 persons were sterilised, 90 per cent of them women. Eugenics was adopted on the Left as a way to create a better 'race', meaning, at that time, 'nation'.

Importantly, eugenicist ideas, including sterilisation of the unfit, were adopted by many feminists before the Second World War. The US birth control campaigner Margaret Sanger was one of them. In 1932 she sought to explain how eugenics could lead to an end to war through preventing overpopulation, particularly of the unfit, which she considered an important cause (Sanger, 1932). These measures included immigration policies to prevent entry of the unfit, segregation of the unfit so that they could not reproduce, and sterilisation. Immigration controls, she said, should keep out 'feebleminded, idiots, morons, insane, syphilitic, epileptic, criminal, professional prostitutes, and others' and a 'stern and rigid policy of sterilization and segregation' should be applied to those who might have 'tainted progeny'. People should, she considered, be given the choice of segregation or sterilisation. The British birth control campaigner, Marie Stopes, too was inspired by eugenicist ideas and concerned to limit the breeding of persons who were not of sufficient 'quality'. She opined in a BBC interview as late as 1957, 'We are breeding rubbish' (quoted in Garrett, 2007: xlii). The extent to which feminists embraced eugenics before the Second World War in the UK is a topic of controversy among historians. There is general agreement that feminists tended to include eugenic language in their theory and practice in order to make themselves more persuasive and easily understood, but their degree of commitment is another matter (Bland, 1995; Makepeace, 2009). However, the absence of criticism, or active support, of the practice of transgendering adults and children, by those who see themselves as progressive or even feminist in the present, should not surprise, as there is a history of such support for similar projects in the earlier period.

Sexual surgeries

Eugenics practice was centred on the performance of sexual surgeries on those considered unfit, and the practice of sterilisation of the unfit in the USA illustrates its scope and acceptability. Two-thirds of the states in the United States passed compulsory sterilisation laws between 1907 and 1937 (Largent, 2008: 65). Sterilisation was not just carried out for eugenic purposes, i.e. to prevent reproduction of defective children, but to punish, and for therapeutic purposes such as changing unacceptable behaviour. The sexual surgeries carried out on those considered unfit included complete castration with removal of the testes, as well as the less invasive practice of sterilisation through vasectomy. Largent explains that, in the United States, amputation of the testes and scrotum was used from the late nineteenth century up to the 1930s to 'treat, punish or control hundreds of rapists, child molesters, and men who engaged in activities associated with homosexuality' (Largent, 2008: 5). He calls this practice 'mutilation', and it was mostly practised on men who were in mental hospitals and prisons. He explains that the reasons given changed over time, going from 'punitive and eugenic' to 'therapeutic and prophylactic' over four decades. The psychiatrists involved in sexual surgeries regularly used them as a 'cure' for women's unacceptable behaviour. At the end of the nineteenth century in the United States, G. Alder Blumer recommended 'gynaecologic surgery' for women patients (Dowbiggin, 1997: 89). He considered that 'insanity was a genital reflex', an idea that was widespread from 1850–1900 and led to the removal of women's wombs and ovaries. In particular he recommended such surgery for women who were loud and vulgar in their language.

One significant connection between the heyday of eugenics and the transgendering of children today is that lesbians and gay men form a constituency that is targeted by both practices. The grim details of the control and punishment of lesbians and gay men by the scientists of sex throughout most of the twentieth century was laid out in the earliest, gay liberation-inspired, history of lesbians and gay men in the United States, Jonathan Katz's *Gay American History* (1976). Katz writes that, 'Lesbians and Gay men have long been subjected to a varied, often horrifying list of "cures" at the hands of psychiatric-psychological professionals, treatments usually aimed at asexualization or heterosexual reorientation' (Katz, 1976: 197). These treatments, which went on well into the second half of the twentieth century, included surgeries such as castration, hysterectomy and vasectomy. Women were subjected in the nineteenth century to surgical removal of the ovaries and of the clitoris, a treatment designed as a 'cure' for various forms of what was called female 'erotomania' and included lesbianism. Lobotomy was performed as late as the 1950s. A range of drug therapies were also used such as the administration of hormones, LSD, sexual stimulants and sexual depressants, alongside other treatments such as hypnosis and electric and chemical shock treatment, and aversion therapy (ibid.). Katz comments that the homosexual victims of sexual surgeries were sometimes 'acquiescent', and sought out treatment, as those requesting to be transgendered do today. Indeed involuntariness is by no means a necessary element in eugenics practices generally. Katz explains that the case histories he examined in his research showed:

> Numbers of these histories concern guilt-ridden, self-hating homosexuals, who have so internalized society's condemnation that they seek out cruel forms of treatment as punishment; they play what can only be termed a masochistic game, in which the doctor is assigned, and accepts, a truly sadistic (as well as remunerative) role.
>
> *(Katz, 1976: 200)*

Katz does not include the transgendering of homosexual men and lesbians within these abusive medical treatments, but Bernice Hausman, in her feminist critique of transgenderism, does (Hausman, 1995). Hausman argues that the treatment of intersexuality and transsexuality in the mid-twentieth century was motivated to a large extent by the desire to reduce the possibility of homosexuality and to create heterosexual citizens.

Despite the similarity between the control of homosexuality in eugenics practice and in transgenderism, this is seldom discussed in the social science literature today. The fact that many of the men and most of the women who seek to transition are homosexual before treatment is, nonetheless, an open secret. Though males seeking to be transgendered may be attracted to women or other men, it is recognised that the women are generally lesbians before they are diagnosed as 'transgender': 'Virtually all females with gender identity disorder will receive the same specifier – Sexually Attracted to Female – although there are exceptional cases involving females who are sexually Attracted to Males' (Mental Health Today, n.d.). Professionals involved in treating gender identity disorder in childhood are aware that three-quarters of the boys referred for diagnosis by their parents will be homosexual or bisexual when they reach adulthood (ibid.). The lawyer and transgender rights activist, Shannon Minter, has provided a compilation of quotations from sexologists and those involved in the creation and implementation of the diagnosis of gender identity that is designed to make evident their desire to prevent the development of homosexuality (Minter, 1999). Minter argues 'If GID in children was not strongly associated with homosexuality in adulthood', it is unlikely that cross-gender behaviours in children 'would have been designated psychiatric disorders or become the focus of an entire clinical field devoted to … "correcting" cross-gender behaviors' (Minter, 1999: 27).

The interest of eugenicists in the control and punishment of homosexuality was a part of their interest in the creation of properly gendered and sexed families and children, an aspect of the movement that relates clearly to the transgendering of children that takes place today. The historian of the US eugenics movement, Alexandra Stern, explains how the eugenics movement shifted focus after the Second World War to concentrate on making families conform to its idea of appropriate gender roles (Stern, 2005). Stern explains that in the 1950s there was less enthusiasm for the more familiar practices of eugenics that were stigmatised by association with Nazism, such as sterilisation, though, as she says, these by no means came to an end, and the laws stayed on the books. Instead eugenicists gravitated towards what was called 'positive' eugenics, concentrating on population control and 'often began to locate the marrow of human differentiation not in racial distinctions … but in sex and gender', such that 'the racism of the 1920s was rearticulated into the sexism of the 1950s' (Stern, 2005: 154). The American Institute of Family Relations (AIFR), which was a main motor of eugenic population policy in the 1950s, and its director, Paul Popenoe, promoted a 'family-centric eugenics that demanded sex and gender uniformity' and promoted the idea that the male/female distinction was the greatest that could exist between two human beings. It was based on evolution, nature and genetics (Stern, 2005: 155). When clients were assessed for counselling by the AIFR, the first step was 'gauging the degree to which their gender identity and comportment corresponded to their anatomical sex' (Stern, 2005: 167). They were then treated on the basis of ideas emanating at that time from 'psychiatry, psychometrics, endocrinology and sex research' (Stern, 2005: 180). This form of eugenics practice is exemplified in the way in which sexologists in this period developed ideas of 'gender' and 'gender identity' and used them in their approach to children they identified as intersex, and in their treatment of transgenderism, a practice that continues today (Hausman, 1995; Meyerowitz, 2002). The avoidance of homosexuality and the construction of robustly heterosexual, and gendered, families, children and adults motivated the sexologists of the period. The continuation of this branch of eugenics throws into question the extent to which the eugenics movement has gone into retreat. Though the acceptability of sterilising some constituencies of the 'unfit' has lessened, sterilisation and sexual surgeries on children identified as transgender is an increasing trend, as this chapter seeks to show. Largent (2008) identifies what he sees as the final death of the American eugenics movement as taking place in the 1980s. It took decades from the 1930s onwards, he explains, to bring it to an end. Opposition to sterilisation of the unfit came from civil rights organisations, and movements 'focusing on race, gender, sexual orientation, class, and physical and mental disabilities' as well as those advocating for the rights of prisoners and mental health patients (Largent, 2008: 140). However, the practice of sterilising children with intellectual disabilities continues in many countries, including the United States. Researchers in Australia found that between 1992 and 1997 there were around 200 sterilisations of young girls performed in Australian hospitals every year (Brady and Grover, 1997). The practice is strongly opposed by disability rights' groups such as Women With Disabilities Australia (WWDA, 2007).

A groundswell of human rights activism against coerced sterilisation of women as a violation of women's reproductive rights is now developing, which uses concepts that could also be applied to the sterilisation of children identified as transgender. The Centre for Reproductive Rights in New York, for instance, considers that coerced sterilisation, that is without full and unpressured consent, should be considered 'cruel, inhumane or degrading treatment or punishment' (Center for Reproductive Rights, 2010). They argue that 'Experts recognize that the permanent deprivation of one's reproductive capacity without informed consent generally results in psychological trauma, including depression and grief' (Center for Reproductive Rights, 2010: 20). The Center points out that the Human Rights Council has stated that coercive sterilisation violates the right to be free from 'torture and CIDT (cruel, inhuman and degrading treatment), as provided for under the ICCPR (International Convention on Cultural and Political Rights)' (Center for Reproductive Rights, 2010: 20). Coercive sterilisation is recognised by the committee that oversees the Convention on the Elimination of All Forms of Discrimination Against Women (CEDAW), the Centre states, as infringing the 'rights to human dignity and physical and mental integrity' (Center for Reproductive Rights, 2010: 20). In relation to children who are transgendered, the question arises of the extent to which they can be seen as uncoerced, considering that their parents, the medical profession, and the courts are advocating this treatment for them, and they are told that it will alleviate their mental distress.

Sterilisation of transgendered children and other long-term adverse health effects

The effects of the drug treatment and sexual surgeries that constitute the transgendering of children are such as to harm their reproductive rights, as well as their bodily integrity and future health, and can therefore be seen as a particularly harmful form of the abuse of children. There are some differences between the sterilisation that forms part of the practice of transgendering children today and the sexual surgeries of the earlier eugenic period. Eugenic sexual surgeries were regularly aimed at sterilisation, rather than having sterilisation as a side effect. But they had other aims too, such as preventing masturbation or criminal behaviour, which resemble the aims of transgenderism today of eliminating unacceptable behaviour, in this case gender non-conformity. Also, in the earlier period, sterilisation was usually non-consensual, whereas the sterilisation carried out as part of treatment for gender identity disorder today is usually seen as an unfortunate side effect of a wanted process. But it should be remembered that homosexual males, in particular, did seek out the sexual surgeries that formed a part of eugenic practice.

Treatment with puberty delaying drugs leads to sterilisation if it is followed with the administration of cross-sex hormones at sixteen years, as the Brill and Pepper handbook on 'transgender' children (2008) explains: 'the choice to progress from GnRH inhibitors to estrogen without fully experiencing male puberty should be viewed as giving up one's fertility, and the family and child should be counseled accordingly' (Brill and Pepper, 2008: 216). For girls, sterilisation is the outcome too because 'eggs do not mature until the body goes through puberty' (ibid.). The issue of fertility, the handbook asserts, may bother parents more than the 'teens', because the latter may think short term and not be able to contemplate much more than getting transgendered in the present (Brill and Pepper, 2008: 220). The handbook speaks of other serious effects of the transgender treatment, such as that birth defects may occur in children born to 'transmen (female-bodied transgenders) taking testosterone prior to pregnancy' (Brill and Pepper, 2008: 219). It also warns that genital surgery can lead to the absence of sexual feeling, and comments that young people may not understand the importance of this (Brill and Pepper, 2008: 220). But, the handbook advises, 'teens' can have sexual surgeries such as the removal of testes or breast removal at any age, not necessarily eighteen, so long as their parents and a surgeon are willing (ibid.). This does seem to contradict the warnings that accompany this advice, about the difficulty 'teens' may have in understanding the implications of such surgeries for fertility and sexual pleasure.

The issue of sterilisation was addressed by the Australian Family Court in the cases involving the treatment of 'Alex', 'Brodie' and 'Jamie'. In each case it was suggested that the child had sufficient understanding to make a decision that could lead to sterilisation, and where they may not fully understand, their parents could make such a decision for them. The judgement in the case involving ten-year-old 'Jamie' explains that he understands he will become sterile, and does this with an interesting contradiction of pronouns and biological sex: 'Jamie is aware that subsequent treatment with female hormones, when she is older, may then affect her capacity for sperm generation' (Family Court of Australia, 2011: 92). But because Jamie 'does not have the level of maturity to be responsible for decisions of such gravity' the parents are given the 'responsibility to make such decisions in consultation with Jamie'.

Children are also quite unlikely to be able to give informed consent to use of the harmful drugs involved in transgender 'treatment'. The drug most commonly used to delay puberty in children is Lupron, a drug approved for the treatment of prostate cancer but commonly used in IVF treatment and to treat endometriosis in women. There is increasing concern among women's health activists about the serious side effects of this drug, with perhaps the most serious in relation to children being loss of bone density. In one study researchers found that women lost as much as 7.3 per cent of their bone density during treatment (Flin, 2008). The drug also causes birth defects and is contraindicated when there is a possibility of pregnancy. Side effects reported to the US Food and Drug Administration by thousands of patients include: tingling, itching, headache and migraine, dizziness, severe joint pain, difficulty breathing, chest pain, nausea, depression, emotional instability, dimness of vision, fainting, weakness, amnesia, hypertension, muscular pain, bone pain, nausea/vomiting, asthma, abdominal pain, insomnia, chronic enlargement of the thyroid, liver function abnormality, vision abnormality, anxiety and others (Flin, 2008). Usage of this drug for delaying puberty in children is 'off label', meaning that it has not been approved for this purpose and is a hazardous and experimental practice. It is particularly problematic to use such a potentially harmful drug to treat the bodies of children who are entirely healthy, and whose only perceived flaw is that they are deemed to have socially unacceptable behaviour.

A particularly serious effect of transgendering children is the distress they are likely to suffer when they change their minds. A British case of a boy who was a poster child for the practice demonstrates the harms. Bradley Cooper came out as a gay man in 2012, two months before the amputation of his penis. He was celebrated as the youngest British 'sex change patient' when he was put on hormones at sixteen, and the National Health Service agreed to pay for the £10,000 amputation surgery that he would have once he reached eighteen (Schlesinger, 2010). Bradley appeared as 'Ria' on chat shows and had gained a certain renown, before, at 18 years old, he changed his mind.

The young hairdresser said that he started to wear women's clothes at twelve when he 'would borrow his mother's lipstick and wear clothes belonging to his three sisters'. After less than a year of living full-time as a woman Bradley decided to de-transition as a result of severe mental distress. He cancelled SRS and stopped taking hormones, saying that 'she has found the changes overwhelming and that they have made her deeply unhappy' (ibid.). Bradley had received a thorough psychological assessment before starting his transition, but nonetheless tried to commit suicide twice during the preceding year, attributing this to the mood swings associated with hormone treatment and distress 'about how alone I am, and how my decision has alienated my family' (Winter, 2012). Bradley became so lonely, he said, that he even entered prostitution for the company. At the time of his decision to de-transition, he was jobless and homeless, sleeping on friends' floors. Bradley hopes to find it easier to have relationships as a gay man: 'She believes she will have better luck in love as a 'trendy' gay man' (ibid.). Cooper's case makes it clear that the psychiatrists cannot know if they are dealing with a genuinely 'transgender' child, and the very serious harms that he suffered should serve to throw doubt on the edifice of 'gender dysphoria'.

Conclusion

In the twenty-first century, decades after sexual surgeries on the 'unfit' for eugenic, punishment and therapeutic reasons were mostly abandoned, a similar practice is increasingly being carried out on children who are considered to be innately 'transgender' because they are disobeying culturally acceptable gender roles. A form of social engineering to force children to conform to rigid gender categories is taking place. The history of sexual surgeries needs to be connected with this contemporary practice in order to cast a more critical light on what is happening today. Ian Dowbiggin, historian of North American eugenics, writes about the way the medical profession adopted the practice of sterilising the unfit in a fashion that could equally be applied to the adoption of the transgendering of children:

> It is a story of human fallibility, of human beings who, when faced with the daunting challenge of caring for emotionally and mentally disabled people, resorted to extreme theories and practices. Most of these men and women were convinced they were absolutely right, even when they might have known better.
>
> *(Dowbiggin, 1997: x)*

Today's transgendering of children is similar to the earlier history of sexual surgeries in that progressive people, including many feminists, feel that this is a reasonable practice, and have not yet begun to criticise it. Feminist research and theory needs to recover the ability to criticise medicine and psychiatry and the way that the scientists of sex treat those who fail to conform to society's norms, if the transgendering of children is to be effectively challenged.

7

A CLASH OF RIGHTS

When gender is inscribed in the law

Transgender activists have been remarkably successful in a short time in their campaign to achieve gender 'rights', an aim that enshrines the protection of 'gender' in the law. As the male-bodied transgender activist Mara Keisling puts it, 'there's never been a social justice movement that has moved this fast … Things are zooming' (Keisling, 2008: 4). This chapter will examine the origins of the campaign for gender rights, and the implications of its success. There is no scope here for a detailed examination of how the law has changed in different countries; rather, the chapter effects a critical examination of what legal recognition of rights to 'gender' means for women in general. The ambitions of transgender activists were set out in 1995 in the United States in the International Bill of Transgender Rights (Frye, 2001). This was not a document that originated in any legislature or had any legal weight, but rather a wish list created by a group of transgender activists at a meeting, and at the time might well have seemed too outlandish to be taken seriously by lawmakers. But its precepts do now form the way in which gender rights have been incorporated into domestic law in many states, and this makes it worthy of careful consideration. It demanded the right to express the 'gender identity' of choice in whatever way the exponent desired, particularly in any spaces previously reserved for women. Since then, equality and human rights legislation has been updated and created in states across the Western world that incorporates the 'right' to express 'gender identity'. As a result, gender, which consists of traditional stereotypes of appropriate behaviour for men and women that regulate male domination and women's subordination, has become a matter of state.

Women's and feminist groups are not invited to consult on such legal changes, as if they would have nothing relevant to say despite the fact that men may, under such legislation, gain the right to be recognised in law as 'women'. Women are the 'absent referent' (Adams, 1990), not officially referred to, even though it is 'women' that the men who wish to express their 'gender rights' seek to personate. There is no suggestion in legislation on the right to gender identity that women will be included in, or advantaged by, the developments. Rather, in an increasingly vigorous feminist challenge, critics argue that such legislation creates two singular difficulties for women's interests (Brennan and Hungerford, 2011). It removes the possibility of women-only spaces, and it promotes gender stereotypes that have long been recognised by feminist theorists as the basic organising mechanism of male domination (MacKinnon, 1989; Jeffreys, 2005).

The creation of the right to 'gender identity' creates a 'clash of rights' in which the rights demanded by one group of people can substantially endanger the rights of another group (Sniderman *et al.*, 1997). In a clash of rights, some adjudication has to be made as to whether the group involved in the rights demand that compromises the rights of another group can be accommodated in human rights norms. An example of the clash of rights is that of campaigners for gay marriage against promoters of the right to religion (Masci, 2009). This kind of clash is about ideologies, wherein the success of the rights demand of one group would restrict the rights sought by another, in this case to marriage and 'family life'. However, in the case of the campaign for the right to gender identity, the challenge is even more problematic and remarkable. The main demanders are from the sex caste of men, the dominant caste whose members are responsible for the violation of women's rights to live, for example, free from violence and the threat of death, to freedom of movement and expression, to freedom from discrimination (Romito, 2008). Moreover, the demanders in this instance do not just claim that they are disadvantaged in their own right, but that they actually are physically members of the female sex caste, women, as in the demand by male-bodied transgenders that they should be able to enter spaces, such as toilets, set aside for women.

The wish list that constitutes the International Bill of Gender Rights (1995) was created by male-bodied persons in the United States who had no experience of being reared in, or treated as, members of the female sex caste, and their biographies reveal them to be unremarkably masculine men. They are men who chose to personate women with various degrees of seriousness as adults. The man who, according to his website, 'authored' the original Bill of Gender Rights in 1990, which became the International Bill of Gender Rights, is JoAnn Roberts, a man whose personation of women is only occasional. Roberts does not claim to be a woman, but a cross-dresser: 'I'm a crossdresser, divorced and remarried with two adult children' (Roberts, 2012), who organises an event for cross-dressers called Beauty and the Beach, 'Crossdresser's Getaway Weekend' (ibid.).

Another significant figure in creating the final document was Phyllis Frye, who is very proud of having been a robust and red-blooded, masculine man.

In a journal article about the Bill, Frye seeks to establish his credentials of having been a most successful and truly manly man before he decided to personate a woman. While, as he puts it 'trying to be a man' he was

> an Eagle Scout, holder of the God & Country Award, Senior Patrol Leader, Brotherhood member of the Order of the Arrow, and a Junior Assistant Scoutmaster. At Thomas Jefferson High School in San Antonio, I was in *A Capella* Choir, Yearbook Staff, Senior Play, lettered twice on the Rifle Team, was ROTC Commander, and was an 'A' student. At Texas A&M University, I was in the Corps of Cadets, Singing Cadets, and completed a B.S. in Civil Engineering and an M.S. in Mechanical Engineering while on four scholarships and one grant. I am a veteran and was honorably discharged as a 1st Lieutenant, U.S. Army in 1972. I obtained, and still retain, a Texas Professional Engineering License in 1975.
>
> *(Frye, 2000: 133)*

Women are quite unlikely to have such a pedigree, but Frye says that he is a woman. He explains,

> As evident from the above accomplishments, I did not become a woman because I could not cut it as a man. I was very successful as a man, but it did not fit my unshakable in-the-gut self-image of who I really was.
>
> *(ibid.)*

He is a lawyer who has 'been legally married to the same woman for twenty-eight years' and has 'a grown child by a previous marriage' (ibid.). In 1992, he founded the International Conference on Transgender Law and Employment Policy (ICTLEP), which drew up the Bill of Gender Rights. He was awarded the 'Creator of Change' Award from the National Gay and Lesbian Task Force (1995) and the Virginia Prince Lifetime Contribution Award, named after the famous cross-dresser, from the International Foundation for Gender Education (1999). Men who promote their rights to 'gender identity' frequently imagine womanhood from an unimpeachably masculine position, such as careers of military heroism (Tur, 2013). The desire of men to trans-gender, such accounts suggest, can be understood as an aspect of deeply conservative and hypermasculine behaviour, rather than demonstrating any commonality with women. It is from such roots, rather than any progressive foundation, that the 'right' to gender emerged.

Without seeking the advice of women, whose stereotypical form these men seek to imitate, Roberts and Frye produced the grandly titled 1995 International Bill of Gender Rights. An examination of these 'rights' shows that they conflict with women's experience. The first right that the Bill proclaims is that 'all human beings have the right to define their own gender identity regardless of chromosomal sex, genitalia, assigned birth sex, or initial gender role' (Frye, 2000: 212). In fact, women do not 'define' their 'gender identity' and 'gender identity' has very little to do with being a woman. Women do not suffer discrimination on the grounds of their 'identity', an 'unshakable in-the-gut-self-image' as Frye describes this, but on the grounds of being of the female sex.

The second right in the Bill is 'The Right to Free Expression of Gender Identity' (ibid.). This seems to mean the right of the male progenitors of the document to wear clothing more usually assigned to women. For women, stereotypical women's clothing is not a right of expression, but enforced, through cultural expectations, legal systems, street harassment, the influence of the sex industry, and workplace and school requirements (Jeffreys, 2005). Another right that these men demand is that of entering spaces set aside by or for women, 'The Right of Access to Gendered Space and Participation in Gendered Activity' (Frye, 2000: 213). Women-only spaces are either set aside on the grounds that women need the safety and security of places where men are not present, or on the grounds that women as a subordinate group need to be able to meet and organise without members of the ruling group present. Until recently, equal opportunity laws have sought to accommodate this understanding by saying that, in some situations, women may indeed exclude men from services and events. In charters of rights and legislation on equality, women are regularly afforded exemptions from the need to not discriminate on the grounds that as a vulnerable group, albeit a majority one, they may need to meet in women-only groups and require spaces such as women-only toilets (Victorian Equal Opportunity and Human Rights Commission, n.d.). This shows recognition of women as a group that needs special treatment. Unfortunately, the demands initiated by male-bodied transgenders and men who cross-dress, because they claim to be 'women' and not men, aim to overturn this recognised exemption for the protection of women's spaces. The other 'rights' in the Bill include 'The Right to Control and Change One's Own Body', 'cosmetically, chemically, or surgically', and the right to access medical treatment to achieve this. Cosmetic surgery has not been understood by feminists to be an issue of women's rights, but as problematic, and based in women's subordinate position (Haiken, 1997; Sullivan, Deborah A, 2001).

Gender rights in international law

The International Bill of Gender Rights did not immediately lead to any gains by transgender lobbyists in relation to international law, but the language and concepts it expresses were increasingly taken up in campaigns to change domestic law in Western countries in the succeeding decades. Before the move to 'gender', domestic laws on what were understood as the rights of 'transsexuals' used the language of sex, not gender, and required persons who wished to change their sex to undertake surgery to become infertile before they could change their status on documents such as their birth certificate. This changed in the 2000s as the notion of 'transsexualism' came to be seen as restrictive, and the move to gender resulted in 'gender rights' covering a broad and vague spectrum of persons was incorporated into legislation on change of status and in anti-discrimination statutes.

The next significant document relating to the right to gender identity that purports to be international came much later, in the Yogyakarta Principles, which arose from a meeting of a 'distinguished group of 29 experts in international law' in Indonesia in 2006, and were formalised in 2007 (Ettelbrick and Zeran, 2010: 30). Though not incorporated into any UN conventions or declarations, the Principles, their promoters argue, have had great effect within the UN, being regularly cited and used as a reference point (ibid.). The Principles cover sexual orientation and gender identity. In terms of sexual orientation, the Principles do seem to constitute an important development for those seeking to challenge laws that still impose harsh punishments on homosexuals in many countries. They form a basis for arguing for the prohibition of the considerable discrimination and violence that lesbians and gay men face, even where homosexuality is not illegal. The problem with the Principles is that they append 'gender identity' rights to rights based on sexual orientation. This is a puzzling conjunction, considering that homophobia has been such an important cause of the construction of the idea of transsexualism and disorders of gender identity in the sexology of the late twentieth century.

Despite this contradiction, the main organisations campaigning for the incorporation of 'gender rights' into law are lesbian and gay ones, including the International Lesbian and Gay Association, the US National Center for Lesbian Rights (NCLR), and the US National Gay and Lesbian Taskforce. The National Center for Lesbian Rights states, 'NCLR is proud to have been the first LGBT legal organization to launch a Transgender Law Project', and this later became the Transgender Law Center (NCLR, n.d.). This development from a supposedly lesbian organisation is surprising, considering that the transgendering of lesbians extinguishes their lesbianism and few other organisations are dedicated to the abolition of the community they represent (Jeffreys, 2003). The main US lesbian and gay organisation, the National Gay and Lesbian Taskforce (NGLTF), also stresses the importance of transgender rights to its core business: 'Transgender people and issues are core to our work at the Task Force. We are proud of our history as one of the first national LGBT organisations to include transgender people in our mission, starting in 1997' (NGLTF, n.d.).

Transgender activists have worked hard to ensure the support of lesbian and gay groups, even going so far as to claim that homosexuality itself is just a form of transgenderism. Phyllis Frye, for instance, explains that he held a workshop at the 1997 'Tenth Annual Creating Change Conference' in San Diego, which was sponsored by the NGLTF, along with Jamison Green and Shannon Minter, 'to ask the question, "Is sexual orientation a subset of gender identity?"'. He argues that 'lesbians, gays and bisexuals are actually the subsets and members of the larger gender identity community' (Frye, 2000: 154–155). This idea is repeated again in a report on 'trans people' in the UK: 'There is a strong argument that much homophobic crime is actually transphobic, as it is a person's gender presentation which attracts attention in public spaces rather than a prior knowledge of their sexual orientation' (Whittle *et al.*, 2007: 55). This seems to be a tenet of transgender activist ideology that is intended to persuade lesbian and gay groups to see a commonality of interest.

Another serious problem with the Yogyakarta Principles is the confusing notion of 'gender' that pervades the document and which its definition of 'sexual orientation' is based upon: 'Sexual orientation is understood to refer to each person's capacity for profound emotional, affectional and sexual attraction to, and intimate and sexual relations with, individuals of a different gender or the same gender or more than one gender' (International Panel of Experts, 2007: note 1). Lesbians and gay men who reject the idea of role playing will have problems with this assumption that homosexuals are attracted to persons on the basis of the same 'gender' rather than the same sex. Some may reject the idea that they have a 'gender', and certainly be concerned as to why they should be assumed to be attracted to a person based on the performance of masculinity or femininity. It is worrying that this degree of profound confusion is at the foundation of the campaign even by lesbian and gay organisations for 'gender' rights. The definition of 'gender identity' in the Principles is broad and vague and reflects queer and transgender theory and essentialist notions of gender:

> each person's deeply felt internal and individual experience of gen-
> der, which may or may not correspond with the sex assigned at birth,
> including the personal sense of the body (which may involve, if freely
> chosen, modification of bodily appearance or function by medical, sur-
> gical or other means) and other expressions of gender, including dress,
> speech and mannerisms.
>
> *(International Panel of Experts, 2007: 6)*

In the Principles, the category of 'sex' is entirely omitted in favour of 'gender'. They state that 'violence, harassment, discrimination, exclusion, stigmatisation' are 'directed against persons in all regions of the world because of their sexual orientation or gender identity, that these experiences are compounded by discrimination on grounds including gender, race, age, religion, disability, health and economic status'. Sex does not appear in this account, and as a result women are expunged, since discrimination against females starts in the womb and is not related to 'gender'. In a feminist and social constructionist understanding, gender is a result and manifestation of the subordination of women as a sex caste, rather than the reason for it.

The fact that 'gender identity' is increasingly defined as a moveable feast may create difficulties for the interpretation of these legal Principles. A major study of those identifying as 'trans' in the UK in 2007 acknowledged that transgenderism does not constitute a defined category, saying that '[t]he categories transvestite, transgender and transsexual are commonly understood as discrete. This research has found that trans people have complex gender identities, often moving from one "trans" category into another over time' (Whittle *et al.*, 2007: 14). The survey found that 44 per cent of respondents not living permanently in their 'preferred gender' 'intended to do so in the future' and this 'has implications for current law which offers some legal protections only for those who are understood as transsexual' (ibid.). This degree of flexibility might be expected to create difficulties for lawmakers, since it implies that the right to be considered a 'woman' in the law, which is how 'gender identity' is generally interpreted, can be wielded by men who 'dress' occasionally or just at weekends. For women, of course, their sex caste status is a full-time and lifelong condition.

Despite their problematic and confusing nature, the Yogyakarta Principles have been seen as a very important development in the human rights domain (Ettelbrick and Zeran, 2010; O'Flaherty and Fisher, 2008). Though they are not binding in international law, they have been understood as 'an authoritative interpretation of international law' (Ettelbrick and Zeran, 2010: 11) and have 'catapulted discussion and action on human rights related to sexual orientation and gender identity to new highs within the United Nations', and they 'provide an important universal definitional point' for 'hundreds of academic papers, bills, resolutions and other documents' (Ettelbrick and Zeran, 2010: 13). Human Rights Watch calls them 'A groundbreaking set of principles on sexual orientation, gender identity, and international law … a landmark advance in the struggle for basic human rights as well as gender equality' (Human Rights Watch, 2007). Unfortunately, 'gender equality' is not possible because 'gender' is a hierarchy, but this assumption by Human Rights Watch that the Principles will somehow advantage women shows the serious confusion that the language of gender has created in the human rights community. The piggy-backing of the right to 'gender' onto lesbian and gay rights has the effect that any advances in lesbian and gay rights will also deepen the clash of rights that the idea of a right to gender creates for women. This is most unfortunate, since there is no doubt that the advancement of rights for lesbians and gay men is of great importance.

An example of the impact of the Principles on policymakers can be found in the 2011 report from the office of the Director-General for Justice of the European Commission, which spelt out the importance of eliminating discrimination on the grounds of 'sex, gender identity and gender expression' (Agius and Tobler, 2011). The report, which is likely to be influential since it emanates from such a source, is based on all the problematic and confusing notions common to queer theory discourse on gender. It states that 'negative attitudes towards trans and intersex people' are often 'directly correlated to the importance that a determinate society places on the binary gender model, as well as the levels of gender stereotypes, sexism and gender inequalities that exist within it' (Agius and Tobler, 2011: 5). A feminist analysis is rather different, and understands the 'gender binary' and inequality based upon biological sex to be the cause of the very concept, 'gender identity', which the report seeks to protect. The report's definition of 'trans' is so broad as to be almost meaningless:

> Indeed the term trans is an umbrella term that includes, but is not limited to men and women with transsexual pasts and people who identify as transsexual, transgender, transvestite/cross-dressing, androgyne, polygender, genderqueer, agender, gender variant or with any other gender identity and gender expression which is not standard male or female, and who express their gender through their choice of clothes, presentation, body modifications, including the undergoing of multiple surgical procedures.
>
> *(ibid.)*

One group of persons that is not included is that quite large group that eschews gender altogether and refuses to obey any of the social demands to demonstrate a particular gender on their persons, many of whom, but not all, are lesbian or gay. They are not 'trans' because they do not fetishise gender in any form, but simply choose to live without it.

The implications of incorporating gender stereotypes in the law

There are two troubling implications of incorporating the protection of 'gender' in the law that will be considered here through the examination of two supposedly pioneering examples of legal change, the UK Gender Recognition Act of 2004 and the Australian Amendment to the Sex Discrimination Act of 2013. The first implication is that when gender is inscribed in law this creates legal protection for the traditional gender stereotypes that originate in the sex caste system. The second is that the increasing vagueness of the category 'gender' enables men to gain protection in law for their impersonation of women, even when they are physically entire, and therefore capable of both raping and impregnating women and girls, and when they are but occasional cross-dressers. Whereas once 'transsexuals' were required to have a diagnosis of gender identity disorder, have performed a real life test of living as the opposite sex and to have undergone physical treatment to alter their bodies, persons claiming protection for their 'gender identities' need to prove none of these things. In many countries, recognition of change of sex or gender still requires evidence of treatment for gender identity disorder, but this is changing. As the definition of those who require protection for their 'gender rights' broadens, national legislation is being created that follows a wider 'de-pathologising' model. An ongoing campaign by transgender activists to enable recognition of changed sex caste status without any diagnosis or treatment is currently under way and is making considerable headway. The 2004 Gender Recognition Act in the UK still requires a diagnosis, but it eschews treatment as a criterion for gaining a certificate of changed status. It is a prime example of the move to 'gender' in legislation; and the confusion around 'gender', in which the Act is mired, leads to some strange outcomes (Jeffreys, 2008).

The UK Gender Recognition Act of 2004

The 2004 Gender Recognition Act (GRA) in the UK was radical for its time. The UK Act goes further than other countries, enabling transgender persons who have undergone surgical treatment to gain new birth certificates and the rights of their, as the GRA puts it, 'acquired gender'. There is, of course, no such thing as a non-acquired gender, but the legislation, and the parliamentary debates at the time, see-saw between seeing 'gender' as just another word for sex, and seeing it as socially constructed. The Act is unusual in enabling transgenders who have had neither surgical nor hormonal treatment to gain recognition in their new 'gender'. The language of 'gender' rather than 'sex' is used in the legislation. Though the Act is apparently about 'gender', a subject that feminists have usually understood to be their own political stamping ground, no women's or feminist groups made submissions in the lead up to this Act. A whole conversation about what constitutes sex and gender and what, for example, a woman is – including the creation of legislation with considerable social and political implications for women – took place offstage as if it were not the concern of women or feminists to be involved in the discussion of these issues.

The Act is the child of an international movement of transgender activists, represented in the UK by organisations such as Press for Change (PFC), the Gender Trust, and the FTM Network. The social acceptability of trans-genderism in the present is suggested by the fact that the two main cam-paigners from PFC, Christine Burns and Stephen Whittle, were awarded an MBE and an OBE respectively for their campaigning efforts for transgender rights and towards the GRA. The 2004 Act is to 'make provision for and in connection with change of gender' (GRA, 2004). The Act defines 'acquired gender' as 'the gender to which the person has changed' or 'The gender in which the person is living'. Under the Act, persons applying for 'recogni-tion' of their 'acquired gender' must appear before a panel that will decide whether to 'recognise' them or not. The panel must grant the application if the following conditions are met by the applicant: they must have or have had 'gender dysphoria'; have performed what is usually called the 'real life' test, i.e. lived in the acquired gender throughout the period of two years ending with the date on which the application is made; and intend to 'continue to live in the acquired gender until death'. Though the problem of transgender regret and the difficulty of any of the aspirants being able to promise not to change their minds were raised in the parliamentary debates, neither was considered to undermine the spirit of legislation which was based on the idea that 'real' transgenders can be recognised and that regrets do not happen. No mechanism was created to allow those 'recognised' under the Act to return and receive a fresh certificate, or series of them in future years, each time they changed their gender identity.

The applicant must provide evidence of their 'acquired gender' in the form of either 'a report made by a registered medical practitioner practising in the field of gender dysphoria and a report made by another registered medical practitioner' or 'a report made by a chartered psychologist practising in that field and a report made by a registered medical practitioner' (GRA: Article 3). Unlike legislation of this kind elsewhere, it does not require that applicants should have undergone medical treatment in the form of hor-mones or surgery, and this can lead to some peculiar consequences. It creates a new situation in which an intact female can become legally male, and may give birth to and raise a child as the 'father' although, according to the UK legislation, the birth certificate should specify that the person who gave birth is the 'mother' rather than the 'father'. It also creates the situation that a man may, with the aid of a certificate recognising him as a woman, enter women-only spaces, which happened in relation to women's prisons in the UK as we will see later in this chapter. This problem for women's security is exacerbated by the fact that such a man may be physically entire.

Though the Gender Recognition Act was radical for its time in not requir-ing drug or surgical treatment to qualify for a certificate of change of 'gender', the international campaign and discussion of transgender rights has moved on considerably in the ensuing decade. This is clear from an examination of the Australian Amendment to the Sex Discrimination Act in 2013, where 'gender identity' is defined so broadly that it represents simply appearance or 'mannerisms' and makes no mention of either diagnosis or treatment. In this legislation gender identity is simply a matter of personal choice and, potentially, subject to change from one moment to the next.

The Australian Sex Discrimination Act Amendment 2013

Law change to incorporate gender rights is moving fast and developing in line with the queer theory approach to gender. The 2013 Amendment to the federal Sex Discrimination Act in Australia adds the categories of sexual orientation, gender identity and intersexuality to those protected from discrimination (Parliament of the Commonwealth of Australia, 2013a). It goes so far as to imply that everyone has a gender, and enables, under 'gender identity', persons to be 'neither male nor female' (Parliament of the Commonwealth of Australia, 2013b). The definition of 'gender identity' is very broad and does not require a diagnosis or treatment, or any period in which the aspirant has to live as the gender they aspire to be, and seems to facilitate any person to claim a 'gender identity' on a temporary or occasional basis: 'gender identity means the gender-related identity, appearance or mannerisms or other gender-related characteristics of a person (whether by way of medical intervention or not), with or without regard to the persons' designated sex at birth' (Parliament of the Commonwealth of Australia, 2013a: 6, Subsection 4 (1)). It is interesting to speculate on what is meant by 'mannerisms', which could perhaps include the behaviour of hair flicking that two of the female partners in Chapter 4 describe their husbands as adopting as they transgendered. This incorporation into law of such finely calibrated measures of socially constructed masculinity and femininity is a new development. The legislation implies that everyone will have a 'gender identity' by defining discrimination on the ground of gender identity as occurring when 'the discriminator treats the aggrieved person less favourably than, in circumstances that are the same or are not materially different, the discriminator treats or would treat a person who has a different gender identity' (Parliament of the Commonwealth of Australia, 2013a: 5B). There is no provision for using as a comparator a person who does not have a 'gender identity', and indeed does not believe in such. In this way the Australian state has now created an assumption that everyone has a gender identity, and the possession of such a quality seems to have become compulsory and unavoidable.

The Amendment breaks new ground by allowing for the possibility that a person may not identify as male or female. According to the Explanatory Memorandum that accompanies the legislation, the definition of 'gender identity' 'provides maximum protection for gender diverse people', a term that introduces a new level of obscurity since the idea of 'gender' relates to a system in which there are only two genders, masculinity for the male, dominant sex caste and femininity for the female, subordinate sex caste; diversity does not apply (Parliament of the Commonwealth of Australia, 2013b: Article 11). The definition includes the way 'a person expresses or presents their gender and recognises that a person may not identify as either male or female'. However, whether the person 'identifies' or not, unless they are intersex, they will be biologically male or female, so the legislation enables the fantasy life of citizens to be protected by the state. It is likely that the 'neither' category will be of most use, immediately, to an Australian man who won a decision in the New South Wales court just as the Amendment was reaching its final stage of going through the legislature, that he could get his birth certificate changed to recognise him as 'neither male nor female' (Bibby, 2013). This decision is being celebrated as path-breaking. In fact Norrie May Welby is a male person who transgendered at the age of twenty-eight and then regretted his decision, but has decided not to identify as male even though he no longer considers himself female. This is probably because he has had his testicles amputated and is, as he puts it, a 'eunuch' (ABC, 2003). He is a man who started out as a gay drag artist before SRS and then, to survive financially, was prostituted by men (ibid.). Welby's situation suggests that the law will constantly have to evolve, on an *ad hoc* basis, to take into account the dysfunction caused by the medical and social acceptance of transgenderism in the first place. Whereas intersex persons may reasonably choose to declare that they are 'neither male nor female', this does not apply to men like Norrie Welby, who are likely to be unambiguously, biologically male but have suffered the confiscation of their genitals by medical professionals licensed by the state.

Once they have accepted the legal validity of 'gender rights', legislators are finding that they have to create more and more vague and confusing language and concepts. There is a slippery slope towards meaninglessness, such as enabling persons who are biologically male or female to realise their fantasies that they are not, with the imprimatur of the state. The full implications of such legislation for women's rights will be elucidated through case law in years to come, but in some jurisdictions decisions are being made under the aegis of 'gender rights' that are clearly very problematic for women's rights to dignity and security. The next section of the chapter will examine the implications of enabling men to exercise their 'gender rights' to enter spaces in which women are particularly vulnerable – women's toilets and women's prisons.

Women-only toilets and the right to dignity

Dignity is an important principle in human rights law. The Universal Declaration of Human Rights opens with the words, 'Whereas recognition of the inherent dignity and of the equal and inalienable rights of all members of the human family is the foundation of freedom, justice and peace in the world' (United Nations, 1948). The entry of male-bodied persons into women's toilets is happening with increasing frequency in the United States in particular, and is being justified successfully with reference to gender rights. This subjects women to the potential for a range of sexually harassing behaviour by men that violates women's right to human dignity. The broad wording of recent documents relating to gender rights creates the possibility that both old-fashioned 'transsexuals' who have gone through reassignment surgery, as well as cross-dressers who engage in their hobby on particular days or weekends, would be able to use women's toilets.

Historically in the west, the availability of women-only toilets has been an important feminist aim, and the *sine qua non* of women's equality (Penner, 2001). Women cannot go out to work or access public space without access to safe toilets. This is still a very considerable problem in countries such as India where there are human rights campaigns about the right to women's toilets, to enable girl children to go to school, as well as to enable women to escape the sexual violence they are vulnerable to when having to defecate or urinate in fields or public places (Yardley, 2012). Presently in the west, however, it does seem that such facilities, which are so crucial to women's well-being and opportunities, are being threatened by the demands of men who cross-dress to access them.

The creation of a 'right' for men to enter women's toilets has, potentially, a number of negative effects, such as the deterrence of women from using them, creating potential health problems, and the forcing of women into the intimate proximity of men, some of whom have a clear interest in the sexual excitements that they can access by violating women's right to human dignity in such places. The danger to women's dignity and security that such entry can occasion is illustrated by the considerable amount of pornography freely available on the web in which men display and exchange photographs they have taken by stealth, through hidden cameras, of women in toilets and locker rooms, defecating and urinating, or naked in showers. This material is a subset of the genre of pornography more usually called 'upskirts', which is the name male porn consumers give to the practice of photographing up women's skirts without their knowledge. Men do this by using cameras on the tips of their shoes on escalators, by having cameras in bags they place on the floor next to women, and, particularly, by putting hidden cameras in women's toilets and shower rooms. The upskirting phenomenon has been recognised as an offshoot of mobile phone technology that enables a new form of sexual harassment and violence against women, and concern about this has led to the introduction of new legislation in several countries to address the issue (Powell, 2009). The men who engage in upskirting are a varied group, including male tennis fans at the Australian Open (ibid.), male school students who uploaded film of a teacher onto the Internet (Epstein, 2012), and even a male urologist. In a case in New York in August 2012, a respected urologist extended his professional interest into a new direction, and was arrested for filming up a woman's skirt on a station platform (Newcomb, 2012). This form of voyeurism includes the direct targeting of women's excretory functions for observation, filming and sound recording.

The offenders who target women in order to gain excitement from the violation of their dignity in this way include men who dress in women's clothes. There is a surprising number of cases in which men wearing women's clothing have been arrested for engaging in behaviour in women's toilets that is harmful to women. The range of acts they engage in includes secret photographing of women using the toilets and showers, peeping at women from adjacent stalls or under stall dividers, demanding that women recognise them as women and becoming aggressive if the women do not, and luring children into women's toilets to sexually assault them. It is not possible to know whether these are men who consider that they are transsexual or transgender or just men adopting women's clothing in order to facilitate their access to women and children, but the problem of allowing men to enter women's toilets persists in either case. The website *GenderTrender* has a useful listing of such arrests in the last few years (GenderTrender, 2011a). In a British case a man dressed up as a 'mannequin with a mask and a wig' to enter a cubicle in the women's toilets in a shopping mall, where he 'performed' an unspecified 'sexual act' (*The Telegraph*, 2011). The twenty-two-year-old man told police he 'found the sound of women on the toilet sexually exciting', and he had filmed women's feet from beneath cubicle doors on his mobile phone and recorded the sound of a flushing toilet. In another case a man dressed as a woman was observed peeping at women and using a cell phone to photograph them in a UC Berkeley women's locker room (Rufus, 2010). In a Little Rock, Arkansas case, a thirty-nine-year-old man wearing women's clothing was arrested after exposing himself and masturbating in front of three children and trying to lure them into the women's bathroom (Newport TV, 2010). He had a long history of indecent exposure. In May 2013 a man wearing 'women's' clothing, who had been using a concealed camera to film women in the women's toilets, was arrested in California (*Daily News*, 2013). There is, of course, no parallel behaviour on the part of women who seek to enter men's toilets to videotape them using the facilities, and men do not need sex-segregated toilets to protect their dignity and security as women do.

The clash of rights that the right to 'gender identity' protection creates is particularly clear in the Colleen Francis case in the United States in October 2012. In this case, Francis, a forty-five-year-old person born male, thrice married, the father of five children, possessed of intact male genitalia, and who lived as a man until 2009, has established the right to use the sauna in the women's locker room at Evergreen State College (Golgowski, 2012). The locker room is used by the girls from two neighbouring high schools and some parents complained that this male-bodied person was naked in the locker room in the presence of their girl children. The college said that it had legally to protect Colleen's right to be naked in the women's locker room, directed the girls to a smaller, less adequate facility and then put up a curtain in the main locker room saying the girls could change behind it. Francis' right to 'gender identity' trumped the rights of those born and raised female. The cases covered here represent just a fraction of those listed on the blogs of transcritical feminists. Moreover, the reported cases are likely to represent the tip of the iceberg of this form of offending by men, since usually women are unaware that they are being recorded or observed.

The right of cross-dressing men to use women's toilets is supported by a supposedly progressive alliance of queer theorists and activists who argue that sex-segregated toilets are unnecessary and irretrievably outdated. One such is Sheila Cavanagh of York University, author of *Queering Bathrooms* (2010). She pooh poohs the idea that 'trans people' could be sexual predators, and says there has been,

> (to my knowledge) no report of a trans person physically or sexually attacking a cisgendered (non-trans) patron in the restroom. It is as though the toilet has become an icon of danger evoked by those who cannot logically substantiate their opposition to trans inclusive legislation.
>
> *(Cavanagh, 2011: 18)*

There is, though, a great deal of evidence that men are violent towards women, across cultures and across history (Romito, 2008), and there is no good reason why men who dress in women's clothing will behave differently. In fact, as we have seen above, there is considerable evidence that there are men who, whether simply cross-dressed or 'transgender', do engage in violence towards women in spaces such as toilets, and such expressions of scorn and derision towards those who point out such uncomfortable truths cannot negate them.

Cavanagh argues for degendered toilets and states, 'Gender inclusive and luxurious toilets are a worthwhile project for the 21st century' (Cavanagh, 2011: 20). Unfortunately, this argument, which is made in pursuit of transgender rights, is beginning to gain ground not just in the rarefied world of queer theory but in local government policy. In 2013 the City Council of Brighton and Hove in the UK announced its intention to degender its public toilets (Ward, 2013). The Council states that it wishes to promote 'gender neutrality' and 'build facilities which are open to all, regardless of sex'. This initiative was to begin with the building of a block with four new lavatories and a cafe. The toilets would have images depicting a man, a woman and a child on the doors. The Council opined that such facilities would be 'more accessible for those who do not identify with the male–female binary' (ibid.). Subsequently, single sex toilets would be progressively phased out. The policy is in response to a demand by a Council working group set up to examine 'issues faced by transgender residents' of the city. The group, the 'Trans Equality Scrutiny Panel', also recommended that titles that referred to gender, such as Mr, Mrs, Miss and Ms, should be banned in order not to offend the transgender community and force them to 'choose between genders'. The Greens Party councillors supported the plan, and, interestingly, it was up to councillors from the conservative side of politics to point out that this was a violation of women's right to security. A councillor from the opposition Tory group argued that '[l]ocal residents, particularly women with children, would much prefer to use separate facilities as apart from anything else, it is safer' (ibid.).

Transgenderism and the prison system

Women's toilets are not the only segregated space in which women are particularly vulnerable to the entry of men who seek to exercise their 'gender rights'. Women's prisons are another space that they are seeking the legal right to enter, and this provides a powerful example of the clash of rights that is created when men's rights to personate women are promoted above the rights of women. Male prisoners in Western countries are using human rights laws successfully to gain access to transgender treatment at public expense in prison, and the right to then transfer to the women's prison. The men who are being given the right to live alongside women in prison include some of those most dangerous to women's safety – men who have been convicted of crimes of grave violence including the murder of women. Men who transgender are more prone to criminal behaviour than other men are. Research from the United States shows that 21 per cent of men who transgender had been sent to prison for any reason, which contrasts with 2.7 per cent of the general American population (Grant et al., 2011). Though the demands of 'transgender' prisoners are still being refused in some jurisdictions, they are increasingly successful, being well supported by gay organisations and major law firms.

In Australia, the transgendering of prisoners is not yet routinely facilitated. If it were, then one candidate would be Australian serial killer, Paul Denyer. Denyer killed three young women in Bayside suburbs of Melbourne, over seven weeks in 1993. He sought during his sentence to 'wear make-up in jail, have a taxpayer-funded sex change and formally alter his name by deed poll to Paula' (Dunn, 2012). He was refused, and in July 2012 exhibited behaviour that showed how unlike a woman he actually was. Police were reported to be investigating four alleged rapes by Denyer of men with intellectual disabilities who were fellow inmates. The Denyer case does illustrate the problems that might occur as a result of the recognition of violent male criminals as 'women' and their transfer to women's facilities. There is no reason that a belief that they are 'women' will alter such men's tendencies to engage in a form of sexual violence that is specifically and clearly male. In another Australian case, in 2012, Derek Lulu Sinden was refused permission in the Queensland courts to start hormone treatment for gender identity disorder. The Queensland Corrections Department argued that the refusal was consistent with its policy of only supplying hormones to men who started to take them before entering the prison system (Smith, 2012). Sinden had been convicted of an attack on seventy-one-year-old Beryl Grace Brown in April 1999, in her home, which caused her to suffer a heart attack and fatal stroke.

Though there is still resistance to enabling male prisoners to transgender in the United States, court judgements in 2011 and 2012 have established the rights of male prisoners to access transgender treatment in the form of both hormones and surgery. In a landmark case in 2011, a man who had a serious history of sexual offences against girl children won the right to hormone treatment in prison (McDermott et al., 2011). Sandy Battista started his violence against girls at a young age. Battista's mother was killed by his father when he was six years old, and he was, allegedly, sexually abused while in the custody of his grandparents. When he was fourteen he assaulted a six-year-old girl, and a year later took another girl child into the woods but did not assault her. In a 1986 case, Battista got caught making obscene phone calls to young girls he picked out of local newspapers, and a decade later, Battista was penalised for keeping pictures of young girls in his jail cell. He was diagnosed as having gender identity disorder in 1997. The law firm, McDermott Will & Emery, which started acting for Battista in his case against the authorities for not allowing him transgender treatment, announced proudly on their website that they were successful in what they consider an important human rights victory, that of enabling him to have hormone treatment. The judge in the case found, in 2011, that denying Battista treatment would constitute 'cruel and unusual punishment which consists of the neglect of her serious medical needs' (ibid.). That precedent was used in the case of another violent male prisoner in the United States in 2012 who was seeking the right not just to hormones but to state funded sex-reassignment surgery (Lavoie, 2012). Robert Kosilev murdered his wife, Cheryl, in 1990, and was living as a woman and taking hormones while in a men's prison at the time of the historic judgement. This case is the first in which a federal judge, Judge Mark

Wolf, has ordered prison officials to provide sex-reassignment surgery for a transgender inmate. The judge ruled that reassignment surgery was the only way to treat 'her' 'serious medical need'. The ruling is expected to set a precedent for other men seeking reassignment in jail.

The question of transfer to a women's prison is intertwined with such decisions, and this 'right' was established in the UK in a court case in 2009, when there was a successful appeal from an unnamed male prisoner to be moved to a women's prison. The petitioner in this case was found guilty in 2001 of the manslaughter of his male lover, who was strangled with a pair of tights, allegedly for refusing to fund the murderer's sex-change surgery. He was sentenced to five years' imprisonment. Five days after his release he attempted to rape a female stranger and was sent back to prison. In order to get gender reassignment surgery the prisoner was told that he must engage in the real life test, that is two years living as a woman, which required transfer to a women's prison. He appealed under the European Convention on Human Rights to be allowed such a transfer. His lawyer told the court that the crimes were all linked to 'a desperation to become a woman'. The judge declared that 'her continued detention in a male prison is in breach of her rights under Article 8 [the right to private and family life]' under the Convention. The man's barrister, Phillippa Kaufmann, referred to the man as a woman and said, 'She lives as a woman amongst men on a vulnerable prisoners' unit and she can't wear what she wants or more than subtle make-up. They are an important statement of her femaleness' (Allen, 2009). The women in the prison where he will be housed will not be told of his identity or of his offence (ibid.). There is a clear clash of rights here, in which a man's right to wear make-up and be housed with vulnerable women who are incarcerated trumps the right of those women to be protected from violent men. The notion of human rights is trivialised thereby.

In response to the judgement, new guidelines were issued for the treatment of prisoners seeking gender reassignment in UK prisons in March 2011, which enabled prisoners to have treatment and to be located in women's prisons. The guidelines state,

> A male-to-female transsexual person with a gender recognition certificate may be refused location in the female estate only on security grounds – in other words, only when it can be demonstrated that other women with an equivalent security profile would also be held in the male estate.
>
> *(Ministry of Justice, 2011)*

The nature of the man's offence and the degree to which he poses a risk to women prisoners is not considered here, only the man's right to personate women while in the company of women is recognised. The integration of men who personate women into women's prisons can be jeopardised by their rejection by women prisoners. In Italy, this was given as a reason to establish a prison especially for transgenders in 2010 (Melloy, 2010). This is an expensive and complex solution, but necessary in response to the problem that although the law recognises these men as women, actual women do not. Aurelio Mancuso, President of Italy's GLBT organisation, Arcigay, explained, 'Housing transgender and male prisoners together is especially problematic. But their relations with female prisoners are also far from straightforward. The women just don't consider them women' (ibid.).

The problems that can arise from housing a man in a women's prison became clear in a Canadian case in 2005, when a violent transsexual had to be removed from free association in the women's jail in which he had been placed on the grounds of his human rights, because of his aggressive behaviour, which had included threatening staff and vandalising the building (Bhardwaj, 2005). Richard Kavanagh, who calls himself Synthia, was placed in a secure facility within the women's prison. Kavanagh was sentenced to life in prison, with no chance of parole for twenty-five years, for the 1987 hammer killing in Toronto of a twenty-three-year-old transsexual prostitute, Leo James Black, also known as Lisa Janna Black. He complained to the Canadian Human Rights commission in 1999 that denial of hormone therapy and surgery constituted discrimination against him. Correctional services in Canada then revised their guidelines to allow surgery for patients who met particular criteria, and this was seen as a landmark decision at the time. Interestingly, Kavanagh's later behaviour was not seen as a reason to exclude men from women's prisons but as a reason to have a separate facility for violent 'women'. Kevin Grabowsky of the Union of Canadian Correctional Officers said that Kavanagh's case illustrates that the correctional service needs to create a special handling unit for violent female offenders, as there is for men, but of course these men who have transgendered are not actually female offenders at all. The doublespeak required in deference to the idea of 'gender rights' can be quite challenging. As the Kavanagh case shows, men who personate women are not just potentially dangerous to women, but to other men who personate women as well.

In another case of a man, who was in the process of 'transition', killing a man with 'gender identity' issues, thirty-four-year-old Nina Kanagasingham, of the UK, was charged with murder in 2010 over the death of the well-known human rights lawyer, Sonia Burgess (*Pink News*, 2010). Sixty-three-year-old Burgess was known to friends, family and work colleagues as both Sonia and David. Kanagasingham pushed Sonia/David Burgess off a station platform at King's Cross in London, where he was killed by an approaching train. Kanagasingham was placed in a men's prison, but after the

2011 guidelines it would seem possible for him to be placed in a women's prison.

Conclusion

It is a serious setback for the journey towards women's equality when states protect 'gender' in their legislation, and proclaim that men's rights to personate women are 'human rights'. This makes 'gender', the mechanism which orders the sex caste system, a matter of state. The appearance and mannerisms of gender, which represent a socially constructed and temporary way of separating persons into dominants and submissives in a hierarchy, are given weight and validity. The criticism of the state recognition of this mechanism of inequality can then be seen as illegitimate and 'transphobic'. Moreover, the recognition of 'gender rights' in a way that enables men to enter women's spaces and claim to be 'women', creates a serious clash of rights. It subordinates the rights of women, persons of the female sex, to dignity, security and privacy, to the rights of (mostly) men who choose to act out a 'gender identity', a state of mind. There are few limits to the categories of men who are gaining the right to do this in a variety of jurisdictions. Sometimes the definition is so broad that it covers men who wish to occasionally cross-dress or those who regret transitioning and now consider themselves neuter. In all cases the category of 'sex' – a very real caste status that women can never escape, and that subjects them to demeaning treatment for their whole lives – disappears in favour of a fantasy in the head of the transgender person.

8

WOMEN'S SPACE AND THE TRANSGENDER CHALLENGE

Written with Lorene Gottschalk

In the last chapter, two previously women-only contexts were examined to show the implications of demands for access to women's toilets and prisons by men who claim to be expressing their 'gender rights'. This chapter examines the implications of such demands in relation to women-only contexts created specifically out of second wave feminism to serve the particular interests of women as a subordinated group. Women's services include refuges/shelters, rape crisis centres, women's health centres – facilities that, though started by volunteers, later acquired state funding. Women's spaces include festivals, marches, women's holiday centres and weekends away, conferences, walking groups that women organise and pay for themselves. The transgender activist movement has demanded access to all of these services and spaces, for persons with male bodies. Where there has been resistance from women and lesbians to these demands, the fallout has been greatly damaging to women's communities. Transgender activists have laid siege to venues, and taken women's services and groups that organise women's social events, to court, in order to enforce access.

The importance of women's services and spaces

Women's services were set up by feminists from the 1970s onwards to serve the interests of women as a subordinate and disadvantaged group. Women's health centres, for example, were created in Australia out of recognition that women's particular needs were neglected in male-dominated health care. They focused upon biologically female bodies, and were sympathetic to women's experience (Kaplan, 1996; Murray, 2002). Shelters/refuges and rape crisis centres and hotlines were set up to enable women to escape and heal from men's violence (Sweeney, 2004). Such women's services are tailored to women's needs and offer mutual support and a forum for women's concerns and consciousness raising. This chapter will address the considerable stresses created within women's communities and the 'women's sector' (women's service organisations) by the determination of male-bodied transgenders to access women's services as workers, clients and members (Price, 2007; Stuart, 2006).

The chapter will also examine the campaigns by transgender activists to enter women's spaces – which were created to enable women and lesbians to socialise and meet politically, without men, in order to articulate their concerns, relax, strengthen bonds, and enjoy women's culture, music, poetry and dance. It will consider the implications of the demand by men who transgender, continue to be heterosexual after transition, and proclaim themselves to be lesbians, to access lesbian-only spaces. The spaces may not just be geographical spaces, but even physical, with some transgenders demanding physical access to the bodies of lesbians, as in the 'cotton ceiling' controversy, in which male-bodied transgenders guilt-trip lesbians who do not want penises in their bodies, with accusations of 'transphobia' (GenderTrender, 2013b).

Some feminists support admission of male-bodied transgenders to services and spaces (McDonald, 2006), while others within women's communities strongly oppose their inclusion, insisting that since they have neither women's biology or experience, they cannot empathise with the experiences of women born and raised female (Greer, 1999; Jeffreys, 2008; Raymond, 1994; Sweeney, 2004). Germaine Greer, for example, accuses male-bodied transgenders of a lack of insight about the extent of their acceptance as women, noting that when 'he forces his way into the few private spaces women may enjoy and shouts down their objections and bombards the women who will not accept him with threats and hate mail, he does as rapists have always done' (Greer, 1999: 74). Very often, splits over the issue of transgender inclusion destroy women's and lesbian groups and lead to the ending of those events that provided women-only social spaces such as lesbian festivals and women's music festivals (McDonald, 2006; Sweeney, 2004; Wales, 1999). Important and necessary facilities for women and lesbians are lost. There is little research that has looked at the implications for women of the campaign by male-bodied transgenders to enter women's or lesbian groups and social spaces. Similarly, there has been little research that examines the implications for women's services, set up to meet women's particular needs, when male-bodied transgenders seek access either as clients or as workers. This chapter includes data from an exploratory study by Lorene Gottschalk that sought to examine the extent to which management staff in women's services in Australia, such as shelters and health centres, are aware of the implications of transgender inclusion, have policies about this, and have experienced attempts by male-bodied transgenders to gain access.

Women-only services and spaces

Women's spaces providing social support and other services were first set up in countries such as Australia, the UK and the United States in the late nineteenth and early twentieth centuries during the first wave feminist movement (Blair, 1984; Freedman, 1979; Kaplan, 1996). Feminists campaigned for such provision again in the 1970s so that, for instance, the Australian government agreed to provide financial assistance to establish and run women's refuges, and by the end of that decade there were over a hundred funded refuges across Australia (Johnson, 1981; Kaplan, 1996; Murray, 2002). Women's health centres that sought to compensate for the male-centredness of the traditional medical profession are also government funded in Australia. The women's health care movement achieved considerable success in drawing attention to women's medical issues previously neglected in medical research, and was responsible for a decline in disease and maternal and neo-natal death rates (Kaplan, 1996). Women-only services such as refuges, centres against sexual assault (CASAs) and health centres fulfilled a desperate need, and the benefits of providing services to meet these needs are well documented (Kaplan, 1996; Lake, 1999).

Historically, when services are mainstreamed, women's special needs become 'invisible' and are frequently neglected (Freedman, 1979; Kaplan, 1996). This occurred in the United States after the first wave feminist movement, when women's spaces were mainstreamed. One result was that the problem of men's violence against women, which was well known in the early twentieth century, had to be 're-discovered' by second wave feminists (Freedman, 1979). Creating women-only space such as women's refuges, women's health centres and women's festivals has been one of the outstanding achievements of the second wave feminist movement (Riger, 1994). In the 1990s, however, women-only space and facilities disappeared to a large extent as a result of the impact of a queer movement, which marginalised lesbianism, and an anti-feminist backlash (Case, 1997; Faderman, 1997). Few women-only spaces still exist, compared with what was available at the height of the second wave feminist movement. The disappearance of women-only spaces has taken place at the same time as a general winding back of all facilities dedicated to women's interests, such as bookstores, publishing, art galleries and cafes. Feminist publishers have mostly disappeared, the shelves dedicated to women's studies in bookstores have been eliminated or merged into 'gender' or cultural studies, and women's studies courses in universities have mostly been abolished or turned into 'gender studies'. At the same time, events previously women-only such as music festivals or marches have become mixed-sex. But, until recently, women's health centres, women's shelters and rape crisis services, and a few festivals and events, remained focused upon women. The transgender challenge is thus directed to the few areas in which a women-only principle has been maintained.

The transgender challenge is an onslaught upon that most important principle of feminism, the necessity of women-only space, in which women separate, by choice, from men. The lesbian feminist philosopher, Marilyn Frye, has characterised the importance of separatism to second wave feminism incisively (Frye, 1983). She explains that,

> Our existence as females not owned by males and not penis-accessible, our values and our attention, our experience of the erotic and the direction of our passion, places us directly in opposition to male-supremacist culture in all respects, so much so that our existence is almost unthinkable within the world view of that culture.
>
> *(Frye, 1983: 145)*

When women forbade male entry into their groups and activities it denied them important goods and sources of power: '[f]emale denial of male access to females substantially cuts off a flow of benefits, but it has also the form and full portent of the assumption of power' (Frye, 1983: 103). The contemporary rage of male-bodied transgenders at being denied entry to women's spaces, and the reluctance of women to give them cause for anger, can be understood with reference to Frye's useful insight that 'conscious and deliberate exclusion of men by women, from anything, is blatant insubordination, and generates in women fear of punishment and reprisal' (ibid.). Men's right of entry is conferred upon them by their position of dominance and women's lack of any right to deny this to them by their subordinate position: 'It is always the privilege of the master to enter the slave's hut. The slave who decides to exclude the master from her hut is declaring herself not a slave' (Frye, 1983: 104). The strength and determination of the transgender challenge, and the anger and vituperation with which it is often conducted, are likely to stem from an understanding of the importance of the principle of separatism to women's freedom. Examples of the transgender challenge in this chapter will begin with the challenge to women-only social space, as exemplified in the Michigan Womyn's Music Festival, and move on to the challenge to women's services.

The transgender siege of the Michigan Womyn's Music Festival

The Michigan Womyn's Music Festival is an iconic women's and lesbian space that, probably for that very reason, became an early target of transgender activism. The festival was first held in 1976 and has been held yearly, for one week, on private land, since that time. It is the oldest and best known women's festival in North America and, with thousands of lesbians attending, has been a most important space for the creation of lesbian culture and community (Fowler, 2001). It provides a geographical space where, for a short period of time, women can get away from constant surveillance and abuse by men in public spaces, and experience an alternative culture free of the slurs and woman hating that abound in malestream popular culture. It would be quite difficult to overstate the value and importance of this festival for lesbian culture and community in particular. Maria Fowler has written about how, from her first attendance in 1995, the festival has represented 'home' to her (ibid.). She explains that the festival was set up to create a positive collective identity for lesbians, and challenges 'dominant constructions about lesbian lives'. For many of the attendees, the festival 'provides a community of resistance' in which they can feel safe to express their lesbianism because they have 'privacy that emerges from the site's spatial and ideological remoteness from the everyday surveillance of the heteronormative gaze' (Fowler, 2001: 53). Fowler quotes one attendee as saying,

> it's a place … where I can feel completely and totally safe; I never have to look over my shoulder, I can go anywhere I want any time of the day or night in any state of dress or undress and never have to worry about anything.
>
> *(Fowler, 2001: 59)*

Festival policy does not permit active questioning about a person's sex or gender, but it excludes self-identified transsexuals, and 'respect for one week of womyn-born womyn space is requested' (Browne, 2011: 249).

Kath Browne says that the festival 'embodies' separatism (Browne, 2011: 248). It allows women to 'live' feminism and 'acts as a way of educating womyn about feminist forms'. Browne explains that nudity is important to the freedom women experience at Michfest because, 'once on the land, away from areas that could be seen by a passerby, Michfest enables women to walk around in various states of dress and undress' (Browne, 2011: 251). Attendees say that this experience can be 'empowering in recognizing the diversity of womyn's bodies and their beauty outside of conventional norms of attractiveness' (ibid.). This was particularly the case in terms of the communal showers under the trees where women did not have to be ashamed of their bodies. Moreover, the festival offers a space where women can be freely loving and affectionate towards one another in ways that heterosexual people take for granted, engaging in 'same-sex intimacies through holding hands, kissing, etc. in all of the festival spaces' free from men's insults and threats of violence (ibid.). These are all activities that women, and lesbians in particular, cannot feel safe or comfortable to engage in when in male company. For all these reasons, transgender activists want access. According to Emi Koyama, author of the 'Transfeminist Manifesto' (Koyama, 2001), the siege of the festival began in 1993 when some transgender activists set up 'Camp Trans' opposite the entrance to the festival to protest the policy of not admitting self-identified transgenders (Koyama, 2006). Camp Trans was repeated in 1994 and then went into abeyance until revived in 1999 as Son of Camp Trans by the activist group Transsexual Menace and the transgender activist organisation, GenderPAC. The founder of both these organisations is the male-bodied transgender, Riki Wilchins, who identifies as a male-to-female-to-male transsexual (Wilchins, 2013). While the original aim of Camp Trans was to get the festival policy changed to admit postoperative transsexuals, by 2002 the stated policy was to gain admission for any self-identified women, which would include any men who identified as women at any time, even when physically entire or just interested in occasional cross-dressing. The campaign by transgender activists went further than just setting up a camp, and included contacting musicians who played at the festival and asking them to boycott it or make public statements against the women-only policy.

They also exploited the 'don't ask' policy to make incursions into the camp and use the facilities. Karla Mantilla wrote in the US feminist newspaper *Off Our Backs* about the damage done to the festival by the intrusion of male-bodied transgenders who entered the communal shower areas, naked and physically entire (Mantilla, 2000). She says,

> If these wannabe 'women' had any understanding of what it is to be a woman in patriarchy they would have respected, not violated, women's space, and they would have understood what a horrific violation it would be for a woman to be confronted with a strange naked biological male, penis and all, when she is unclothed and vulnerable.
>
> *(ibid.)*

The concern of the transgender activists with their own 'liberation', she argues, came 'at the expense of women trying for just one week in one remote corner of the United States to feel completely safe from male violence' (ibid.). After male-bodied transgenders chose to enter the festival, Mantilla says that 'the feeling of complete safety from men and patriarchal rape culture' was 'eroded' because women attendees knew that 'a man' could always be there. Mantilla comments that the determination of male-bodied transgenders to enter the space shows how deeply 'threatening' women's separatism is to men, and that more such spaces are needed, not fewer. The transgender challenge, she says, is a 'rebellion against women's rebellion' and works against 'the liberation of women from patriarchy'; it is straightforward anti-feminism by social conservatives.

In 2010 the tactics of transgender activists who entered the festival became particularly violent and aggressive. A member of the security crew, who says she did not question anyone's 'gender', described how Camp Trans set up Camp Tranarchy, and 'vandalized the festival and threatened festival goers' (Dirt from Dirt, 2010a). A flyer being distributed by the activists showed a rather extraordinary degree of woman hating: 'A hot load from my monstrous tranny-cock embodies womanhood more than the pieces of menstral [*sic*] art your transphobic cunts could ever hope to create'. Women at the camp recorded a range of violent incidents they were subjected to. One said that her car was vandalised and a chemical sprayed on both door locks. There was gunfire one night from the Camp Trans area, waterlines were cut and tyres slashed, shower plumbing was damaged and banners destroyed. Tents were painted with 'Fuck fest' and 'Real women have cocks'. Women spoke of being traumatised, suffering post-traumatic stress disorder, and not feeling safe to attend the festival again (Dirt from Dirt, 2010b). The transgender siege has not been entirely successful, however. There have been numerous reports from the 2012 festival that, as a reflection of a strengthening new wave of feminism, women are becoming much more organised in their opposition to the male-bodied transgender incursions, using signs, T-shirts and chants to show these men that they are not welcome on the land (GenderTrender, 2012).

Lesbian spaces

The Michigan Women's Music Festival survives as a nominally women-only space at this time. Most other women's spaces have not been so lucky and have experienced legal challenges, or folded under the pressure to admit male-bodied transgenders. A wide variety of women's activities have exploded under this pressure, including women's walking groups and reading groups, but, most importantly, facilities designed to provide the beating hearts of lesbian community – lesbian centres – have been stricken by controversy. One example of this damage is the Sydney Lesbian-Space Project. During 1993 lesbians had raised around $250,000 to buy a lesbian community centre in Sydney, Australia. They wanted a women's space but with a focus on lesbian culture and community (Kline, 2006). However, male-bodied transgenders who identified as lesbians had contributed to the fund raising on the understanding that they would be included. After a lesbian event in Brisbane was severely disrupted by the presence of male-bodied transgenders, the Lesbian-Space collective felt it necessary to introduce a policy to exclude them. The new policy was strongly disputed by women who supported the right of male-bodied transgenders to be in women's spaces and irreconcilable conflict erupted, with the result that the Lesbian-Space Project was abandoned and the issue was never resolved.

Transgender entryism caused the demise of the first and historically significant lesbian centre in Canada, too. The Vancouver Lesbian Connection (VLC) was run from its inception in 1985 by a collective, and offered services such as a library of women's resources, a place to spend time, recreation facilities and space for events. The VLC has iconic status in Canada's lesbian and gay history and became 'the template for lesbian community centres in other cities' (DiMera, 2011). It was destroyed as a result of the entryism of a male-bodied and physically entire transgender, Mamela, who had been a volunteer with the Gay and Lesbian Centre from 1995, and learnt there of the existence of the VLC. Mamela was attending the University of British Columbia gender clinic and described himself as a radical lesbian feminist with a female gender consciousness. He was initially refused inclusion in the VLC on the grounds of having been raised as a male, but persisted, and after much debate the VLC agreed to include men who transgender so long as they identified as lesbians, with the result that Mamela was admitted in 1996. This change in policy was soon regretted. According to collective members, Mamela's behaviour was quite disruptive, including harassment of staff and volunteers, using resources without permission, answering the crisis line without training, and sexually propositioning staff and volunteers. The VLC eventually revoked Mamela's membership on the grounds of aggressive and sexually offensive behaviour, at which point he filed a complaint against the VLC with the British Columbia Human Rights Tribunal in 1999. In the Tribunal's decision, Mamela's complaint was upheld and the VLC was ordered to pay $3,000 in compensation for injury to his 'dignity, feelings and self-respect'. But the decision came after the VLC had disbanded, having been unable to raise money for legal costs, and having had neither time nor energy to fight for the right to 'women-only space' (Wales, 1999). The effect of this transgender challenge was to destroy a most important resource for lesbians.

The transgender challenge to women's services has been even more effective because these services are now usually state funded, and their staff – especially when seeking to comply with legislation that enshrines the right of male-bodied transgenders to be understood as 'women' – are likely to comply with transgender demands more readily lest they lose their financial viability. Transgender activists campaign to get women's organisations and services to adopt trans-inclusion policies that enable male-bodied persons, with or without intact male genitalia, to gain access.

The experience of the women's sector

As a result of transgender entryism, women's services in many countries are having to devise policies to deal with a new problem. When the services were set up in earlier decades, male-bodied transgenderism was a much less significant phenomenon in size and in legal clout. Rape crisis centres and women's refuges were straightforwardly woman-centred. As they were increasingly mainstreamed, regulated and funded by states, they had to defend their women-only status, which some were unable to maintain. But others gained exemptions from equal opportunity legislation that enabled them to maintain women-only workforces and clientele. These achievements are now endangered by the demands of male-bodied transgenders who, through claiming to be women rather than men, are able to circumvent such exemptions. The issue of transgender inclusion can be seen as a beachhead for the inclusion of men as workers and clients. Once male-bodied transgenders, particularly those with penises intact, are included, the exclusion of men who do not cross-dress or transition becomes one simply of where the line to men's inclusion is drawn. The principle is likely to be overturned. This is not the case, interestingly enough, in the UK, where the Equality Act 2010 enables women's services to specifically exclude men who transgender in certain circumstances (Women's Resource Centre, 2011: 6).

In Australia there is no such legal exemption for the exclusion of male-bodied transgenders, and an Australian study, conducted through interviews with nineteen women managers of CASAs, women's shelters and women's health centres, sheds useful light on the implications of trans inclusion. Interviews centred on these women's views about, and experiences of dealing with, the issue (Gottschalk, 2009). They reveal considerable determination to protect the women-only nature of their services, but the issue of transgenderism caused some dissension. Their views depended upon whether the interviewees saw male-bodied transgenders as 'women' or not, and on whether they had direct experience of trans inclusion. In the interviews, the women's opinions about a safe space for women were explored, and the way in which their beliefs about men and male-bodied transgenders as employees and clients, aligned with their philosophy. Interviewees from CASAs are identified as CASA1, those from women's health centres as WH1, those from refuges as WR1, and so on.

The importance of women-only space

Most of the organisations in the study were committed to providing women-only space. Their stated mission is to provide a service for women, by women – though some did also provide services for men – and a minority were prepared to employ men, although only one did so at the time of the interview. The interviewees were unanimous in their opinion that their service provided a safe space for clients. In the case of CASAs and domestic violence refuges, the concern was safety from perpetrators, who were overwhelmingly men. In the case of women's health centres, it was a safe space for women to discuss sensitive health issues with female health professionals who were specially trained to deal with women's health and wellbeing needs. Thus the organisations tended to be staffed by women, with men often specifically and sometimes legally excluded, through exemptions under equal opportunity legislation. The interviewees show an expertise and wisdom that has developed over many years of dedication to serving the needs of women for security, privacy and dignity.

The following comments from interviewees show the emphasis they placed on a service provided for women, where they could have their needs met and share experiences in a safe environment free from male domination. CASA5 stated,

> Our clients are women only, [our service is] run out of a 'women's house' so it is a strictly women-only space. Even with trades people all efforts are made to find female tradies. All staff are women – we have exemption under EEO [Equal Employment Opportunity].

WH1 shows a sensitive awareness of the importance of a women-only environment:

> One of the things I am most aware of personally is the potential for somebody who has experienced violence or who is experiencing violence ... and they walk over the threshold here they do feel safe ... so you would not want to jeopardise that. [Our shelter has a] long tradition of being women focused and over those years we've developed an expertise around women, physical, emotional and social health issues and because we're a women-only staff as well there's a lot of interaction and safety. It is a cooperative female environment in which to work, safe from men.

Interviewees also saw women's space as providing an important consciousness raising forum for women, allowing women to share stories and experiences of violence and to learn about the institutionalisation of male dominance. CASA5 explains that women's space,

> gives them a voice ... to learn that it [male violence] is not the women's problem in that they are not at fault. It empowers women. Usually

women are dominated by men in the wider world … if men are present, women feel disempowered given that they are victims of male violence.

One interviewee, WR2, said that even a male tradesperson changed the atmosphere in a women's refuge in a problematic way, undermining the feeling of safety,

> but I know whenever we've had like a male servicing the photocopier, or something like that, suddenly it just feels like there's some underlying tension in the place in terms of having clients here … and somehow the dynamics just feel differently.

Employing transgender workers

Where centres had formal employment policies, these focused on whether or not they would employ men, and made no mention of men who transgender. Some had non-discrimination policies and were open to employing men as well as women, though generally most employees were women. Five of the interviewees had formally applied for a legal exemption and were able to legally discriminate against men in their services, while others had an informal policy to exclude the employment of men but had not formalised that exclusion legally. Some interviewees commented on the fact that clients, including male clients, overwhelmingly preferred a female counsellor. As CASA1 explained, 'It is women workers by demand. Even male clients prefer a woman counsellor even though they can ask for a male. We have had three requests for a male counsellor in the past four years'.

Where centres had applied for a legal exemption to allow them to employ women only, they had not usually considered the issue of employing male-bodied transgenders. The opinions about trans inclusion differed significantly and depended entirely on whether they believed male-bodied transgenders to actually be women, and whether or not they placed importance on the different socialisation experiences of women born and raised female from those born and raised male but identifying as women in adulthood. A minority of interviewees (four) said they would prefer to exclude male-bodied transgenders, recognising the different socialisation that women and men experience, as CASA2 explained:

> We have a strong women-only policy … MTFs have different experiences and stories growing up in a culture that defines masculinity and femininity … We would not employ a transgender as a counsellor. But it has never been discussed or addressed or challenged.

An important factor that influenced the interviewees' opinions about the employment of male-bodied transgenders was whether or not they had previous experience with such persons, either as workers or as clients. Two of the centres represented by the interviewees had employed men who had transgendered as workers. One of these interviewees was CASA5, who had spoken strongly in support of women-only space and whose personal belief was that a male-bodied transgender was not a woman. She states,

> We have had an experience with a trannie. It is an issue in this organisation. The biggest thing is the lack of consensus about what is a woman … Men who claim they are women inside have no idea of what it is to be a woman.

The experience that CASA5 had with a male-bodied transgender worker had resulted in strong disagreement among the staff, which the centre was attempting to resolve: 'there is a lot of debate and the issue remains contentious'.

Male-bodied transgenders as clients

It was more common for the centres to have policies about whether or not to accept male-bodied transgenders as clients and the implications of accepting them differed depending on the type of service offered. Women's health centre staff are specially trained to understand and manage health concerns that are peculiar to women. They are not trained to deal with issues around sex-reassignment surgery and hormone treatment, nor are they trained in the special mental health issues experienced by male-bodied transgenders, which include the trauma of questioning gender identity, coming out as transgender, transitioning and adjusting to life as a man who has transgendered. Training staff and making resources available to male-bodied persons is, inevitably, a diversion of energies and funds away from women's health. All of the women's health centres in this study admitted only clients whom they considered to be female, but for some this included male-bodied transgenders. Those who accepted male-bodied transgenders did so in the belief that a man who identifies as a woman is a woman, despite not having a woman's anatomy and possibly having a penis. For the same reason they excluded female-bodied transgenders, in the belief that a woman who identifies as a man is a man, despite having a woman's anatomy. Female-bodied transgenders, however, do suffer from the same health issues as women who do not transgender, as well as the harms created by surgery and hormones, and may thus be more easily treated in a women's facility. One interviewee, WH2, explained that though she would have preferred not to include male-bodied transgenders because of the different health issues involved, she feared that any other course would lead to loss of funding, since state funding agencies had policies against such discrimination.

The centre that WH1 represented rejected female-bodied transgenders who presented with female health issues but were prepared to accept male-bodied transgenders, for whose health needs they had no training or expertise. WH1 explained that her centre had been approached by a transgender support group who asked them to help male-bodied transgenders to monitor their hormone treatment, and offered help with information about transgenderism as well as advice on developing a policy. WH1 admitted that, at the time the policy was formed, there was 'some robust discussion around feminism, violence against women and what it is to be a woman'. From the discussions, WH1 gained the impression that most of the workers at the centre agreed that male-bodied transgenders should be included. However, an email interviewee who had worked at the centre at the time said that the conflict experienced by the workers, who had polarised, was severe. She had been present during discussions with male-bodied transgender representatives and when she asked them why they did not go to a transgender support group to have their needs met, one of them 'held forth about wanting to be accepted as a woman and wanting to be among women … to see his identity confirmed by being among women'. Expertise in transgender health, it seems, was less important than gaining access to women-only services, and gaining the important goal of getting women staff to recognise them as 'women'. Attendance and employment in women's services serve a particular function for men who transgender that has nothing to do with the purposes for which those services were established, that is, the opportunity to have their 'womanhood' affirmed.

The issues involved in including male-bodied transgenders as clients in women's domestic violence refuges/shelters and rape crisis centres are different from those in women's health centres. The perpetrators of such violence against women are men, and these facilities offer space in which women can feel safe, free of any threat from male abusers or the triggering effects of seeing and being dealt with by men. Though male-bodied transgenders also suffer violence, the perpetrators are unlikely to be women and, though they may wish to be in spaces from which men who have not transgendered are absent, this should not be at the expense of the needs of women survivors. The interviewees in the study had mixed feelings. One interviewee, WR2, when asked about transgender clients, immediately replied, 'No we're very clear that it is only women and children we work with', but she then thought further about her reply, and said, 'Aahh I think if she identifies as a woman ahh I think she'd meet the criteria.' CASA5 felt unsure of how to respond on the issue of male-bodied transgender clients: 'The male and female experience of socialisation is different ... I feel conflicted and confused about where I stand. It brings up contradictory things for me, very complicated.' In the end she re-affirmed the need for retaining women-only spaces on the basis that male-bodied transgenders were not, in fact, women. She suggested that separate services should be provided for transgenders. Unfortunately, for male-bodied transgenders, such separate services may not be acceptable because they would not satisfy the need for affirmation as a 'woman' that a women-only service can provide. One of the services offered by CASAs and women's refuges was group-discussion therapy facilitated by a skilled counsellor, and it was in relation to this important facility that concerns about male-bodied transgenders mixing with women clients was greatest. CASA5 said, 'it would take away the safe space for some (women)'. CASA6 had experience of attempts to run mixed groups and felt that her women clients would object to the presence of male-bodied transgenders, so they would have to have the choice of separate groups that did not contain them, a development that would require extra funding and resources.

The experience of WR1 illustrates the problems that can arise with male-bodied transgender clients. WR1's centre has a non-discrimination policy, and their clients are referred from mainstream health services and the police. So they feel they have no choice but to accept whoever is referred to them. WR1 had a person referred to the centre as a woman, who presented in women's clothing. Staff realised through mannerisms and an Adam's apple that this person was either a cross-dresser or a man who had transgendered. However, because he had been referred, and because of anti-discrimination laws, they felt they had no choice but to accept him as a client. They originally placed him in one of the accommodation units with women, but the women complained and said they 'did not want someone with a penis with them'. One said, 'I'm not going in there, he's got a penis.' The transgender client could not be placed with women and children, and had to be placed on his own in a unit for six weeks, which had the effect of denying space to women, and prioritising the needs of this man over those of women who needed refuge. The workers at the refuge found the situation stressful as they did not know how to deal with it and were afraid of breaking the law by discriminating. In the end they were forced to discriminate against women and in favour of a male-bodied person with entire male genitalia. Trans-inclusion policy in the case of this refuge, which was set up to service women's needs, led to the subordination of women's interests to those of a person raised male and with male biology.

Trans-inclusion policies

As a corollary to changes in legislation that recognise male-bodied transgenders as women who may then access women's services, transgender activists have created best practice guides to train providers on how to welcome these male persons. These manuals can be quite instructive as to the lack of understanding, on the part of their authors, of the way that the subordination of women works. One manual, created by transgender activists from Canada – which has been influential and is provided as a resource on human rights and equality websites, trades union websites and lesbian and gay websites, for instance – argues that women should not be concerned for their safety around male-bodied transgenders because they are no more likely to pose a risk to women in a shelter than any other 'women' (Darke and Cope, 2002). The Trans Inclusion Policy Manual states that 'there is no evidence to suggest that trans … women are more verbally or physically abusive than other women' (Darke and Cope, 2002: 84). In fact there is a great deal of evidence to suggest that men, whether they choose to transition or not, are violent towards women (Romito, 2008), but the authors circumvent this difficulty by identifying male-bodied transgenders as 'women', and therefore no longer members of the class of persons that is violent towards women. This stratagem does not work, unfortunately, because there is also much evidence that men who seek to transgender can be counted in the ranks of rapists and murderers of women, as we saw in the last chapter.

The Canadian manual, having tossed aside the issue of women's safety, goes on to consider, rather more sympathetically, the problems of the male-bodied transgenders themselves in shelters or refuges, such as the anxiety they might feel about 'privacy' if they still have penises. The manual states that most accommodation will have single bathrooms. If the person with a penis has to share a room with a woman, then a 'temporary screen' could be erected so that the penis will not be visible when they are changing clothes. It is not acceptable, though, says the manual, for the transgender person to be asked to change clothing in the bathroom. It is, perhaps, surprising that the issue of vulnerable, and often traumatised, women in shelters not wishing to see penises is not the focus here, but the feelings of the person *with* the penis. The manual states that requiring a transgender person to use a single room is 'akin to segregation' and unacceptable. There is no excuse for such segregation, it says, just because a woman might be traumatised by violence and find a transgender person triggering because of their masculine characteristics. The authors suggest that having to deal with masculine characteristics in their bedroom might be helpful to a woman who has suffered violence from men, because '[p]art of a survivor's healing process is to learn to differentiate her abuser from others with a similar characteristic: whether it's the muscular arms of a non-trans woman or the curly red hair of a trans-woman' (Darke and Cope, 2002: 86). Male-bodied transgenders can help women, we are told, to get over their concerns about having unknown men as their intimate companions. The manual expostulates, in an authoritarian tone, 'The law is clear on this one: the discomfort of others does not justify discrimination.' In this way, the safety and dignity of women is subordinated to the comfort of men who have an *idée fixe* that they are, themselves, women.

The manual addresses the crucial question that is most likely to be relevant to women's safety, of whether a woman can request not to be housed in a double room with a male-bodied transgender. The answer it gives is that she cannot do so, and she is forced either to share with a male-bodied transgender or exit the facility. The most intimate fraternisation with a person with male biology, and most likely a penis, is entirely compulsory for her. The manual compares the situation to that of a woman refusing to share with a 'lesbian, or a woman of colour, or an Aboriginal woman', all persons of female biology who do not represent the class of persons that is violent towards women, and concludes, 'If a resident would rather leave than sleep in the same room as a lesbian, a trans-woman, or an old woman, then that is her choice.' In other words, she is seen as choosing to be homeless, and voluntarily abandoning her place of refuge because she is too prejudiced to remain (Darke and Cope, 2002: 87).

The manual gives the same cruel and insensitive advice for dealing with a recalcitrant woman who does not want to be counselled on her issues of violence and rape by a male-bodied transgender:

> You can deal with this situation in the same way you would if a service-user said she is not going to talk to a woman who has a disability, or to a woman she 'knows' is a lesbian. You can remind her that it is against the law for your organization to discriminate and that all staff are well-qualified to provide services.
>
> *(ibid.)*

The traumatised woman is to be guilt-tripped by accusations that she is discriminatory and prejudiced, and threatened into compliance. This sort of incongruous rhetoric, designed to force women to room, shower and consort with men who cross-dress, or male-bodied transgenders, has not had the effect of making all women's services, particularly those that retain feminist personnel and principles, agree to admit male persons. In fact, in the case of Vancouver Rape Relief, a significant victory was achieved for women's right to women-only services. This case may signify that the ambitions revealed in the Canadian manual will not be realised, since it establishes the right of women's anti-violence services, in particular to reject men who transgender from their organisations.

A male-bodied transgender on the rape crisis hotline? Vancouver Rape Relief

An important test case took place in relation to trans inclusion on a rape crisis hotline, the case of Vancouver Rape Relief and Women's Shelter (VRRWS). One of the services offered by VRRWS is a twenty-four-hour rape crisis line that, at the time of the transgender challenge, received approximately 1,500 calls each year from women who had experienced sexual assault including rape, incest, other forms of violence and sexual harassment from men. In 1995 VRRWS refused training to a male-bodied and postoperative transgender, Nixon, who sought to become a counsellor at the centre, but was recognised as a man on the basis of his appearance (Mathen, 2004). VRRWS's position was that women must feel safe with the persons providing services to them and that such safety was compromised if a woman, who was a victim of male violence, is offered a service by a man or a person who had not always been a woman and was raised as a male (Mayeda, 2005).

Though refused training as a peer counsellor, Nixon was invited to support the centre in another capacity, such as participating in fund raising. Nixon insisted on being a peer counsellor and filed a Human Rights Complaint. VRRWS sought a negotiated settlement, but Nixon was determined to legally win the right to be a counsellor. Nixon's argument was that all persons must be assessed individually in relation to the service or employment that was being offered. If he had won, as VRRWS founder Lee Lakeman points out, this would have opened the doors to men to be seen as qualified for all positions in any women's organisation (Murphy, 2012). It potentially also sets a precedent for the dominant group, e.g. white, middle class, male, to take positions on bodies that represent indigenous or ethnic minority groups.

In January 2002, the Tribunal decision went in favour of Nixon on the grounds that VRRWS had not proven that 'experience as a girl and woman was necessary to becoming a peer-counsellor to raped and battered woman'. In August 2003, the British Columbia Supreme Court conducted a judicial review of the Tribunal decision, and set it aside in favour of VRRWS. Nixon appealed in 2005 to the British Columbia Court of Appeal and in December 2005 the Court unanimously decided in favour of VRRWS, which is now permitted to restrict their selection of volunteers to exclude those born biologically male and brought up as males, and the shelter has the right to determine its own membership (Sisyphe, 2005). The decision from the British Columbia Supreme Court (BCSC) in December 2003 has set a precedent. It has already been cited in forty-two decisions of the Tribunal and the BCSC (Sisyphe, 2005). The case has also been used in Canada by indigenous Canadians to argue, successfully, that they had the right to exclude a non-aboriginal man who applied for a position as an executive director of an indigenous organisation. The Nixon v. Vancouver Rape Relief case caused deep divisions in the feminist and lesbian communities of Canada, and poisoned the political atmosphere.

When women's services enable transgender access they can lose their women-only status, and have to abandon the objectives which they were founded to address. For instance, the women's health service in San Francisco founded by famous lesbian activists Del Martin and Phyllis Lyon and established to provide health care and health education for women, especially for lesbians, has changed its name from *Lyon Martin Women's Health Services* to *Lyon Martin Health Services* as it now also provides health care for transgender people (Lyon Martin Health Services, 2008).

Identity politics and service provision

There are other categories of persons with 'identities' that do not match their bodies, besides transgenders, which are creating online communities and demanding rights. This could potentially create problems for other forms of service provision, when services targeted at particular disadvantaged groups become subject to demands from persons who have a purely psychological identification with those constituencies. Staff at facilities and services targeting people with disabilities might face somewhat similar dilemmas to those running women's shelters, in terms of the best use of resources, if policies required them to accept transableists as clients. Transableists, after all, are able-bodied persons who consider that they have the identities of persons with disabilities, and they may not need support in quite the same way as those people who actually have disabilities do. In cases where a male-bodied transgender is also personating a person with disabilities, it may be that the work and diversions of energy required to serve the needs of someone with cumulative layers of delusion will seem an unreasonable use of resources.

A transableist featured in an episode of *National Geographic's* Taboo series, Chloe Jennings-White, is also a male-bodied transgender (Jennings-White, n.d.). Chloe lives as a paraplegic in a wheelchair, but does not have a disability. The documentary does not mention that Chloe is not female and only deals with one of the personations, transableism, involved. Chloe (Clive) is a scientist with a Cambridge University PhD, whose hobby is one most usually engaged in by able-bodied persons, rock climbing (ibid.). He was a married heterosexual man with two children before embarking on his career of impersonation. It is interesting to consider whether, if Chloe were to request a place in a specialised housing unit for persons with disabilities, accommodation would be made. The problem of identification with disability, race, sex, by persons, mainly men, who do not have the experience or physiology associated with those categories, is a growing one and not just related to transgenderism.

The most intimate of women's spaces – women's bodies

The most important space for women is their bodies. It is men's invasion and occupation of women's physical selves that has been identified by feminists as the foundation of women's subordination. Men have, historically, sold and swapped women as property in marriage and prostitution so that their bodies can be used for sex and reproduction (Lerner, 1987). The attempt to wrest control of their bodies from individual men and from patriarchal laws and institutions has been perhaps the most important underlying impetus for feminist activity, because without such control women have no chance to access any other forms of freedom. Abortion has been key to feminist activism, as a woman who cannot control reproduction becomes simply a vehicle for the purposes of others. Similarly, a woman's right to define her own sexuality, to select only herself as a sexual partner, to choose celibacy, or to choose to relate sexually to carefully selected others, has been understood as central to women's right to self-determination. It is perhaps not surprising, then, that male-bodied transgenders, in line with the generations of men who have sought to control women's bodies, consider that this is an important space to occupy.

The right of women to sexual self-determination is directly contradicted in the attempt by some transgender activists to force women to open up their vaginas for sexual use by these men's penises. In an extraordinary example of what political scientist Carole Pateman calls the male right of access, some transgender activists are now seeking to guilt-trip lesbians into allowing penises into their bodies (Pateman, 1988). This is taking place through a campaign to demolish what these transgender activists call the 'cotton ceiling', a term that is based upon the feminist understanding that women in public life face a 'glass ceiling' that prohibits access to men's inner sanctums. The 'cotton ceiling', a term invented by the transgender porn actor, Drew Deveaux, comprises women's underpants, which create a barrier against penetration by the penises of male-bodied transgenders (Garmon, 2012). The idea that the reluctance of women and lesbians to service these penises is a problem to be taken seriously and overcome, has achieved such acceptability that the very malestream organisation, Planned Parenthood, facilitated a workshop on the 'cotton ceiling' at their conference in Toronto, called 'Pleasures and Possibilities', in 2011. This workshop was for male-bodied transgenders only, that is a space from which women were excluded, at which these men could discuss tactics to get into the bodies of lesbians or 'cis' women in general who were resistant to their charms (Planned Parenthood, 2011).

The workshop was called 'Overcoming the Cotton Ceiling: Breaking Down Sexual Barriers for Queer Trans Women' and run by transgender activist, Morgan Page (Page, 2011). The workshop description states,

> Overcoming the Cotton Ceiling will explore the sexual barriers queer trans women face within the broader queer women's communities through group discussions and the hands-on creation of visual representations of these barriers. Participants will work together to identify barriers, strategize ways to overcome them, and build community.
>
> *(Page, 2011)*

The campaign relies on guilt-tripping, in which women who resist are accused of transphobia or transmisogyny, in an attempt to induce them to admit unwanted penises to their bodies. In the cotton ceiling campaign, women's right to sexual self-determination is redefined as a form of discrimination against male-bodied persons, which deserves to be zealously opposed. The male-bodied transgender activists who campaign to gain access to women's bodies in this way call their penises 'lady sticks'. The origins of this rather surprising term are informative. It is commonly used in transgender pornography, in which men with penises are prostituted for the sexual pleasure of male consumers. Thus, one transgender porn website, Shemale Models Tube, has this description of one of the male-bodied transgenders in a porn video: 'Ms. Meat is a horny girl who loves getting her lady stick sucked off all day long' (Shemale Models Tube, n.d.). It is, however, unreasonable to expect that lesbians and feminists should suspend disbelief in order to facilitate the sexual fantasy lives of these men with penises. The quite basic demands by women that they should have the right to a self-defined sexuality and choice in who they love are too important.

Conclusion

The practice of separating from men to create political and social space was fundamental to feminism from the 1970s onwards. Similarly, the creation of services targeted specifically at women was a triumph of that era and has had very important results in improving women's health and safety. Estelle Freedman argued, as far back as 1979, that women-only spaces were crucial to feminism in the early twentieth century too: 'The decline of feminism in the 1920s can be attributed in part to the devaluation of women's culture in general and of separate female institutions in particular' (Freedman, 1979: 524). The transgender challenge has been a significant factor in the demise of the spaces and services that second wave feminism created. Along the way it has caused serious internal strife in feminist and lesbian communities, which has diverted time, energy and resources and led to disillusionment and some despair. If women's services and spaces, which are fundamental to the possibilities of feminist revival in the present, are to continue or be created anew, then the right of women to gather without men, whether those are men who have transgendered or not, has to be promoted and respected.

CONCLUSION

The abolition of gender

The 'gender' belief system, that is, the idea that there are essential differences between women and men, forms the justification and sorting system for women's subordination. This book has focused on one problematic product of this system in the present, transgenderism, and sought to show its harms, and it has argued that 'gender', as it is encapsulated in transgenderism, hurts many. The transgenders themselves are hurt by regimes of hormonal and surgical treatments that may not reduce their suicidality, and are likely to lead to pain, physical harms and social isolation. They are hurt, too, by being sold a myth, the idea that they can be changed into a different sex through such means, and that this is a reasonable ambition. As the regretters point out, there is real tragedy in having lost body parts, as well as partners, contact with family and children, and suffering loneliness and isolation as a result of the peddling of this myth by the 'transsexual empire' of endocrinologists, surgeons, psychologists and some psychiatrists.

At this time, the 'transsexual empire' consists of far more than medical professionals. Myriad other personnel and organisations have become involved in peddling this pernicious idea, including many lesbian and gay organisations, liberal feminist groups, student organisations, even educators, who consider, for instance, that such an entity as the 'transgender child' exists. Meanwhile, the serious unhappiness of those children, men and women who feel desperate enough to pursue the harms of transgenderism are neglected. The treatment of transgenderism is iatrogenic, in that it purports to enact a cure for a problem of severe psychological distress, but in fact creates new harms and neglects the underlying malady in favour of quackery. All of those who collude with the myth of transgenderism, whether they be queer or 'feminist' academics, or lesbian and gay law centres, need to take some responsibility for the harms that they are supporting. For those in lesbian and gay, and feminist communities who might say that they have nothing to do with transgenderism and just try to avoid the subject, perhaps because they fear the damage to their reputations, I would say that it is past time to take this hugely harmful phenomenon seriously. As this book has sought to show, the harms are so egregious that it is not ethically acceptable to turn away.

Gender, in the form of transgenderism, hurts in many ways that do not just pertain to transgenders themselves. It hurts the wives, partners and family members of men and women who transgender, causing them acute distress and loss so severe that some researchers are prepared to call this post-traumatic stress disorder. It hurts, too, the feminist movement, and threatens the gains feminists have fought for in the creation of women-only services and spaces. The very few women-only spaces that still exist, such as the Michigan Womyn's Music Festival, are subjected to campaigns of bullying and intimidation. It undermines and causes huge confusion in feminist academia and feminist theory, to the extent that the biological reality of women's lives, on the basis of which, and through which, females are relegated to subordinate status is disappeared, relegated like the dinosaur to history and museums.

Gender hurts, too, in terms of the time, energy and resources that are required to provide legal reform, facilities, and services to support those who have been transgendered. School, college and university counsellors are trained in and expected to employ transgender ideology and politics (Gendered Intelligence, 2009–2013). City councils and workplaces are required to access training and instigate policies that comply with transgender logic. The UK government's Equality and Human Right Commission website, for instance, contains guides for employers, schools, health care and social work staff on providing services for and working with transgenders (Equality and Human Rights Commission, n.d.). Schools, colleges and local councils face demands for transgender facilities, which often involve the abolition of important women-only spaces such as toilets. Youth services, prisons, shelters and many other services are required to employ this logic too. All these institutions and personnel are being required to learn new language, much of which, such as the term 'cis', relegates women – those who are biologically female – to a secondary status, as just one kind of woman, which is, in transgender logic, privileged over those men who travel under the illusion that they – persons born and raised as males and with male biology – are themselves 'women'.

But the gender in transgenderism is positive for those who gain financially from it, such as the medical professionals, counsellors, psychologists, endocrinologists, surgeons, pharmaceutical companies. It is also positive for a burgeoning online industry of providers of accoutrements, breast binders, wigs, man-size high-heeled shoes, and of advice, for example how to wear constraining 'feminine' clothing and imitate 'feminine' posture. It is positive for the considerable industry of transgender pornography and prostitution that is directed towards male cross-dressers and all men who are titillated by material involving men with breast implants and penises, or men being forced to wear corsets, and so forth. It is positive, for those who do 'diversity' training, who instruct businesses and public services to suspend their concerns about transgenderism and comply with the right to 'gender identity', no matter how this affects the rights of women. There is much money to be made from the transsexual empire.

The gender in transgenderism is positive for the support and maintenance of the gender scaffolding that upholds the edifice of male domination. In this way transgenderism is hostile to the rights of all women. Gender functions as a sorting system for male domination, identifying the subordinates and the dominants. It also provides the bars of the cage that imprison women in their daily lives. In the name of 'gender', girls and women grow up controlling their movements, taking up little space, being careful to show men and boys deference lest they be attacked for man hating, or being bra-burning bitches. They treat their bodies as objects to be transformed for men's gaze with make-up and cosmetic surgery; show off areas that fashion dictates should be naked: chests, bum cracks, backs, stomachs; constrain their movement with tight clothing and shoes that harm and distort feet and cause pain. All these are practices that maim the ambitions and desires of girls and women.

Transgenderism supports the idea that there is something natural and inevitable about gender. This is despite the fact that feminists, and women in general, constantly challenge 'femininity' in their actions and appearance. Transgender activists do not appreciate these challenges and seek to enforce their view that the protection of femininity should be the goal of feminism against clear evidence that many women, lesbians in particular, want no part of it. Gender functions as an ideological system that justifies and organises women's subordination and for this reason it must be dismantled. Women and girls cannot access full humanity and the rights and opportunities of full human status (MacKinnon, 2005) while the idea that there are personality traits and appearance norms that are naturally and essentially associated with girls and women still has social currency and serves to control and limit their lives.

The exhaustion of the category 'transgender'

The scope of the transgender empire may be reaching its peak, as transcriticism is increasing at a fast pace both within activist feminism and from wives and regretters. There is an increasing groundswell of criticism of the concept and practice of transgenderism from a newly invigorated radical feminist movement. Moreover, the idea of transgenderism has become so vague and general that the category is in danger of being exploded. The old idea that men possessed of a gender identity disorder could be effectively separated off from men who cross-dressed has been seriously undermined by a burgeoning development of men who claim to be women but retain their penises, and, like Virginia Prince, elect only to take hormones; and from men who say that transgender treatment should be seen as cosmetic surgery that anyone can choose. Some transgender activists seek to include all lesbians and gay men within the category transgender. The term is fast losing any distinctive meaning.

The claims of transgender activists to 'rights' for their gender identities are in imminent danger of being discredited by a proliferation of rather more unusual identity politics online, which are presently trying to build movements and rights-based political campaigns. Identity politics has been criticised by feminist theorists as emanating from the conservatism and extreme individualism that began under neo-liberal political regimes from the 1980s onwards (McNeil, 1996). Identity politics replaced structural political analysis, and meant that people could claim identities that were seen to arrive from the heavens rather than from the power structures of sex, race and class. Identity politics was consonant with the politics of supposedly empowered consumerism that this political period represented. Identities, and the paraphernalia that supported them, were consumed, rather than being seen as constructed out of forces of oppression (Davis, 2011). This analysis is well suited to many of the identities that have resulted from the setting up of personal blogs through Tumblr and led to online communities of persons who consider themselves to have the identities of other races, known as transethnics, or to be half human and half animal, therians, or fictional characters, fictives, or nonhuman, otherkin. The 'Dragon Man', O. Scribner, has provided a useful historical map of the development of the otherkin community, for instance (Scribner, 2012). They adopt the political approach of transgenderism, claiming that they are discriminated against at work for being wolves or gnomes, and that people do not understand them and marginalise and exclude them. Max Read, in his article for the online magazine *Gawker* about this phenomenon, quotes a Tumblr personality who seeks to keep up with the more unusual trends in identity: 'The relationship between legitimate social justice activists and delusional weirdos is ever-changing and gives fascinating insights into how activist communities work' (Read, 2012). Online social activists who have accepted that persons should have human rights based on their 'identities', rather than on the basis that they are members of oppressed groups, can have difficulty knowing where to draw the line. The politics of these more unusual identities are based on transgenderism, but there is considerably more scepticism online about how much respect should be paid to them. Claims by men that they are really women meet with a more sympathetic response than claims by a white woman that she has always been a Korean cat (Read, 2012).

Transableism, an identity politics of persons who want to have limbs amputated, or their backs broken so that they can be paraplegics, now has quite a considerable presence online and some support among medical professionals who consider that the desire for amputation should be respected and have named it Body Integrity Identity Disorder (BIID) (Davis, 2011; First and Fisher, 2012). The medical ethicist, Carl Elliott, argues that in fifty years' time both transgenderism, and its less respectable cousin, transableism, will both seem shocking and retrograde (Eliott, 2000, 2003). As he says, 'Fifty years ago the suggestion that tens of thousands of people would someday want their genitals surgically altered so that they could change their sex would have been ludicrous' (Elliott, 2003: 230). In another fifty years the cultural conditions may once again not be sympathetic to the idea of transgenderism or to BIID. The idea that bodies should be altered by the medical profession as a matter of 'right', because their owners consider they would prefer to be another sex or to have a disability, will likely seem extraordinary and seriously harmful.

It is puzzling that men who claim to be women have achieved so much more public acceptance and legal support, when those engaging in activities that are not necessarily very different are not receiving such affirmation. It is likely to be the acceptance of the essential nature of gender that creates the nest bed for the acceptance of transgenderism. The idea of 'gender', because it is seen as natural and necessary and indeed underwrites the social formation of male dominant societies, can be understood as acceptable even when it appears in unusual places or persons. Gender in any form is more acceptable and understandable than the absence of gender. The removal of arms and legs, self-castration and voluntary blindness are not supported by such a profoundly embedded belief system and can be identified as unreasonable, in a way that the pursuit of body modification to create a simulacrum of womanhood on a male body is not.

Feminism and the end of gender

If the growing new wave of feminism has more success in challenging the edifice of gender than previous stages in women's emancipation have had, transgenderism will disappear. 'Gender difference' is both based upon and used to explain women's material inequality. When that inequality is challenged, the requirement that women should behave as subordinates will be undermined too, because the fact that women take up little space and keep their knees together is the appearance correlate of the fact that they make only two-thirds of the money that a man does in his lifetime. When women are not under pressure to wear the clothing of subordinates, then their attire will have less appeal to men's masochism, and the variety of transgenderism that results from men's interest in cross-dressing will have no rationale. At present appearance norms for women represent their lower status and thus constraint, inability to move easily through high heels, revelation of flesh, shaving and painting signify womanhood and offer to men all the delights of self-abasement when they adopt them. Cross-dressing by men will not make sense in a future when flat shoes and trousers can be worn by either sex, and there is no clothing redolent of subordination that supplies the thrill of submission.

The new wave of feminism promises greater movement towards a future that is not so tightly structured around the worship of aggressive masculinity and the institution of heterosexuality, and this may make it less imperative for those men who presently transgender to avoid being homosexual to do so. It may remove the social stigma that propels them to change their bodies in order to love the same sex. For lesbians and other women who seek to avoid the low wages, social denigration and enforced humiliation of becoming 'feminine', and who may want to love other women without social disapproval, greater sex equality will remove the motivation to transition. A world in which there is less violence by men towards girls and women will provide less reason for women to wish to vacate the female bodies in which they have been abused. Being a girl or woman will not be a liability.

But the new wave of feminism must confront new challenges. Transgender activists are waging a struggle for the survival of their ideology, which involves online abuse and campaigns of harassment, public assaults upon feminists and campaigns to prevent feminist freedom of speech and association. The opponents are mostly men who consider they are really women, and in male-dominated societies, men are powerful and have authority. Their sexual proclivities are protected, so that pornography and prostitution are preserved by governments to seduce male citizens and acquire their votes. Male sexual interests created out of women's subordination are zealously respected. But the new wave of feminism must confront new challenges from the medical and institutional support of gender, too. Support for transgenderism is government policy in the UK (Equality and Human Rights Commission, n.d.). In a science fiction twist, the state now oversees the construction and maintenance of sex role stereotypes, through the UK legislation in which a panel of experts adjudicates on the 'gender' of applicants for 'gender recognition certificates' (Jeffreys, 2008). This is a long way from the heady days of the 1970s, when the feminist project was to eliminate what were then called sex roles. State policy is now wedded to the construction of 'gender' and the most insulting caricatures of womanhood, to the extent of accepting that these should be inflicted upon children, through guidelines on transgender children from the UK's National Health Service. I can remember in the early

1970s when I was in the National Union of Teachers women's group in Manchester, UK, that our foremost task was the removal of sex role stereotyping from school textbooks. Janet, we considered, should not be restricted to helping her mother in the kitchen while John got to tinker with the family car. All that optimism seems a long time ago now. States, legislatures, much of the feminist academy, and lesbian and gay organisations are involved in a gender protection racket. The new wave of feminist activism that seeks to abolish gender is on a direct collision course with the protection of gender. There will be interesting times ahead.

REFERENCES

ABC (2003, 11 August). Enough rope with Andrew Denton. Australian Broadcasting Corporation. www.abc.net.au/tv/enoughrope/transcripts/s927538.htm

Adams, Carol J. (1990). *The Sexual Politics of Meat*, New York: Continuum

Agius, Silvan and Tobler, Christa (2011 June). Trans and intersex people. Discrimination on the grounds of sex, gender identity and gender expression. Network of legal experts in the non-discrimination field. European Commission: Director-General for Justice. www.refworld.org/pdfid/4fdedde32.pdf

Allen, Vanessa (2009, 5 September). Transsexual killer and attempted rapist wins 'human rights' battle to be moved to women's prison, London: *The Daily Mail*. www.dailymail.co.uk/news/article-1211165/Transexual-prisoner-wins-High-Court-battle-moved-womens-jail.html

Alleyne, Richard (2011, 15 April). Puberty blockers for children considering sex change, London: *The Telegraph*. www.telegraph.co.uk/health/healthnews/8454002/Puberty-blocker-for-children-considering-sex-change.html

Angelsforum (2012, 7 October). In the *Sun*. MtoF has regrets. http://79.170.40.33/angelsforum.co.uk/phpforum/viewtopic.php?f=2&t=23423

APA Task Force (2007). American Psychological Association Task Force on the sexualization of girls. American Psychological Association. www.apa.org/pi/women/programs/girls/report-full.pdf

Asscheman, H., Gooren, L.J.G. and Eklund, P.L.E. (1989). Mortality and morbidity in transsexual patients with cross-gender hormone treatment. *Metabolism*, 38 (9): 867–73

Atlas Strawberries (2012). About. http://atlasstrawberries.tumblr.com/about

Bailey, Michael (2003). *The Man Who Would Be Queen*, Washington, D.C.: Joseph Henry Press

Bailey, J. Michael and Triea, Kiira (2007). What many transgender activists don't want you to know. *Perspectives in Biology and Medicine*, 50 (4): 521–34

Barrow, Becky (2012, 7 November). Women earn 1/2 million pounds less than men: even for identical jobs the pay gap's still huge. *Mail Online*. www.dailymail.co.uk/news/article-2228984/Women-earn-1-2m-lifetime-men-Even-identical-jobs-pay-gaps-huge.html

Batty, David (2004, 31 July). Mistaken identity. *The Guardian*. www.guardian.co.uk/society/2004/jul/31/health.socialcare

Batty, David (2007a, 25 May). Sex change doctor guilty of misconduct. *The Guardian*. www.guardian.co.uk/society/2007/may/25/health.medicineandhealth2

Batty, David (2007b, 25 May). Russell Reid inquiry. Key figures. *The Guardian*. www.guardian.co.uk/uk/2007/may/25/health.society

Batty, David (2013, 6 January). Doctor under fire for alleged errors prescribing sex-change hormones. *The Guardian*. http://guardian.co.uk/society/2013/jan/06/transexualism-gender-reassignment-richard-curtis

Bauer, Robin (2008). Transgressive and transformative gendered sexual practices and white privileges: the case of the dyke/trans BDSM communities. *Women's Studies Quarterly*, 36 (3–4): 233–53

Benvenuto, Christine (2012a). *Sex Changes. A Memoir of Marriage, Gender, and Moving On*, New York: St. Martin's Press

Benvenuto, Christine (2012b, 3 December). Staying in the same town as my ex. *Kveller, A Jewish Twist on Parenting*. Now only available at GenderTrender. http://gendertrender.wordpress.com/2012/12/06/censored-by-trans-activists-staying-in-the-same-town-as-my-ex-by-christine-benvenuto/

Bhardwaj, Ajay (2005, 14 October). Violent transsexual shipped out: Killer transferred from jail after threatening staff. *UCCO-SACC*. www.ucco-sacc.csn.qc.ca/ScriptorAdmin/scripto.asp?resultat=649498P

Bibby, John (2013, 1 June). Please, just call me Norrie, this is a whole new agenda. Melbourne, Australia: *The Age*. http://theage.com.au/national/please-just-call-me-norrie-this-is-a-whole-new-agenda-20130531-2nhmo.html

Billings, Dwight B. and Urban, Thomas (1982). The socio-medical construction of transsexualism: an interpretation and critique. *Social Problems*, 29 (3): 266–82

Blair, Karen J. (1984). The limits of sisterhood: the woman's building in Seattle, 1908–21. *Frontiers: A Journal of Women's Studies*, 8 (1): 45–52

Blanchard, Ray (1991). Clinical observations and systematic studies of autogynephilia. *Journal of Sex and Marital Therapy*, 17 (4): 235–51

Blanchard, Ray (2005). Early history of the concept of autogynephilia. *Archives of Sexual Behavior*, 34 (4): 439–46

Bland, Lucy (1995). *Banishing the Beast: Feminism, Sex and Morality*, London: Penguin Books

Bono, Chaz (2011). *Transition: Becoming Who I was Always Meant to Be*, New York: Dutton

Bodlund, O. and Kullgren, G. (1996). Transsexualism – general outcome and prognostic factors: a five-year follow-up study of nineteen transsexuals in the process of changing sex. *Archives of Sexual Behavior*, 25: 303–17

Bower, Herbert (2001). Gender identity disorder in the DSM-IV classification: a critical evaluation. *Australian and New Zealand Journal of Psychiatry*, 35: 1–8

Boyd, Helen (2004). *My Husband Betty: Love, Sex and Life with a Crossdresser*, Berkeley, CA: Seal Press

Boyd, Helen (2007). *She's Not the Man I Married: My Life with a Transgender Husband*, Berkeley, CA: Seal Press

Brady, Susan M. and Grover, Sonia (1997). The sterilisation of girls and young women in Australia: a legal, medical and social context. Canberra, Australia: Human Rights and Equal Opportunity Commission. www.wwda.org.au/brady.htm

Brennan, Cathy and Hungerford, Elizabeth (2011). 'Gender identity' legislation and the erosion of sex-based legal protections for females. radicalhub.com/2011/08/01/gender-identity-legislation-and-the-erosion-of-sex-based-legal-protections-for-females/

Brill, Stephanie and Pepper, Rachel (2008). *The Transgender Child. A Handbook for Families and Professionals*, San Francisco, CA: Cleis Press

Brodrib, Somer (1992). *Nothing Mat(t)ers. A Feminist Critique of Postmodernism*, Melbourne, Australia: Spinifex Press

Brown, Nicola, R. (2007). Stories from outside the frame: intimate partner abuse in sexual-minority women's relationships with transsexual men. *Feminism and Psychology*, 17 (3): 373–93

Brown, Nicola, R. (2009). 'I'm in transition too': sexual identity renegotiation in sexual-minority women's relationships with transsexual men. *International Journal of Sexual Health*, 21: 61–77

Brown, Nicola, R. (2010). The sexual relationships of sexual minority women partnered with trans men: a qualitative study. *Archives of Sexual Behaviour*, 39: 561–72

Brown, Elspeth (2011). Feeling archive: partners as transphobic. http://elspethbrown.tumblr.com/post/20288979119/partners-as-transphobic

Browne, Kath (2011). Lesbian separatist feminism at Michigan Womyn's music festival. *Feminism and Psychology*, 21 (2): 248–56

Bucar, Elizabeth and Enke, Anne (2011). Unlikely sex change capitals of the world: Trinidad, United States, and Tehran, Iran, as twin yardsticks of homonormative liberalism. *Feminist Studies*, 37 (2): 301–28

Bullough, Vern L. (2006). Legitimizing transsexualism. *International Journal of Transgenderism*, 10 (1): 3–13.

Burris, Barbara (1973). Fourth world manifesto. In Anne Koedt, Ellen Levine and Anita Rapone (eds), *Radical Feminism*, New York: Quadrangle Books, pp. 322–57

Butler, Judith (1990). *Gender Trouble. Feminism and the Subversion of Identity*, New York: Routledge

Butler, Judith (2004). *Undoing Gender*, New York: Routledge

Buxton, Amity (2006). When a spouse comes out: impact on the heterosexual partner. *Sexual Addiction and Compulsivity: The Journal of Treatment and Prevention*, 13 (10): 317–32.

Califia, Pat (1994). *Public Sex: the Culture of Radical Sex*, San Francisco, CA: Cleis Press

Cameron, Laura (2013). How the psychiatrist who co-wrote the manual on sex talks about sex. *Motherboard*. http://motherboard.vice.com/blog/heres-how-the-guy-who-wrote-the-manual-on-sex-talks-about-sex#ixzz2SSORkDVM

Card, Claudia (ed.) (1991). *Feminist Ethics*, Lawrence, KS: University of Kansas Press

Case, Sue-Ellen (1997). Toward a butch-feminist retro future. In *Heller, Dana (ed.), Cross-Purposes: Lesbians, Feminists and the Limits of Alliance*, Bloomington, IN: Indiana University Press, pp. 205–20

Cavanagh, Sheila L. (2010). *Queering Bathrooms. Gender, Sexuality, and the Hygienic Imagination*, Toronto, Canada: University of Toronto Press

Cavanagh, Sheila L. (2011). You are where you urinate. *The Gay and Lesbian Review*, July–August: 18–20

Center for Reproductive Rights (2010). Reproductive rights violations as cruel, inhumane or degrading treatment or punishment: a critical human rights analysis, New York: Centre for Reproductive Rights. http://reproductiverights.org/sites/crr. civicactions.net/files/documents/TCIDT.pdf

Chapman, Donna and Caldwell, Benjamin (2012). Attachment injury resolution in couples when one partner is trans-identified. *Journal of Systemic Therapies*, 31 (2): 36–53

Chase, Lisa (2011). Wives' tales: the experiences of trans partners. *Journal of Gay and Lesbian Social Services*, 23, Issue 4: 429–51

Chiland, Colette (2004). *Transsexualism. Illusion and Reality*, London: Sage

Chin, Angelina (2012). *Bound to Emancipate: Working Women and Urban Citizenship in Early Twentieth-Century China and Hong Kong (Asia/Pacific/Perspectives)*, Lanham, MD: Rowman & Littlefield

Clements-Nolle, Kristen, Marx, Rani and Katz, Mitchell (2006): Attempted suicide among transgender persons. *Journal of Homosexuality*, 51 (3): 53–69

Comfort, Alex (1972). *The Joy of Sex. A Gourmet Guide to Lovemaking*, London: Quartet

Cook-Daniels, Loree (1998a). Transpositioned. *Circles Magazine*. www.elspethbrown. org/sites/default/files/imce/cook-daniels_trans-positioned1998_0.pdf

Cook-Daniels, Loree (1998b). Dancing with snipers. http://elspethbrown.org/sites/default/files/imce/cook-daniels_dancing_with_snipers.doc

Connell, R.W. (2005). *Masculinities*, Cambridge, UK: Polity Press

Connell, Raewyn (2012). Transsexual women and feminist thought: toward new understanding and new politics. *Signs*, 37 (4): 857–81

Connell, Raewyn (2011). Transgenderism and feminism. Lecture. African Gender Institute. http://soundcloud.com/african-gender-institute/professor-raewyn-connell

Coveney, Lal (1979). Transsexuals in the women's liberation movement. Paper for the Rad/Rev Conference, Leeds, 22–23 September 1979. Lesbian Archive collection, Glasgow Women's Library. Box no: LAIC 1/3

Crossdresserswives.com (n.d.a, accessed 19 December 2012). Founder's story. www. crossdresserswives.com/revision/foundersstory.html

Crossdresserswives.com (n.d.b, accessed 19 December 2012). Bill of Rights. www. crossdresserswives.com/revision/billofrights.html

CSGS (2011). Postposttranssexual: transgender studies and feminism. Center for the Study of Gender and Sexuality at New York University. www.csgsnyu. org/2010/10/postposttranssexual-transgender-studies-and-feminism/

Culture Lab (2013). Women and society CFP. Culturelab. Annenberg School for Communication, University of Pennsylvania. http://culturelab.asc.upenn. edu/2013/05/20/women-society-cfp/

Daily News (2013, 14 May). Police: Palmdale man dressed as woman in restroom arrested. Los Angeles: *Daily News*. www.dailynews.com/news/ci_23244297/police-palmdale-man-dressed-woman-restroom-arrested

Daly, Mary (1978). *Gyn/Ecology. The Metaethics of Radical Feminism*, Boston, MA: Beacon Press

Darke, Julie and Cope, Allison (2002). *Trans Inclusion Policy Manual for Women's Organizations,* Vancouver, BC: Trans Alliance Society

Davis, Jenny (2011). Prosuming identity: the production and consumption of transableism on Transabled.org. *American Behavioral Scientist,* 56: 596–617

Day, Elizabeth (2005, 9 October). Richard, the first transsexual GP, was Vanda, the miner's daughter. www.telegraph.co.uk/news/uknews/1500262/Richard-the-first-transsexual-GP-was-Vanda-the-miners-daughter.html

De Beauvoir, Simone (1973, first published 1949). *The Second Sex,* New York: Vintage Books

Delphy, Christine (1993). Rethinking sex and gender. *Women's Studies International Forum,* 16 (1): 1–9

Delphy, Christine and Leonard, Diana (1992). *Familiar Exploitation: A New Analysis of Marriage in Contemporary Western Societies,* London: Polity Press

D'Emilio, John (1998, first published 1983). *Sexual Politics, Sexual Communities,* Chicago: Chicago University Press

Department of Health (2008). *Medical Care for Gender Variant Children and Young People: Answering Families' Questions,* London: National Health Service. www.gires.org.uk/assets/DOH-Assets/pdf/doh-children-and-adolescents.pdf

Devor, Holly (1994). Transsexualism, dissociation, and child abuse: an initial discussion based on nonclinical data. *Journal of Psychology and Human Sexuality,* 6 (3): 49–72

Devor, Holly (1999). *FTM. Female-to-Male Transsexuals in Society,* Bloomington and Indianapolis, IN: Indiana University Press

Devor, Aaron (2002). Who are 'we'? Where sexual orientation meets gender identity. *Journal of Gay and Lesbian Psychotherapy,* 6 (2): 5–21

Dhejne, C, Lichtenstein, P, Boman, M., Johansson, A.L., Langstrom, N. and Landen, M. (2011). Long-term follow-up of transsexual persons undergoing sex reassignment surgery: cohort study in Sweden. US National Library of Medicine. National Institutes of Health. PLoS One. 2011 Feb 22;6(2):e16885. doi: 10.1371/journal.pone.0016885. www.ncbi.nlm.nih.gov/pubmed/21364939

DiMera, Matthew (2011, 31 March). Gay places that matter. Gay spaces. Suggestions from Vancouver's gay archivist. www.xtra.ca/public/Vancouver/Vancouver_plaques_project_lacks_gay_sites-9954.aspx

Dirt from Dirt, The (n.d.). The dirt from dirt blog. http://dirtywhiteboi67.blogspot.com/

Dirt from Dirt (2010a, 12 September, accessed 17 January 2013). Trans (male) violence – Camp Trans and Michfest 2010, Part 1. http://dirtywhiteboi67.blogspot.com.au/2010/09/trans-male-violence-camp-trans-and.html

Dirt from Dirt (2010b, 15 September, accessed 17 January 2013). Trans (male) violence – Camp Trans and Michfest 2010, Part 2. http://dirtywhiteboi67.blogspot.com.au/2010/09/trans-male-violence-camp-trans-and_15.html

Doan, Laura (2001). *Fashioning Sapphism. The Origins of a Modern English Lesbian Culture,* New York: Columbia University Press

Dowbiggin, Ian Robert (1997). *Keeping America Sane. Psychiatry and Eugenics in the United States and Canada, 1880–1940,* Ithaca, NY and London: Cornell University Press

Dreger, Alice D. (1998). 'Ambiguous sex' – or ambivalent medicine? Ethical problems in the treatment of intersexuality. *The Hastings Center Report,* 28 (3): 24–35

Dreger, Alice D. (2011, 22 June). Trans advocates. *The Stranger*. www.thestranger. com/seattle/trans-advocates/Content?oid=8743338

Drescher, Jack (2002). An interview with GenderPAC's Riki Wilchins. *Journal of Lesbian and Gay Psychotherapy*, 6 (2): 67–85

Drspiegel.com (accessed, 19 February 2013). www.drspiegel.com/facial-feminization-ffs/

Duffy, Maureen (1966). *The Microcosm*, London: Hutchinson

Dunn, Mark (2012, 26 July). Serial killer Paul Denyer quizzed on four jail rapes in six weeks. Melbourne: *Herald Sun*. www.heraldsun.com.au/news/law-order/killer-paul-denyer-quizzed-on-jail-rapes/story-fnat7jnn-1226435264343#mmpremium

Dunne, Gillian A. (2000). *Lesbian Lifestyles: Women's Work and the Politics of Sexuality*, Basingstoke and London: Macmillan

Dykstra, Laurel A. (2005). Trans-friendly preschool. *Journal of Gay and Lesbian Issues in Education*, 3 (1): 7–13

Dynes, Wayne (1992). Wrestling with the social boa constrictor. In Stein, Edward (ed.). *Forms of Desire. Sexual Orientation and the Social Constructionist Controversy*, London: Routledge, pp. 209–38

Ekins, Richard (1997). *Male Femaling. A Grounded Theory Approach to Cross-dressing and Sex-changing*, London: Routledge

Ekins, Richard (2005). Virginia Prince: transgender pioneer. *International Journal of Transgenderism*, 8 (4): 5–15

Ekins, Richard and King, Dave (2010). The emergence of new transgendering identities in the age of the internet. In Hines, Sally and Sanger, Tam (eds). *Transgender Identities: Towards a Social Analysis of Gender Diversity*, New York: Routledge, pp. 25–42

Elliott, Carl (2003). *Better Than Well: American Medicine Meets the American Dream*, New York: W.W. Norton and Company

Ellis, Henry Havelock (1927, first published 1897). *Studies in the Psychology of Sex Vol. 2. Sexual Inversion*, Philadelphia, PA: F.A. Davis

Endocrine Society (2009). Endocrine treatment of transsexual persons: an endocrine society clinical practice guideline. Chevy Chase, MD, USA. www.endo-society.org/guidelines/final/upload/Endocrine-Treatment-of-Transsexual-Persons.pdf

Enke, A. Finn (ed.) (2012). *Transfeminist Perspectives in and beyond Transgender and Gender Studies*, Philadelphia, PA: Temple University Press

Enke, A. Finn (2012a). The education of little cis. Cisgender and the discipline of opposing bodies. In Enke, Anne (ed.), *Transfeminist Perspectives in and beyond Transgender and Gender Studies*, Philadelphia, PA: Temple University Press, pp. 60–77

Enke, A. Finn (2012b). Introduction. Transfeminist perspectives. In Enke, Anne (ed.), *Transfeminist Perspectives in and beyond Transgender and Gender Studies*, Philadelphia, PA: Temple University Press, pp. 1–15

Epstein, Steven (1992). Gay politics, ethnic identity: the limits of social constructionism. In Edward Stein (ed.). *Forms of Desire. Sexual orientation and the social constructionist controversy*, London: Routledge, pp. 239–94

Epstein, Emily Anne (2012, 11 May). Students arrested after they 'filmed upskirt video of their teacher and posted it on YouTube'. *Daily Mail*. www.dailymail.co.uk/news/article-2142748/Students-arrested-filmed-upskirt-TEACHER-posted-YouTube.html

Equality and Human Rights Commission (n.d., accessed 3 June 2013). Transgender additional resources. www.equalityhumanrights.com/advice-and-guidance/your-rights/transgender/transgender-additional-resources/

Erhardt, Virginia (ed.). 2007. *Head Over Heels: Wives Who stay With Cross-dressers and Transsexuals*, New York: Routledge

Ettelbrick, Paula L. and Zeran, Alia Trabucco (2010, 10 September). The impact of the Yogyakarta Principles on International Human Rights Law Development. A study of November 2007–June 2010. ARC International: Yogyakarta Principles in Action. www.asiapacificforum.net/support/issues/sexual_orientation/downloads/yogyakarta-principles/Yogyakarta_Principles_Impact_Human_Rights_Law.pdf

Facialfeminizationsurgery.info (n.d., accessed, 19 February 2013). Facial feminization surgery. www.facialfeminizationsurgery.info/

Faderman, Lillian (1997). Afterword. In *Heller, Dana (ed.). Cross-Purposes: Lesbians, Feminists and the Limits of Alliance*, Indianapolis, IN: Indiana University Press, pp. 221–29

Family Court of Australia (2004, 13 April). Re Alex (hormonal treatment for gender identity disorder) Fam. CA 297. www.austlii.edu.au/au/cases/cth/FamCA/2004/297.html

Family Court of Australia (2008, 15 May). Re Brodie (special medical procedure) Fam. CA 334. www.austlii.edu.au/cgi-bin/sinodisp/au/cases/cth/FamCA/2008/334.html?stem=0

Family Court of Australia (2011, 6 April). Re Jamie (special medical procedure) Fam. CA 248. www.austlii.edu.au/cgi-bin/sinodisp/au/cases/cth/FamCA/2011/248.html?stem=0

Female to Male (n.d., accessed 22 May 2013). Metoidioplasty. www.femaletomale.org/female-to-male-surgery/metoidioplasty/

Fine, Cordelia (2010). *Delusions of Gender. The Real Science behind Sex Differences*, Sydney: Allen and Unwin

First, M.B. (2004). Desire for amputation of a limb: Paraphilia, psychosis, or a new type of identity disorder. *Psychological Medicine*, 35: 919–928

First, Michael and Fisher, Carl E. (2012). Body integrity identity disorder: the persistent desire to acquire a physical disability. *Psychopathology*, 45: 3–14

Flin, Susan K. (2008). Lupron – what does it do to women's health. *National Women's Health Network*. http://nwhn.org/lupron%C2%AE-%E2%80%93-what-does-it-do-women%E2%80%99s-health

Foucault, Michel (1978). *The History of Sexuality, Volume 1: An Introduction*, New York: Pantheon

Fowler, Maria (2001). Sexual social scripts and the re-imaginings of community identity. *Ethnologies*, 23 (1): 45–61

Freedman, Estelle (1979). Separatism as a strategy: female institution building and American feminism, 1870–1930. *Feminist Studies*, 5 (3): 512–519

Frye, Marilyn (1983). *The Politics of Reality: Essays in Feminist Theory*, Trumansburg, NY: The Crossing Press

Frye, Phyllis (2000), The International Bill of Gender Rights v. The Cider House Rules: transgenders struggle with the courts over what clothing they are allowed to wear on the job, which restroom they are allowed to use on the job, their right to marry, and the very definition of their sex, *William & Mary Journal of Women and the Law*, 7: 133–216

Frye, Phyllis (2001). History of the International Conference on Transgender Law and Employment Policy, Inc. www.transgenderlegal.com/ictlephis1.htm

Futterweit, Walter (1998). Endocrine therapy of transsexualism and potential complications of long-term treatment. *Archives of Sexual Behavior*, 27 (2): 209–26

Gage, Carolyn (2010 February). The inconvenient truth about Teena Brandon. *Trivia: Voices of Feminism*. Issue 10. www.triviavoices.com/issue-10-are-lesbians-going-extinct-1.html

Garber, Marjorie (1997). *Vested Interests. Crossdressing and Cultural Anxiety*, London and New York: Routledge

Gardiner, Jill (2003). *From the Closet to the Screen. Women at the Gateways Club, 1945–85*, London: Rivers Oram Press

Garmon, Savannah (2012, 27 January, accessed 25 July 2012). Requiem for a dialogue. www.prettyqueer.com/2012/01/27/requiem-for-a-dialogue/

Garrett, William (2007). *Marie Stopes: Feminist, Eroticist, Eugencist*, San Francisco, CA: Kenon Books

Gender Menders (n.d.). Social outreach of the Gender Identity Awareness Association. Archived version at: http://pandora.nla.gov.au/tep/56567

Gender Spectrum (n.d.b), accessed 16 April 2012). www.genderspectrum.org/

GenderTrender (n.d.a). http://gendertrender.wordpress.com/

GenderTrender (2011, 4 March). Men who love the ladies' restroom. http://gendertrender.wordpress.com/2011/03/04/men-love-the-ladies-restroom-this-week-in-the-news/

GenderTrender (2011a, 13 February, accessed 20 May 2013). Male to eunuch, asexuality and gender nullification. http://gendertrender.wordpress.com/2011/02/13/male-to-eunuch-asexuality-and-gender-nullification/

GenderTrender (2012, 15 August). Letter from Michfest 2012: 'Man on the land'! http://gendertrender.wordpress.com/?s=michfest

GenderTrender (2013, 18 January). Tweeting Suzanne Moore: A random sample. http://gendertrender.wordpress.com/2013/01/18/tweeting-suzanne-moore-a-random-sample/

GenderTrender (2013b, 17 March). Cotton ceiling this week. http://gendertrender.wordpress.com/2013/03/17/the-cotton-ceiling-this-week/

Gendered Intelligence (2009–2013). Trans awareness training. http://genderedintelligence.co.uk/professionals/training

Golgowski, Nina (2012). Parents' outrage as transgendered woman is permitted to use the women's locker room 'exposing himself to little girls'. *Mail Online*. www.dailymail.co.uk/news/article-2227562/Colleen-Francis-Outrage-transgendered-woman-permitted-use-college-womens-locker-room-exposing-himself.html

Goth, Amber (2012, 29 August). Transgendered author being attacked and slandered – attempt to censorship through intimidation. http://amber-goth.blogspot.co.uk/?zx=6b1b1eef54cc40dd

Gottschalk, Lorene (2003). Same-sex sexuality and childhood gender non-conformity: a spurious connection, *Journal of Gender Studies*, 12 (1): 35–50

Gottschalk, Lorene (2009). Transgendering women's space: a feminist analysis of perspectives from Australian women's services. *Women's Studies International Forum*, 32 (3): 167–78

Gottschalk, Lorene and Newton, Janice (2003). Not so gay in the bush: 'coming out' in regional and rural Victoria. University of Ballarat, Vic: School of Behavioral and Social Sciences and Humanities. http://researchonline.ballarat.edu.au:8080/vital/access/manager/Repository/vital:2516;jsessionid=53F64AAE0C63856C0B8F10 9AFE3B1627

Grant, Jaime M., Mottet, Lisa A., Tanis, Justin, Harrison, Jack, Herman, Jody L. and Keisling, Mara (2011). Injustice at every turn: A report of the National Transgender Discrimination Survey. Washington, D.C.: National Center for Transgender Equality and National Gay and Lesbian Task Force

Gray, Stephen (2012, 14 March). In photos: Germaine Greer glitter-bombed for trans comments. *Pink News*. www.pinknews.co.uk/2012/03/14/in-photos-germaine-greer-glitter-bombed-for-trans-comments/

Green, Jamison (1999), 'Look! No, don't!'. In More, Kate and Whittle, Stephen (eds), *Reclaiming Genders. Transsexual grammars at the fin de siecle*, London and New York: Cassell, pp. 118–31

Green, Jessica (2011, 19 April). London transgender conference cancelled after trans complaints. *Pink News*. www.pinknews.co.uk/2011/04/19/london-transgender-conference-cancelled-after-trans-complaints/

Greer, Germaine (1999). *The Whole Woman*, Milson's Point, NSW: Doubleday

Hage, J.J. (2000). Ovarian cancer in female-to-male transsexuals: report of two cases. *Gynecologic Oncology*, 76: 413–15

Haig, David (2004). The inexorable rise of gender and the decline of sex: social change in academic titles, 1945–2001. *Archives of Sexual Behavior*, 33 (2): 87–96

Haiken, Elizabeth (1997). *Venus Envy: A History of Cosmetic Surgery*, Baltimore, MD: The Johns Hopkins University Press

Hakeem, Az (2007). Trans-sexuality: a case of the 'Emperor's New Clothes'. In Morgan, David Howell and Ruszcynski, Stan (eds). *Lectures on violence, perversion and delinquency*, London: Karnac Books, pp. 179–92

Hakeem, Az (2012). Psychotherapy for gender identity disorders. *Advances in Psychiatric Treatment*, 18: 17–24

Halberstam, Judith (1998). *Female Masculinity*, Durham and London: Duke University Press

Halberstam, Judith and Hale, C. Jacob (1998). Butch/FTM border wars: a note on collaboration. *GLQ: A Journal of Lesbian and Gay Studies*, 4 (2): 283–5

Harding, Sandra (ed.). (2004). *The Feminist Standpoint Theory Reader*, New York and London: Routledge

Harne, Lynne (2011). *Violent Fathering and the Risks to Children*, Bristol, UK: Policy Press

Hausman, Bernice L. (1995). *Changing Sex. Transsexuality, Technology, and the Idea of Gender*, Durham and London: Duke University Press

Herald Staff (2012, 13 September). Children's hospital doc arrested on child porn charge. http://bostonherald.com/news/regional/view/20220913childrens_hospital_doc_arrested_on_child_porn_charge

Hewitt, Jacqueline K, Paul, Campbell, Kaslanna, Porpaval, Grover, Sonia, Newman, Louise K and Warne, Garry. (2012). Hormone treatment of gender identity disorder in a cohort of children and adolescents. *Medical Journal of Australia*, 196: 578–81

Heyer, Walt (2011). *Paper Genders*, Make Waves Publishing

Heyer, Walt (2013). *Sex Change-It's Suicide: a Whistleblower Speaks Out*, Create Change Independent Publishing

Heyer, Walt (n.d., accessed 16 April 2013). Sex change regret. www.sexchangeregret. com/

Hoagland, Sarah (1988). *Lesbian Ethics: Towards New Value*, Palo Alto, CA: Institute of Lesbian Studies

Hollis (2013, 18 May, accessed 19 July 2013). Taking steps towards trans allyship. *Earth First! Newswire*. http://earthfirstnews.wordpress.com/2013/05/18/taking-steps-towards-trans-allyship

Horizon (2000). Complete obsession. *BBC*. www.bbc.co.uk/science/horizon/1999/obsession_script.shtml

Hudson (n.d.., accessed 26 May 2013). Hudson's FTM resource guide. www.ftmguide.org/links.html#info

Human Rights Watch (2007, March 27). 'Yogyakarta Principles': a milestone for lesbian, gay, bisexual, and transgender rights. Experts set out global standards for sexual rights and gender equality. www.hrw.org/news/2007/03/25/yogyakarta-principles-milestone-lesbian-gay-bisexual-and-transgender-rights

Iantaffi, Alex and Bockting, Walter O. (2011). Views from both sides of the bridge? Gender, sexual legitimacy and transgender people's experiences of relationships. *Culture, Health and Sexuality*, 13 (3): 355–70

Illich, Ivan (1975). The medicalization of life. *Journal of Medical Ethics*, 1 (2): 73–7

International Panel of Experts (2007). The Yogyakarta Principles. Principles on the application of international human rights law in relation to sexual orientation and gender identity. www.yogyakartaprinciples.org/principles_en_principles.htm

Ira (2010, 6 September). Chest binding 101.Transguys. http://transguys.com/features/chest-binding

Irving, Dan (2012). Elusive subjects: notes on the relationship between critical political economy and trans studies. In Enke, A. Finn (ed.). (2012). *Transfeminist Perspectives in and beyond Transgender and Gender Studies*, Philadelphia, PA: Temple University Press, pp. 153–69

ISNA (n.d., accessed 16 July 2013). Intersex society of North America. www.isna. org/

Jeffreys, Sheila (1989). Butch and femme now and then. In Lesbian History Group (eds). *Not a Passing Phase: Reclaiming Lesbians in History 1840–1985*, London: The Women's Press, pp. 158–87

Jeffreys, Sheila (1990). *Anticlimax: A Feminist Perspective on the Sexual Revolution*, London: The Women's Press

Jeffreys S. (2000). 'Body art' and social status: cutting, tattooing and piercing from a feminist perspective. *Feminism and Psychology*, 10 (4): 409–29

Jeffreys, Sheila (2003). *Unpacking Queer Politics*, Cambridge, UK: Polity

Jeffreys, Sheila (2005). *Beauty and Misogyny: Harmful Beauty Practices in the West*, London: Routledge

Jeffreys, Sheila (2006). Judicial child abuse: The family court of Australia, gender identity disorder, and the 'Alex' case. *Women's Studies International Forum*, 29: 1–12

Jeffreys, Sheila (2008). They know it when they see it: the UK Gender Recognition Act 2004. *Journal of Politics and International Relations*, 10 (2): 328–345

Jeffreys, Sheila (2012). Who cooked Adam Smith's dinner? In Pettman, Ralph (ed.). *Handbook on International Political Economy*, Singapore: World Scientific Publishing, pp. 285–302

Jeffreys, Sheila (2012a, 29 May). Let us be free to debate transgenderism without being accused of 'hate speech'. *Guardian*. www.guardian.co.uk/commentisfree/2012/may/29/transgenderism-hate-speech

Jennings, Rebecca (2006). The gateways club and the emergence of a post-second world war lesbian subculture. *Social History*, 31 (2): 206–25

Jennings-White, Chloe (n.d., accessed 22 January 2013). Ascent List for Chloe Jennings-White. www.peakbagger.com/climber/ClimbListC.aspx?cid=4163

Johnson, Vivien (1981). *The Last Resort: A Women's Refuge*. Ringwood, Vic: Penguin Books

Joslin-Roher, Emily and Wheeler, Darrell (2009). Partners in transition: the transition experiences of lesbian, bisexual and queer identified partners of transgender men. *Journal of Lesbian and Gay Social Services*, 21 (1): 30–48

Kamo, Yoshinori (2000). 'He said, she said'. Assessing discrepancies in husbands' and wives' reports on the division of household labor. *Social Science Research*, 29: 459–76

Kaplan, Gisela (1996). *The Meagre Harvest. The Australian Women's Movement 1950s to 1990s*, St. Leonards, NSW: Allen and Unwin

Katz, Jonathan (1976). *Gay American History: Lesbians and Gay Men in the USA*, New York: Avon Books

Keisling, Mara (2008). Fighting for transgender rights. *Contemporary Sexuality*, November, 42 (11): 4–9

Klaich, Dolores (1974). *Woman Plus Woman: Attitudes towards Lesbianism*, New York: Simon and Schuster

Koyama, Emi (2001, accessed 20 July 2013). The transfeminist manifesto. http://eminism.org/readings/pdf-rdg/tfmanifesto.pdf

Koyama, Emi (2006.). Whose feminism is it anyway? The unspoken racism of the transinclusion debate. In Stryker, Susan and Whittle, Stephen (eds). *The Transgender Studies Reader*, London and New York: Routledge, pp. 697–705

Kurdek, Lawrence A. (2007). The allocation of household labor by partners in gay and lesbian couples. *Journal of Family Issues*, 28 (1): 132–48

Kveller (2012, 5 December). A note to our readers. www.kveller.com/blog/parenting/a-note-to-our-readers/

Lake, Marilyn (1999). *Getting Equal: the History of Australian Feminism*, St Leonards, NSW: Allen and Unwin

Langer, Susan J. and Martin, James I. (2004). How dresses can make you mentally ill: examining gender identity disorder in children. *Child and Adolescent Social Work Journal*, 21 (1): 5–23

Largent, Mark A. (2008). *Breeding Contempt. The History of Coerced Sterilization in the United States*, New Brunswick, NJ: Rutgers University Press

Laura (n.d., accessed 22 August 2011). Laura's playground. Transgender children. http://www.lauras-playground.com/transgender_transsexual_children.htm

Lavoie, Denise (2012, 4 September). Judge orders sex change for mass murder convict. http://bigstory.ap.org/article/judge-orders-sex-change-mass-murder-convict/

Lawrence, Anne (2004). Autogynephilia: a paraphilic model of gender identity disorder. *Journal of Gay & Lesbian Psychotherapy*, 8 (1–2): 69–87

Lawrence, Anne A. (2007). Becoming what we love. Autogynephilic transsexualism conceptualized as an expression of romantic love. *Perspectives in Biology and Medicine*, 50 (4): 506–20

Lawrence, Anne A. (2008). Shame and narcissistic rage in autogynephilic transsexualism. *Archives of Sexual Behavior*, 37: 457–61

Leriche, Albert, Timsit, M.O., Morel-Journel, N., Bouillot, A., Dembele, D. and Ruffion, A. (2008). Long-term outcome of forearm flee-flap phalloplasty in the treatment of transsexualism. *BJU International* (Formerly *British Journal of Urinology*), 101 (10): 1297–300

Lerner, Gerda (1987). *The Creation of Patriarchy*, New York: Oxford University Press

Lev, Arlene Istar (2004). *Transgender Emergence. Therapeutic Guidelines for Working with Gender-variant People and their Families*, Binghamton, NY: The Haworth Press

Lev, Arlene Istar (2008). More than surface tension: femmes in families. *Journal of Lesbian Studies*, 12 (2–3): 127–44

Levine, Martin P. (1998). *Gay Macho: The Life and Death of the Homosexual Clone*, New York: New York University Press

Lucassen, Leo (2010). A brave new world: the left, social engineering, and eugenics in twentieth-century Europe. *Irish Review of Social History*, 55 (2): 265–96

Luecke, Julie C. (2011). Working with transgender children and their classmates in pre-adolescence: just be supportive. *Journal of LGBT Youth*, 8 (2): 116–56

Lyon Martin Health Services (2008). Our mission. www.lyon-martin.org

Mackinnon, Catharine A. (1989). *Toward a Feminist Theory of the State*, Cambridge, MA: Harvard University Press

Mackintosh, Mary (1968). The homosexual role. *Social Problems*, 16 (2), 182–92

McConville, James and Mills, Eithne (2003). Re Kevin and the right of transsexual persons to marry in Australia. *International Journal of Law, Policy and the Family*, 17 (3): 251–74

McDermott, Will and Emery (2011, 26 May). McDermott scores major win in landmark transgender rights case. www.mwe.com/news/uniEntity.aspx?xpST=News Detail&news=9678

McDonald, Myfanwy (2006). An other space: between and beyond lesbian-normativity and trans-normativity. *Journal of Lesbian Studies*, 10 (1–2): 201–14

McHugh, Paul (1992). Psychiatric misadventures. *American Scholar*, 61 (7): 497–510

McHugh, Paul (2004). Surgical sex. *First Things. A Journal of Religion, Culture and Public Life*, pp. 34–8

McNeil, Sandra (1996). *All the Rage. Reasserting Radical Lesbian Feminism*. Harne, Lynne and Miller, Elaine (eds). London: The Women's Press

Makepeace, Clare (2009). To what extent was the relationship between feminists and the eugenics movement a 'marriage of convenience' in the interwar years? *Journal of International Women's Studies*, 11 (3): 66–80

Mallon, Gerald P. (2009). *Social work practice with transgender and gender variant youth*, London: Routledge

Mantilla, Karla (2000, April). Men in ewes' clothing: the stealth politics of the transgender movement. *Off Our Backs*, 30 (4): 5

Masci, David (2009, 21 May). *A Clash of Rights? Gay Marriage and the Free Exercise of Religion*, Washington, D.C.: The Pew Forum on Religion and Public Life. www.pewforum.org/Gay-Marriage-and-Homosexuality/A-Clash-of-Rights-Gay-Marriage-and-the-Free-Exercise-of-Religion.aspx

Mathen, Carissima (2004). Transgendered persons and feminist strategy. *Canadian Journal of Women and the Law*, 16 (2): 291–396

Mayeda, Graham (2005). Re-imaging feminist theory: transgender identity, feminism and the law. *CJWL/RFD*, 423–72

Melloy, Killian (2010, 15 February). *Italy to Open World's First Jail for Transgendered Prisoners*, Boston, MA: The Edge. www.edgeboston.com/index.php?ch=news&sc=&sc2=news&sc3=&id=102325

Mental Health Today (n.d.). DSM-4 (n.d.) *Mental Health Today*. www.mental-health-today.com/gender/dsm.htm

Meyer, I.H. (1995). Minority stress and mental health in gay men. *Journal of Health and Social Behavior*, 36: 38–56

Meyer, Jon (1982). Theory of gender identity disorders. *Journal of the American Psychoanalytical Association*, 3: 21–36

Meyer, Jon and Reter, Donna J. (1979). Sex reassignment. Follow up. *Archives of General Psychiatry*, 36 (9): 1010–15

Meyerowitz, Joanne (2002). *How Sex Changed. A History of Transsexuality in the United States*, Cambridge, MA: Harvard University Press

Millett, Kate (1972). *Sexual Politics*, London: Abacus, Sphere Books

Ministry of Justice (2011). *Care and Management of Transsexual Prisoners*, Ministry of Justice. UK: National Offender Management Service

Ministry of Justice (2012). Gender recognition certificate statistics, July to September 2011. Ministry of Justice Statistics Bulletin. www.justice.gov.uk/downloads/statistics/tribs-stats/grp-statistics-july-sept-11.pdf

Minter, Shannon (1999). Diagnosis and Treatment of Gender Identity Disorder in Childhood. *Sissies and Tomboys: Gender Nonconformity and Homosexual Childhood*, New York: New York University Press, pp. 9–33

Money, John, Jobaris, Russell and Furth, Gregg (1977). Apotemnophilia: two cases of self-demand amputation as a paraphilia. *The Journal of Sex Research*, 13 (2): 115–25

Moore, Eva, Wisniewski, Amy and Dobs, Adrian (2003). Endocrine treatment of transsexual people: a review of treatment regimens, outcomes, and adverse effects. *The Journal of Clinical Endocrinology and Metabolism*, 88 (8): 3467–73

Moore, Suzanne (2013, 9 January). I don't care if you were born a woman or became one. *The Guardian*. www.guardian.co.uk/commentisfree/2013/jan/09/dont-care-if-born-woman

More, Kate (1999). Never mind the bollocks 2. An Interview with Judith Butler. In More, Kate and Whittle, Stephen (eds) (1999). *Reclaiming Genders. Transsexual grammars at the fin de siecle*, London and New York: Cassell, pp. 285–302

Morgan, Robin (1978). Lesbianism and feminism: synonyms or contradictions? In Morgan, Robin, (ed.). *Going Too Far*, New York: Vintage

Murphy, Meghan (2012, accessed 5 November). Rape Relief v. Nixon, transphobia, and the value of women-only space. An interview with Lee Lakeman. *Feminist Current*. http://feministcurrent.com/5033/rape-relief-v-nixon-transphobia-and-the-value-of-women-only-space-an-interview-with-lee-lakeman/

Murray, Suellen (2002). *More than Refuge: Changing Responses to Domestic Violence*, Crawley: University of Western Australia Press

My Husband's Panties (2005, accessed, 4 June 2013). My husband's panties blogspot. http://myhusbandspanties.blogspot.co.uk/

Nagoshi, Julie L., Brzuzy, Stephan/Stephanie and Terrell, Heather K. (2012). Deconstructing the complex perceptions of gender roles, gender identity, and sexual orientation among transgender individuals. *Feminism and Psychology*, 22 (4): 405–22

National Geographic (2011). Secret lives. National Geographic Channel. http://channel.nationalgeographic.com/channel/taboo/galleries/taboo-secret-lives-photo-gallery/#chairbound-by-choice-46559

NCLR (n.d.). Transgender law, San Francisco, CA: National Center for Lesbian Rights. www.nclrights.org/about-us/

Newcomb, Alyssa (2012, 4 August). Doctors accused of filming unsuspecting women may have risked careers over 'compulsion'. *ABC News*. http://abcnews.go.com/US/doctors-accused-filming-women-risked-careers-compulsion/story?id=16928588

Newport TV (2010, 10 March). Update: Friends of man arrested for sexual indecency are shocked. www.fox16.com/mostpopular/story/Update-Friends-of-man-arrested-for-sexual/d/story/ehozQqRzrEmKVIfjZgGHLQ

Newton, Esther (1984). The mythic mannish lesbian: Radclyffe Hall and the new woman. *Signs*, 9 (4): 557–5

NGTLF (n.d.). Transgender issues. Washington, D.C.: National Lesbian and Gay Taskforce. www.thetaskforce.org/issues/transgender

NHS (2007). A guide to hormone therapy for trans people, London: Department of Health. www.qahc.org.au/files/shared/docs/trans_hormone_therapy.pdf

Noble, Bobby (2012). Trans. Panic. In Enke, A. (ed.). *Transfeminist Perspectives in and beyond Transgender Studies*, pp. 43–59

NoGoingBack (2013, accessed 16 May 2013). *No Going Back*. http://groups.yahoo.com/group/nogoingback/

Nuttbrock, Larry, Hwahng, Sel, Bockting, Walter, Rosenblum, Andrew, Mason, Mona, Macri, Monica and Becker, Jeffrey (2010). Psychiatric impact of gender-related abuse across the life course of male-to-female transgender persons. *Journal of Sex Research*, 47 (1): 12–23

NWSA (2013). National Women's Studies Association. Constituency Groups. www.nwsa.org/content.asp?pl=19&sl=75&contentid=75

O'Flaherty, Michael and Fisher, John (2008). Sexual orientation, gender identity and international human rights law: Contextualising the Yogyakarta Principles. *Human Rights Law Review*, 8 (2): 247–48

Owens, Jared (2011, 16 April). Judge agrees with boy who identifies as a girl. *The Australian*. www.theaustralian.com.au/news/nation/judge-agrees-with-boy-who-identifies-as-a-girl/story-e6frg6nf-1226039973338

Page, Morgan (2011, accessed 25 July 2012). Overcoming the cotton ceiling. http://pleasureandpossibilities.com/programming/workshop-descriptions/

Pande, Rohini (2006). Son preference and daughter neglect in India: What happens to living girls, ICRW: International Centre for Research on Women. www.icrw.org/publications/son-preference-and-daughter-neglect-india

Parliament of the Commonwealth of Australia (2013a). Sex Discrimination Amendment (Sexual Orientation, Gender Identity and Intersex Status) Bill 2013, Canberra, Australia: The Parliament of the Commonwealth of Australia. House of Representatives. http://parlinfo.aph.gov.au/parlInfo/download/legislation/bills/r5026_aspassed/toc_pdf/13090b01.pdf;fileType=application%2Fpdf

Parliament of the Commonwealth of Australia (2013b). Sex Discrimination Amendment (Sexual Orientation, Gender Identity and Intersex Status) Bill 2013. Explanatory Memorandum. Canberra, Australia: The Parliament of the Commonwealth of Australia. House of Representatives. http://parlinfo.aph.gov.au/parlInfo/download/legislation/ems/r5026_ems_1fcd9245-33ff-4b3a-81b9-7fdc7eb91b9b/upload_pdf/378454%20.pdf;fileType=application%2Fpdf#search=%22legislation/ems/r5026_ems_1fcd9245-33ff-4b3a-81b9-7fdc7eb91b9b%22

Parsons, Talcott (1951). *The Social System*, London: Routledge and Kegan Paul

Pateman, Carole (1988). *The Sexual Contract*, Cambridge, UK: Polity Press

Penelope, Julia (1993). *Lesbian Culture. An Anthology: The Lives, Work, Ideas, Art and Visions of Lesbians Past and Present*, Berkeley, CA: The Crossing Press

Penner, Barbara (2001). A world of unmentionable suffering: women's public conveniences in Victorian London. *Journal of Design*, 14 (2): 35–43

Pepper, Rachel (2012). *Transitions of the Heart. Stories of Love, Struggle and Acceptance by Mothers of Gender Variant Children*, Berkeley, CA: Cleis Press

Perovic, S., Stanojevic, D. and Djordjevic, M. (2005). Vaginoplasty in male-to-female transsexuals using penile skin and urethral flap. *International Journal of Transgenderism*, 8 (11): 43–64

Persson, Diane, J., (2009). Unique challenges of transgender aging: implications from the literature, *Journal of Gerontological Social Work*, 52: 633–46

Pfarrer, Steve (2012, 5 December). Gender change and a family's undoing. *Amherst Bulletin*. www.amherstbulletin.com/artsleisure/2942204-95/benvenuto-husband-gender-book

Pfeffer, Carla (2008). Bodies in relation – bodies in transition: lesbian partners of trans men and body image, *Journal of Lesbian Studies*, 12 (4): 325–45

Pfeffer, Carla (2010). 'Women's work'? Women partners of transgender men doing housework and emotion work, *Journal of Marriage and Family*, 72 (1): 165–83

Pink Paper (2010, 1 November). Trans woman remanded in male prison over tube death. London: *Pink News*. www.pinknews.co.uk/2010/11/01/trans-woman-remanded-on-charge-of-murdering-trans-lawyer-sonia-burgess/

Pitts, Victoria (2001). Visibly queer: body technologies and sexual politics. *The Sociological Quarterly*, 41 (3): 443–63)

Planned Parenthood (2011, accessed 25 July 2012). Pleasures and possibilities. http://pleasureandpossibilities.com/programming/workshop-descriptions/

Powell, Anastasia (2009). New technologies, unauthorised visual images and sexual assault. Australian Institute of Family Studies Newsletter. ACSSA Aware 23. www.aifs.gov.au/acssa/pubs/newsletter/n23pdf/n23c.pdf

Price, Sarah (2007). Transsexual fights for her lesbian rights. *Australian Woman Network,* www.w-o-m-a-n.net/home/node/920

Prince, Virginia (2005a, first published 1967). The expression of femininity in the male. *International Journal of Transgenderism,* 8 (4): 21–7

Prince, Virginia (2005b, first published 1978). The 'transcendents' or 'trans' people. *International Journal of Transgenderism,* 8 (4): 39–46

Prosser, Jay (1998). *Second Skins. The Body Narratives of Transsexuality.* New York and Chichester, UK: Columbia University Press

Raymond, Janice (1986). *A Passion for Friends: Towards a Philosophy of Female Friendship.* Boston, Massachusetts: Beacon Press

Raymond, Janice (1994, first published 1979). *The Transsexual Empire: The Making of the She-Male,* New York: Teachers College Press Columbia University

Read, Max (2012, 9 June). From otherkin to transethnicity: your field guide to the weird world of Tumblr identity politics. *Gawker.* http://gawker.com/5940947/from-otherkin-to-transethnicity-your-field-guide-to-the-weird-world-of-tumblr-identity-politics

Reilly, Philip R. (1991). *The Surgical Solution. A History of Involuntary Sterilization in the United States,* Baltimore and London: The Johns Hopkins University Press

Rich, Adrienne (1993, first published 1982). Compulsory heterosexuality and lesbian existence. In Abelove, H., Barale, M.A. and Halperin, D.M. (eds), *The Lesbian and Gay Studies Reader,* London: Routledge, pp. 227–54

Riger, Stephanie (1994). Challenges of success: stages of growth in feminist organizations. *Feminist Studies,* 20 (2): 225–300

Riska, Elianne (2003). Gendering the medicalization thesis. *Advances in Gender Research,* 7: 61–89

Roberts, JoAnn (2012, accessed 19 January 2013). I'm JoAnn Roberts. www.cdspub.com/jar.html

Roberts, JoAnn (2013). Beauty and the beach. www.cdspub.com/batb.html

Roberts, JoAnn (n.d., accessed 19 January 2013). Misson statement. Transgender Renaissance Association. www.ren.org/

Romito, Patrizia (2008). *A Deafening Silence. Hidden Violence against Women and Children,* Bristol, UK: The Policy Press

Rudd, Peggy (1999). *My Husband Wears My Clothes. Crossdressing from the perspective of a wife,* TX: PM Publishers

Rufus, Anneli (2010, 12 October). Cross-dressing peeper infiltrates Cal women's locker room, California, USA: *East Bay Express.* www.eastbayexpress.com/92510/archives/2010/10/12/cross-dressing-peeper-infiltrates-cal-womens-locker-room

Russell, Donald Hayes (1968). The sex conversion controversy. *New England Journal of Medicine,* 279: 535–6

Russell, Heath (2013). Out here in the redwoods: Season 2, Episode #2. http://archive.org/details/AH-out_here_in_the_redwoods_season_2_ep2

Sabante, Cindel (2013). *My Husband, My Panties.* www.kobobooks.com/ebook/My-Husband-My-Panties-Feminization/book-g_6GU3U-okiICtoKrIf8nA/page1.html

Sanger, Margaret (1932, April). A plan for peace. *Birth Control Review,* pp. 107–8. www.issues4life.org/pdfs/1932_peaceplan_margaretsanger.pdf

Savannah (2013, 14 March). Getting with girls like us: a radical guide to dating trans* women for cis women. *Autostraddle*. www.autostraddle.com/getting-with-girls-like-us-a-radical-guide-to-dating-trans-women-for-cis-women-160269/

Schilt, Kristen (2006). Just one of the guys? How transmen make gender visible at work. *Gender and Society*, 20 (4): 465–90

Schilt, Kristen and Wiswall, Matthew (2008). Before and after: gender transitions, human capital, and workplace experiences. *The B.E. Journal of Economic Analysis and Policy*, 8 (1): 1–28

Schlatterer, K., von Werder, K. and Stalla, G.K. (1998). *Transsexualism and Osteporosis. Experimental and Clinical Endocrinology and Diabetes*, 104: 413–19

Schlesinger, Fay (2010, 24 January). Boy, 16, to become Britain's youngest sex change patient after NHS agrees to pay for £10,000 operation. *Mailonline*. www.dailymail.co.uk/news/article-1245697/Boy-16-sex-change-operation-NHS.html

Scribner, O. (2012, last modified 8 Sept. 2012, accessed 3 May 2013). Otherkin timeline: The recent history of elfin, fae, and animal people, v. 2.0. in The Art and Writing of O. Scribner. www.frameacloud.com/otherkin_and_therianthropes/otherkin_timeline

Scum-o-rama (2012, 29 March). MTF trans bored over woman-centric feminism. http://scumorama.wordpress.com/2012/03/29/mtf-trans-bored-over-reproductive-rights-centered-feminism/

Seil, David (2002). Discussion of Holly Devor's who are 'We'? *Journal of Lesbian and Gay Psychotherapy*, 6 (2): 23–34

Serano, Julia (2007). *Whipping Girl. A Transsexual Woman on Sexism and the Scapegoating of Femininity*, Berkeley, CA: Seal Press

Shemale Models Tube (n.d., accessed 17 March 2013). Thick black T-girl. http://shemalemodelstube.com/galleries/thick-black-tgirl-ms.-meat-gets-sucked-off-5271.html

Sissification (n.d.a, accessed 14 April 2013). The sissification guide. http://thesissificationguide.blogspot.co.uk/?zx=2989241eef5be06d

Sissification (n.d.b, accessed 14 April 2013). Sissification/feminization artwork http://pinterest.com/pleasant_one/sissification-feminization-artwork/

Sissy School (n.d.). Welcome to sissy school, a place just for sissies! www.sissyschool.com/

Sisyphe (2005, 15 December). Rights of equality-seeking organizations protected. Sisyphe.org. http://sisyphe.org/spip.php?breve532

Smith, Anthony (2012, 25 July). 'Granny-killer' refused hormones in prison. *Gay News Network*. http://gaynewsnetwork.com.au/news/northern-territory/7973-granny-killer-refusedhormones-in-prison.html

Sniderman, Paul M., Fletcher, Joseph F., Russell, Peter H. and Tetlock, Phillip E. (1997). *The Clash of Rights: Liberty, Equality, and Legitimacy in Democratic Pluralism*, Cambridge, MA: Yale University Press

Solomon, Sondra E, Rothblum, Esther D., and Balsam, Kimberley F. (2005). Money, housework, sex and conflict: same-sex couples in civil unions, those not in civil unions and heterosexual married siblings. *Sex Roles*, 52 (9/10): 561–75

Sorella, Lucille (n.d., accessed 24 May 2013). Femme secrets. Feminine body language secrets. http://feminizationsecrets.com/part1/

Spack, Norman (2008). Foreword. In Brill, Stephanie and Pepper, Rachel. *The Transgender Child. A Handbook for Families and Professionals*, San Francisco, CA: Cleis Press

St. John, Leith (2010, 20 January). Interview: Stephanie Brill and Rachel Pepper. *Lambda Literary*. www.lambdaliterary.org/interviews/01/20/the-transgender-child-by-stephanie-brill-rachel-pepper/

Stafford, Diane (2011). Precocious puberty (early puberty). Boston Children's Hospital. www.childrenshospital.org/az/Site1474/mainpageS1474P0.html

Stanford University (n.d., accessed, 5 March 2013). What are health concerns for trans men? http://vaden.stanford.edu/health_library/TransmenHealthConcerns.html

Stern, Alexandra (2005). *Eugenic Nation. Faults and Frontiers of Better Breeding in America*. Berkeley and Los Angeles, CA: California University Press

Strange, Kelly (2012, 27 November). 'I'm tired of doing my hair and make-up': Pensioner, 75, who became a woman in sex change operation 23 years ago wants to be a man again. *The Daily Mail*. www.dailymail.co.uk/news/article-2239120/Gary-Norton-75-woman-sex-change-operation-23-years-ago-wants-man-again.html#ixzz2M3Otkqc9

Stryker, Susan (2008). *Transgender History*, Berkeley, CA: Seal Press

Stryker, Susan and Whittle, Stephen (eds) (2006). *The Transgender Studies Reader*, London: Routledge

Stuart, Jaimie (2006). In another bracket: trans acceptance in lesbian utopia. *Journal of Lesbian Studies*, 10 (1/2): 215–29

Stulhofer, A, and Ajdukovic, D. (2011). Should we take anodyspareunia seriously? A descriptive analysis of pain during receptive anal intercourse in young heterosexual woomen. *Journal of Sex and Marital Therapy*, 37 (5): 346–58

Sullivan, Deborah A. (2001). *Cosmetic Surgery: The Cutting Edge of Commercial Medicine in America*, New Jersey: Rutgers University Press

Sullivan, Nikki (2001). *Tattooed Bodies: Subjectivity, Textuality, Ethics, Pleasure*, Connecticut and London: Praeger

Summers, Anne (2013). *The Misogyny Factor*, Sydney, NSW: New South Publishing

Susan's.org (2007, 16 March). Transsexual regret. Dennis. www.susans.org/forums/index.php/topic,11302.msg82555.html#msg82555

Susan's.org (2012, 13 October). 'I had NHS sex swap to be a woman – now I'm 75 I want them to put my tackle back'. www.susans.org/forums/index.php/topic,127922.0.html

Sweeney, Belinda (2004). Trans-ending women's rights: the politics of trans-inclusion in the age of gender. *Women's Studies International Forum*, 27 (1): 75–88

Sweeney, Mark (2013, 14 January). *The Observer* withdraws Julie Burchill column as editor publishes apology. *Guardian*. www.guardian.co.uk/media/2013/jan/14/observer-withdraws-julie-burchill-column

Szasz, Thomas (1960). The myth of mental illness. *American Psychologist*, 15: 113–18

The Telegraph (2009, 4 February). World's youngest sex-change operation. www.telegraph.co.uk/news/worldnews/europe/germany/4511986/Worlds-youngest-sex-change-operation.html

The Telegraph (2011, 18 April). Man dressed like 'mannequin' spies on ladies in toilet Sydney, *The Daily Telegraph*. www.dailytelegraph.com.au/mannequin-man-spies-on-ladies-in-toilet/story-e6freuy9-1226040998448

Tenpenny, Joshua and Cascio, Justin (2002, 2 July). Driving spikes through your dick (and other, less dramatic do-it-yourself genital modification techniques for FTMS). www.trans-health.com/2002/ftm-genital-modification/

ThaiMed (n.d.). Facial feminization surgery. www.thaimakeover.com/transgender-srs-thailand/facial-feminization-ffs-bangkok.html

They say this never happens (2012). 'Die cis scum'. http://theysaythisneverhappens. wordpress.com/die-cis-scum/

Thom, Ben and Weeks, Harri (2010). Transgender guide for NHS Acute Hospital Trusts. Royal Free Hampstead. www.royalfree.nhs.uk/pdf/trasngender_booklet_low%20res.pdf

Thompson, Denise (2001). *Radical Feminism Today*, London: Sage

T-Kingdom (n.d., accessed, 20 February 2013). www.t-kingdom.com/

Transguys (2010, 6 September). Chest binding 101. http://transguys.com/features/chest-binding

Tur, Bob (2013, 12 June). Famed chopper pilot to become a woman. Interview with Bob Tur. *TMZ*. www.tmz.com/2013/06/12/bob-tur-transgender-woman-zoe/

TYFA (n.d., accessed 22 August 2011). Trans Youth Family Allies. www.imatyfa. org/

Tyler, Meagan (2011). *Selling Sex Short: The Pornographic and Sexological Construction of Women's Sexuality in the West*, Newcastle-Upon-Tyne, UK: Cambridge Scholars Press

United Nations (1948). Universal Declaration of Human Rights. Geneva. www. un.org/en/documents/udhr/index.shtml

United Nations (1979). Convention on the Elimination of All Forms of Discrimination Against Women. www.un.org/womenwatch/daw/cedaw/

Valentine, David (2007). *Imagining Transgender. An Ethnography of a Category*, Durham and London: Duke University Press

Victorian Equal Opportunity and Human Rights Commission (n.d. accessed 18 March 2013). Discrimination: special measures. www.humanrightscommission. vic.gov.au/index.php/exceptions-exemptions-and-special-measures/special-measures

Vida, Ginny (ed.). (1978). *Our Right to Love: A Lesbian Resource Book*. Englewood Cliffs, N.J.: Prentice Hall

Wales, Melody (1999). The finest lesbian feminist artist. *Xtra West*, 163: 21–2

Ward, Victoria (2013, 17 February). A city council has scrapped male and female public lavatories in favour of 'gender neutral' facilities so as not to alienate the transgender community. UK: *The Telegraph*. www.telegraph.co.uk/news/uknews/9876127/ Public-lavatories-to-become-gender-neutral.html

Waring, Marilyn (1989). *If Women Counted. A New Feminist Economics*, London: Macmillan

Weeks, Jeffrey (1977). *Coming Out. Homosexual Politics in Britain from the Nineteenth Century to the Present*, London: Quartet

Weiss, Jillian T. (2007). The Lesbian Community and FTMs. *Journal of Lesbian Studies*, 11 (3–4): 203–11

Welle, Dorinda L, Fuller, Sebastian S., Mauk, Daniel and Clatts, Michael C. (2006). The invisible body of queer youth: identity and health in the margins of lesbian and trans communities. *Journal of Lesbian Studies*, 10 (1–2): 43–71

Weyers, S, Verstraelen, H., Gerris, J., Monstrey, S, Santiago Gdos, S, Saerens, B, De Backer, E., Claeys, G., Vannerchoutte, M., Verhelst, R. (2009). Microflora of the penile skin-lined neovagina of transsexual women. *BMC Microbiology*, 9 (102): 180

Whittle, Stephen, Turner, Lewis and Al-Alami, Maryam (2007). Engendered penalties: transgender and transsexual people's experiences of inequality and discrimination. The Equalities Review. A research report commissioned by the Equalities Review. UK: Crown Copyright, 2007

Wilchins, Riki (2013, 7 February). Op-ed: 'It's the women's room!' and other bathroom complications. *The Advocate*. www.advocate.com/commentary/2013/02/07/op-ed-its-womens-room-and-other-bathroom-complications

Wilson, Ian, Griffin, Chris and Wren, Bernadette (2002). The validity of the diagnosis of gender identity disorder (child and adolescent criteria). *Clinical Child Psychology and Psychiatry*, 7 (3): 335–51

Winter, Katy (2012, 29 October). 'I was born a boy, became a girl, and now I want to be a boy again': Britain's youngest sex swap patient to reverse her sex change treatment. *Daily Mail*. www.dailymail.co.uk/femail/article-2224753/Ria-Cooper-Britains-youngest-sex-change-patient-reverse-treatment.html#ixzz2Kv2nf0Er

Winters, Kelley (2011). The proposed gender dysphoria diagnosis in the DSM-5. http://gidreform.wordpress.com/2011/06/07/the-proposed-gender-dysphoria-diagnosis-in-the-dsm-5/

Wittig, Monique (1992). *The Straight Mind and Other Essays*. Boston, MA: Beacon Press

Women's Resource Centre (2011). Women only services: making the case, London: Women's Resource Centre. http://thewomensresourcecentre.org.uk/wp-content/uploads/making_the_case_for_women_only.pdf

Woodhouse, Annie (1989). *Fantastic Women: Sex, Gender and Transvestism*, Basingstoke, UK: MacMillan Education

Worcester, Nancy A. (2013). Menstruation activism: is the personal still political? *Sex Roles*, 68: 151–154

Writing Group for the Women's Health Initiative Investigators (2002). Risks and benefits of estrogen plus progestin in healthy postmenopausal women. *JAMA* 288: 321–33

WWDA (Women with Disabilities Australia) (2007, accessed 16 April 2012). Policy and Position Paper: The development of legislation to authorise procedures for the sterilisation of children with intellectual disabilities. www.wwda.org.au/polpapster07.htm

Yardley, Jim (2012, 14 June). In Mumbai, a campaign against restroom injustice. *The New York Times*. www.nytimes.com/2012/06/15/world/asia/in-mumbai-a-campaign-against-restroom-injustice.html?pagewanted=all&_r=0

Yogyakarta Principles (2007). Principles on the application of international human rights law in relation to sexual orientation and gender identity. www.yogyakartaprinciples.org/principles_en.htm

Young, Toby (2013, 14 January). Here is Julie Burchill's censored *Observer* article. http://blogs.telegraph.co.uk/news/tobyyoung/100198116/here-is-julie-burchills-censored-observer-article/

Zimmerman, Bonnie (2008). A lesbian-feminist journey through queer nation. *Journal of Lesbian Studies*, 11 (1–2): 37–52

Zola, Irving Kenneth (1972). Medicine as an institution of social control. *Sociological Review*, 20: 487–503

Zucker, Kenneth J. and Spitzer, Robert L. (2005). Was the gender identity disorder of childhood diagnosis introduced into DSM-III as a backdoor maneuvre to replace homosexuality? A historical note. *Journal of Sex and Marital Therapy*, 31: 31–42

INDEX